NEW THEATRE VISTAS

STUDIES IN MODERN DRAMA
VOLUME 7
GARLAND REFERENCE LIBRARY OF THE HUMANITIES
VOLUME 1840

STUDIES IN MODERN DRAMA
KIMBALL KING, *Series Editor*

JOE ORTON'S COMEDY
OF THE LAST LAUGH
by Andrew Gallix

THEATRE UNDER DECONSTRUCTION?
A Question of Approach
by Stratos E. Constantinidis

THE PINTER ETHIC
The Erotic Aesthetic
by Penelope Prentice

PAST CRIMSON, PAST WOE
The Shakespeare–Beckett Connection
edited by Anne Marie Drew

BARNESTORM
The Plays of Peter Barnes
by Bernard F. Dukore

NEW THEATRE VISTAS
Modern Movements in International Theatre
edited by Judy Lee Oliva

NEW THEATRE VISTAS
MODERN MOVEMENTS IN INTERNATIONAL THEATRE

EDITED BY
JUDY LEE OLIVA

GARLAND PUBLISHING, INC.
NEW YORK AND LONDON
1996

Copyright © 1996 by Judy Lee Oliva
All rights reserved

Library of Congress Cataloging-in-Publication Data

New theatre vistas : modern movements in international theatre / [edited by] Judy Lee Oliva.
    p.   cm. — (Studies in modern drama ; v. 7)
  ISBN 0-8153-1670-4 (alk. paper)
    1. Theater.   I. Oliva, Judy Lee, 1952–   . II. Series.
PN2037.N44   1996
792—dc20   95-30422
                                                                        CIP

Printed on acid-free, 250-year-life paper
Manufactured in the United States of America

Dedication
For Bob Cothran

This book is dedicated to my colleague, Scenic Designer, Bob Cothran. I feel honored to work with someone whose joy and curiosity about life, people, and theatre embodies a kind of universal creative ethic so rare and so profound and one that the contributors to this book have experienced and write about so passionately. If in a lifetime one can meet an individual who can connect the prose with the passion; who can make the soul take flight--they will know what it is to be an artist. Bob holds dreams in his hands, delights in the fantasy, and crafts a moment never to be forgotten.

Contents

Acknowledgments	ix
General Editor's Note	xi
Introduction Judy Lee Oliva	xiii

Crossing Boundaries: Directing Gay, Lesbian,
    and Working-Class Theatre in Scotland
    Richard Trousdell
	3

Belgian/American Theatre Exchanges:
    Reflections and Bridges
    Suzanne Burgoyne
	25

Stanislavsky Meets Shepard at the Shchepkin Bonnie Gould	43
On the Edge: Utrecht, Netherlands 1993 Susan Vaneta Mason	59

Maybe Theatre Is Born: Directing Student
    Theatre in Communist and
    Post-Communist Poland
    Kathleen Cioffi
	73

The Politics of *The Professional*: Connecting
    the Prose with the Passion
    Dennis Barnett
	89

Vestiges of Control: Censorship and Society in
    Contemporary Egyptian Theatre
        Kenneth Robbins   105

Year of Improvising in the Balkans
        Vivian K. Mason   119

After the Visit, the Ruins
        Ned Bobkoff   135

East Meets West Meets Hamlet:
    Get Thee to a Noh Master
        Jonah Salz   149

Kuando 1991: A New Beginning
    A Ritual Pilgrimage
        Alexandra B. Bonds   165

Israel's Rina Yerushalmi and Her Directorial
    Experiments in Spatial Interrelations
        Yael Nir   183

Diablomundo and the Royal Hunt:
    The Shadow and the Sun
        Judy Lee Oliva   197

List of Contributors   217

Acknowledgments

I wish to thank Pam Allen for her patient and careful formatting of the book and for her moral support throughout this project. The departmental staff at the University of Tennessee deserve mention for help with the international correspondence, and for helping me deal with the computer challenges that this kind of project inherently meets. Those special people include: Sue Dodd, Shari Taylor, Sharon Ward and Kelli Blair. I am especially grateful to Barbara Korner and Greg Kunesh, my colleagues at other universities who read and offered commentary in the initial stages of my writing. My colleagues at the University of Tennessee share my enthusiasm for international theatre. I am particularly thankful to Bob Cothran, with whom I shared many insightful discussions about theatre and the collaborative process. Above all, I am thankful to my husband Bruce, who reminds me of the important things in life and who remains my source of inspiration.

General Editor's Note

This volume in Garland Publishing's Studies in Modern Drama collects essays on contemporary theatre which reveal the changing face of the world, as well as challenges to the boundaries of traditional stage production. Authors examine familiar texts in new settings, discovering what editor Judy Lee Oliva calls "the effect of cultural-specific gestures, stances and the nuance of words," so that audiences and critics are forced to recognize stereotypes and reevaluate older critical methods.

Topics range from directing gay and working-class theatre in Scotland to producing American and British drama in Holland, Belgium, and Poland. New voices in the theatre are heard, and old ones are put to new tests. What remains is the power of performance to inspire emotional and intellectual response. Writers, directors, costume designers, producers, and critics provide an uncommon range of perspectives to the changing roles of theatre in an increasingly global community.

Professor Oliva holds an M.F.A. in Directing and a Ph.D. in Theatre and Drama from Northwestern University. She is presently teaching at the University of Tennessee and has contributed numerous articles to *Theatre Journal, Theatre Topics,* and *Theatre History Studies.* A book on English playwright David Hare, published in 1991, *David Hare: Theatricalizing Politics* is a comprehensive study of the first two decades of Hare's career. A descendant of the Chickasaw tribe, Oliva has a special interest in Native American Performance, thereby continuing her research into the impact of performance on international culture.

Kimball King

Introduction

As the world continues to change its boundaries—new countries emerging from the ruins of the old, new names evolving from old countries, and old names replacing new countries—traditions are shifting, changing, or struggling to survive. This re-charting and re-mapping of the world has opened up previously restricted and censored theatrical institutions and has allowed for unprecedented exchange possibilities. These thirteen original essays on international theatre projects document the process of the theatrical endeavor created while meeting the additional challenges encountered in different cultures, unfamiliar terrain, and unstable political and social climates. However, without exception, the contributors of *New Theatre Vistas* note the collective empowerment of the theatre aesthetic, which in their eclectic experiences, transcends language barriers, economic instability, and social traditions.

The central focus of all the essays in this collection is on process. However the narrative style of each is necessarily disparate, dependent upon the nature of the project and the role of the individual authors. While some contributors conducted their work in the professional theatre, most projects were realized in academic institutions. While some experimented with original texts, other contributors worked on classics such as *Hamlet* or *Woyzeck*. Most of the projects explored contemporary American or English play texts, including work by Sam Shepard, Arthur Miller or Peter Shaffer, to name a few. Two of the projects were done in America, and only one project, Burgoyne's, developed into an actual exchange. Her chapter details the Belgian and American production of Paul Willems's *It's Raining in My House*. The eclectic style of this collection is also a product of the particular kind of role that each contributor served. Though most are theatre educators, they functioned in various artistic capacities: as directors, dramaturgs, designers, observers and participants. The essays embrace a wide range of theatrical exploration, from a Russian-language production of *Curse of the Starving Class* by theatre students from the Shchepkin Institute at the Maly Theatre, to Israel's Rina Yerushalmi's experiments in spatial interrelations on productions of *Hamlet* and *Woyzeck* with her professional company, The Itim Ensemble. Some chapters offer a significant discussion of text as in Jonah Salz's description of the Noho Group's extrapolation of *Hamlet* reworked as *Ophelia*. Richard Trousdell elaborates on the creation of text, particularly cognizant of the dichotomy of people in plays and plays in people as he recounts the process of American collaborators on a project about an American-Scottish relationship. Dennis Barnett's discussion of Yugoslavian playwright Dusan Kovacevic's play, *The Professional*, complements his account of the performance issues that he encountered in his portrayal of the main character in the American premiere of the play.

Stylistic issues aside, other differences are apparent in the form of the essays. The narratives are by intent more personal and follow a more flexible form than more traditional "scholarly" collections. These international projects made a profound impact on all those involved and each contributor required a somewhat different format to describe his experience. Whereas Vivian Mason relied on the diary entries of her Bulgarian students to best express the aesthetic energy of her work with them; director Ned Bobkoff relates his personal reactions to the activities in the Turkish marketplace and then uses those observations to serve as an ongoing metaphor in the creation of the play *The Visit*.

No matter what style or form the essays manifest, the issues that emerge pervade the very nature of theatre itself; the humanity that it takes to create art is illuminated during the struggle and that struggle is universal, albeit multifarious. The collective observations regarding the process of creating theatre in the international, multicultural arena contribute greatly to our ultimate understanding of theatre as a universal art form. These first hand accounts of crossing cultural, political and aesthetic boundaries enumerate some exemplary lessons for both theatre practitioners and educators. There are lessons to be learned about cultural stereotypes and how we see each other's stereotypes. The contributors to *New Theatre Vistas* became aware of culture-specific gestures, stances and the nuances of words. Many times they had to unlearn and reevaluate their aesthetic values and standards. Their goal was often one of translating intercultural vocabulary into theatre. They had to find analogies between cross-cultural experience. The problems that they encountered in order to create theatre in unique circumstances were constant reminders of inherent prejudices. They learned that there

Introduction

could be no assumptions regarding logic, beliefs, training or behavior, without consequences. The writers in this collection became aware that along with the newfound freedom in many European countries came a newfound fear. Student actors who grew up in a communist regime with rigid dictated control found it difficult to exhibit spontaneity and to express the actual joy they felt while acting. Long-standing traditions grounded in religious ritual became more meaningful when practiced alongside contemporary events. And censorship took on additional meanings in the light of multicultural perspectives. The political nature of art often prevailed, when, for example, acquiring props for a production meant resorting to bribery and illegal tactics.

In Susan Mason's essay she concludes that these experiments in international theatre projects are "pioneering work for which no manuals or maps exist." However, perhaps this collection of essays will provide some guidelines for future projects; they will no doubt stimulate thought regarding not only how we do theatre but why. Though no one essay serves as a model to produce international theatre, as a collective whole *New Theatre Vistas* does offer a new "vista" by which to "view" theatre—as an art that creates a global human community.

Judy Lee Oliva
University of Tennessee

New Theatre Vistas

Crossing Boundaries:
Directing Gay, Lesbian, and Working-Class Theatre in Scotland
by
Richard Trousdell

The Pride of the Clyde[1]

The River Clyde flows through Glasgow, dividing the city center on the north bank from the devastated "Gorbals" working-class districts on the south. Like the river for which it is named, the Clyde Unity Theatre of Glasgow reflects class issues that divide the city, a common Scottish identity that binds it together, and the focused energy that carries the city's creative life out into the country and beyond.

Aileen Ritchie and John Binnie founded Clyde Unity Theatre in 1986 and, as co-creators of its twenty or so productions, they have made it Scotland's leading radical touring theatre company. Both Ritchie and Binnie had wanted to be actors, but not by playing what they saw as stereotypical roles in Scotland's commercial theatre. Ritchie, a large woman and a feminist, knew that she would likely be cast in subsidiary parts as "mother, wife, or whore,"[2] where women are seen only in relation to men. Binnie, a working-class gay man, knew that if he were to be cast at all he would have to change his accent and pretend to be straight.

Instead, they decided to start their own theatre that would not hide issues vital to them "as young Scots growing up and living in modern Glasgow."[3] Starting from who and what they were, Ritchie and Binnie hoped to reach beyond Glasgow's center to a neglected Scottish audience in public housing schemes, unemployed worker centers, old-age pensioner homes, and small town venues throughout the country:

Our two main areas of work--touring with new Scottish plays and community-based devised shows--share the same goals. We aim to use entertainment to make people question their own attitudes towards social issues, such as sexuality, health, race and the position of women in Scottish society. Or, more simply, we are committed to a form of theatre which puts ordinary Scottish characters on stage without resorting to stereotypes such as "the hardman" and "his girlfriend." In our productions we aim to use comedy and emotive writing to present a picture of society which celebrates the Scottishness which unites us while promoting the right of the individual to be different.[4]

The American Connection

The assertive Scottish identity of Clyde Unity Theatre has strong cross-cultural roots. Ritchie and Binnie modelled their theatre in part on the old Glasgow Unity Theatre, a left-wing, social action group of the 1940s and 1950s that toured original plays to working-class venues and produced Scotland's first openly gay play, *Lambs of God* by Benedict Scott in 1948.[5] As Binnie knew from research he did for his senior thesis at the University of Glasgow, the original Glasgow Unity Theatre found inspiration in the example of America's Group Theatre. In aligning itself with an international theatre movement, the new Clyde Unity Theatre not only connected to its Scottish roots, but also adopted goals of social activism, popular audience development, and collaborative methods at the heart of America's most famous theatre of social consciousness.

A more contemporary American influence on Clyde Unity is the impact of Broadway and Hollywood musicals. The mythology of Judy Garland and Mickey Rooney is a direct source for Clyde Unity plays such as *Beyond the Rainbow, MacWizard Fae Oz,* and *Wee'uns in the Wid.*[6] The Garland & Rooney "can-do!" spirit is also mirrored in Ritchie & Binnie's self-presentation as a team of feisty outsiders who use energy, determination and show biz smarts to challenge the establishment. Clyde Unity's extensive borrowing from American pop culture points to a central theme in their work about how American ideas shape Scottish life.

American songs are featured extensively in Clyde Unity productions, signalling the Company's retro style as well as its taste for cross-cultural parody. In their most frequently performed play, *Killing Me Softly*, a beguiling American ballad is played off against the fact of AIDS, making clear that what kills softly in Scotland isn't a song, but rather shame about one's sexuality. The emotional power of American music is even more the subject of Binnie's award-winning *Beyond the Rainbow*. In it, the character of Judy Garland reveals the techniques she uses to sell the famous song she secretly loathes. In the process, she disenchants a Scottish fan who has tried to escape the ordinary facts of his life by living the fantasy of hers. To an American, these examples suggest that Clyde Unity has a love-hate relationship with its American connection. On the one hand it pays tribute to American glamor and accomplishment, but on the other it offers a strong critique of American sentimentality, materialism, and self-preoccupation. To a Scot, like playwright John Binnie, the theme has a somewhat different meaning:

> Our critique of America isn't really about America, but more about Hollywood. I love the movies, . . . and Hollywood's so powerful, and magical--and I'm interested [in] how that dream factory affects Scotland. It transports us, and stimulates and excites us. But sometimes, we can get so caught up in it, that we forget our own real lives. Hollywood makes the American Dream so potent, but I think so few people understand what it is to be Scottish. Our culture is often disparaged, or ignored.[7]

New Directions

Given Clyde Unity's focus on Scottish-American themes, it was perhaps inevitable they would invite two Americans to join the Company. Actor Joan Jubett and I were chosen for their 1993 Edinburgh Festival season because we had staged the 1991 American premiere of Binnie's *Killing Me Softly* at the University of Massachusetts, and so we were known and trusted. A deeper and less explicit reason for our invitation was that this tight-knit Company sensed it was changing and needed to change, but it wasn't sure how. Its growing success, for example, meant that Binnie and Ritchie's individual careers--his in writing, hers in film--were starting to take off and to carry them beyond Clyde Unity. Would new eyes from the outside help them to see where they were going and to clarify the new direction in which the Company ought to move? And if they could no longer be with Clyde Unity full-time, could someone else step in and make sense of their work?[8] Maybe; it was worth a try.

Bobbie:	We've forgotten one thing.
Mari:	What?
Elspeth:	The school's show.
Bobbie:	You'll have to come back from adult responsible-hood to join us for one last time.
Ruth:	My part would have to be stunning for me to come out of retirement.
Mari:	And the show would have to have a social function.
Bobbie:	But what can we do?
Elspeth:	Improvise!
All:	Improwhat?
Elspeth:	Don't take it too seriously.
Bobbie:	I'm scared.
Ruth:	Same here.
Mari:	Don't be. We'll hold hands.[9]

When the World Was Young

A major goal of our cross-cultural work, then, proved to be a traditional one: to see if an outside perspective could help reveal a native process more clearly. There were two projects for collaboration. First, we were going to revise and restage *When the World Was Young*, an early play from Clyde Unity's repertory that was a company favorite, but which they felt had never fully worked in production. The play's first half--Binnie's autobiographical account of growing up gay in a small Scottish town--was funny and tender, but then the plot became issue-heavy as the action shifted to the grownup lives of its characters. Could we help shape a new ending that would somehow pull the play's comic and serious threads together? Until this project, no Clyde Unity play had ever been interpreted by outside sources. Normally, each of its productions is written for a core company of two men and two women--most of whom act, write, and direct--and is then worked out on-the-spot by the playwright, acting as director. In this way, "playwriting," "acting," or "directing" are overlapping functions at Clyde Unity rather than exclusively defined roles. Now, for the first time, the Company was interested to see how an outside director would interpret one of its plays. Among other things, they hoped I would bring a more psychologically oriented approach to *When the World Was Young*--what they called my American "Method" style--as one way to refashion the work and find its ending. Sometimes working in another culture means getting stuck with the labels for your own--and then trying to see if they fit.

A second project, which mirrored the actual relationship Joan Jubett and I had to the Company, was to help devise a wholly new play about the pain and promise of cross-cultural contact. As is often the case with Clyde Unity projects, this one had a story line and a title, *Accustomed to Her Face*, but no script. What Binnie had in mind was a life-changing love story between an American and a Scot in which the lovers would separate before either was fully transformed. In that way, *Accustomed to Her Face* could raise questions about personal and cultural change without pretending it had all the answers. The characters would be a young, openly lesbian American student named Erin and a working-class Scottish woman called Basher, who thought she was straight. A third character, Basher's flatmate, Maxy, would flesh out the play's working-class world and provide an obstacle. By exposing these disparate characters to a whirlwind summer romance, the play would bring to full boil the issues of culture, sex, and class that had simmered long at the core of Clyde Unity's work.

As Binnie intended, the play would also break new ground. It would be the Theatre's first work with a lesbian subject, a theme to which the Company was strongly committed. Given the sexual politics of the 1990s, however, this was a tricky subject for a male playwright-- even a gay one--to attempt. He knew from the start that he would have to rely heavily on collaboration with Ritchie and his sister, Company actor Mari Binnie, if he were to depict truthfully the all-female subject he had in mind. He also knew he would have to move beyond his usual autobiographical methods in order to extend himself imaginatively into the lives of lesbian friends and witnesses. Despite the considerable political and artistic risks involved in such a project, the Company was eager to move forward.

> Basher: *Whit the fuck's happenin'? It's fuckin' brilliant. It's the fuckin' ye see. So fuckin' good. I thought I'd tried everything--but naw. . . . I don't wanna*

talk about it. Some men get turnt on at the thought a' two women daein' it fir them--well, they can forget it. She's mine, no their's.

Accustomed to Her Face

There was another way in which the new play project might prove cathartic that none of us realized at first. By bringing in American collaborators on a project about an American-Scottish relationship, we would be entering a Pirandellian world in which parts of our life together might suddenly turn up in the evolving text and be reflected back to us in a new and startling light. As the improvisations of rehearsal began to show us, American collaborators were important to this project like lightning rods that could capture and illuminate Clyde Unity's charged preoccupation with things American. This important and deeply felt agenda was not clear to any of us when we started our work together.

Erin:	Fascinating countryside.
Maxy & Basher:	In't it?
Erin:	Let me pay for the gas.
Maxy:	Sure, 4.50.
Basher:	Don't take it.
Maxy:	It's money I'm entitled to.
Basher:	You've plenty.
Maxy:	I'm no' a bastardin' charity.
Basher:	Naw. You're a tight cunt.
Erin:	Such language.
Basher:	. . . 'is oor language.
Erin:	It's not politically correct.
Basher:	Who gees a fuck? There's the sewage.
Erin:	Oh. . . uhuh.

Accustomed to Her Face

Culture Shock

The first thing we had to learn about working in Glasgow was that we were not in Edinburgh. Although Scotland's two leading cities are only an hour apart by train or car, their respective citizens define themselves as being worlds apart in class, style, and outlook. Edinburgh defines itself as royal and classical; Glasgow stamps its image as proletarian and post-industrial. In reality, Glasgow and Edinburgh have equally posh suburbs and equally bleak public housing "estates." But conventionally, Edinburgh is old Scotland, the romance of yesterday, while Glasgow is young Scotland, the tough-minded present. These vigorously maintained differences are distilled in the accents of the two cities. The speech of Edinburgh is familiar to American ears as the lilting accent of plays like *The Prime of Miss Jean Brodie*. The Edinburgh accent reflects a genteel, middle-class Scottish tradition that is strongly influenced by its connection to England and the English.

Glaswegian speech, on the other hand, is resistant to English influence; it is working-class Scots: glottal, slurred, and salty. It falls on American ears as barely English at all, a misapprehension most Glaswegians would take as a mark of pride. In plain-dealing Glasgow, which seems to be reinventing itself at every moment, culture shock hits immediately because its tough language, like its jarring redevelopment, forces you to pay attention, listen up, and not ride along on old assumptions.

> *Maxy:* Do you want a shag? *(SHE AND BASHER LAUGH).*
> *Erin:* Is that a type of haircut?
> *Basher:* No, a ride. *(MORE LAUGHTER)*
> *Erin:* In a car on the wrong side of the road?
> *Basher:* A fuck!
> *Erin:* Oh . . . .
>
> *Accustomed to Her Face*

In practical terms, working in Glasgow meant we had to work hard to understand literally what people were saying. It took even longer to catch the sound of strong inner attitudes about Scottishness or class that appear in the guise of self-deprecation and mock rudeness. As it turned out, Glaswegian irony was often aimed at perceived American habits of self-involvement, earnestness, and being polite.

> *Erin:* *(ARRIVING)* I arrived -- exhausted.
> *Basher:* Tanned, obnoxious, American. . . . And we hid to meet her.
> *Maxy:* 'Cos her fuckin' mam wis friends wi' ma fuckin' mam.
> *Basher:* 40 fuckin' years ago.

Erin: *So kind of you to meet me.*
Maxy: *And she expected us to look after her, ferry her aboot.*
Basher: *She wis in fir a shock.*

Accustomed to Her Face

Like the character of Erin, I had much to learn about working in Scotland. At first, it was more a question of what I had to unlearn, because many of my assumptions about directing were of no use to the task at hand. Pre-production planning, for example, which I took to be a cornerstone of good collaboration, has little place in Clyde Unity's creative agenda. Grants do have to be written on time, and there are always deadlines to meet. But as a touring company playing mostly one-night stands, Unity never knew what to expect. In a well-equipped venue, the company might be able to do a production as planned; in another they might need to adjust their effects and blocking to a fixed layout in a florescent-lit recreation hall. With audiences who already know their work--"our audience" as Mari Binnie proudly calls them--Unity can do their most controversial plays full length and workshop their issues afterwards. With a new audience--like ones who greet them with "Oh, are youse the poufs [i.e., queers]?"--the company may have to adjust the playing of whole scenes on-the-spot to acknowledge and overcome signs of audience resistance. On the road, they never know.

In such a context, a director's usual control of the agenda through production effects, fixed ground plans, and detailed blocking is on pretty shaky ground. Of course, directors are always improvising in any situation, but the degree of spontaneous invention required by Clyde Unity's circumstances is what I had to notice, especially in how it fostered collaboration. When no one knew what to expect, everyone was on the same footing because no one uniquely had the power of a prearranged solution. I came to see preplanning as a luxury of rich theatres with power bases and substantial resources to be conserved, controlled, or defended. Poor theatres like Clyde Unity have to be more quick-witted because everyone's inventiveness and judgment are on the line all the time--not just a director's.

The Road to Edinburgh

When we begin our work early in July, John Binnie and I have time only for a quick talk over lunch. We swap ideas about the ending of *When the World Was Young* and he describes his latest thoughts about the new play. When we start rehearsals a week later, a new end scene for *When the World Was Young* was ready to try, but only three pages of *Accustomed to Her Face* were actually written. With just three weeks between us and two openings at Edinburgh, there wasn't any time to waste. Nevertheless, John Binnie asked us all to take time to meet one another by saying aloud the three things we most liked and most disliked about ourselves. This mostly funny, sometimes moving, public exposure was our welcome into a group whose trust is based on being open about one another's strengths and weaknesses. Its message was that our honest interaction was the work and not just a preparation for it. In ways we couldn't yet know, the quality of our lives together was the medium of John's playwriting. We came first, the words came later.

What did become clear immediately was that *Accustomed to Her Face* needed to take priority over the revival of *When the World Was Young*. As guest director for *When the World Was Young*, I worried about that choice. But with a finished script in hand, and a known directing task ahead, I thought that the actors and I had enough rehearsal time to make the revised play work. *Accustomed to Her Face* was another matter: not only did the new play need to be devised virtually from scratch, it was also the Company's Edinburgh Festival premiere piece that critics would use to gauge Clyde Unity's standing. Moreover, since none of us knew what the new play might prove to be, we didn't know how we ought to work at it day-by-day. John Binnie was "directing" in the sense of writing the play in rehearsal using the actors and the space as his medium. Binnie invited me to "help devise" the production--mainly, I assumed, as a source for its American bits-- but I hadn't a clue what "devising" really meant. Flying so totally in the dark was scary, especially when the thrill of the unknown encouraged me to let go of old routines, and to trust in what I might discover. *Accustomed to Her Face* became the major focus in our rehearsals because it demanded the most of us all and forced me to move beyond my usual skills as a director toward new ones I couldn't yet see. For half of each rehearsal day, I could do my usual directing thing with *When the World Was Young*. For the rest of the time, just like everyone else, I'd have to find out what to do, by seeing what needed to be done.

At first, I functioned mostly like an assistant director to Binnie by giving supportive feedback on early improvisations and by suggesting a few myself. But when it came to trying to develop material into some sort of meaningful action or structure--a director's usual strong suit--it was almost always better if I held back my ideas and let the playwright lead the way, even when he wasn't sure where he was going. Usually a director's virtue lies in being clear and articulate; now, I had to learn *not* to give feedback when I sensed that longer stewing was more important than any quick directorial fix. My staging expertise was another redundant virtue. John Binnie sketches his dramatic ideas in exact physical detail, not just in words. For him, writing and staging are the same thing and happen simultaneously. Often, in fact, a physical action suggested the words, and no words survived if they couldn't be vividly staged. However dark and tentative the process, it was clear that John Binnie was "writing" a physical production and not just a script.

For most of our rehearsals, then, I found myself functioning like a silent witness to a creative act that was happening on its own, but which needed someone like me whose sole task was to watch it happen.[10] The playwright was busy directing; the actors were busy improvising; I was the only one free to watch the whole process. Usually, what makes me a good director is my full engagement with the work; now my attentive detachment is what seemed to make me valuable. In one sense, I was a necessary observer whose presence both threatened and validated an unfolding experiment. In another sense, I functioned like a good dramaturg, a trusted friend of the production who made tactful suggestions about text, mediated the production dialogue, and kept track of the production's logic--or lack of it--as it developed. When asked, I sometimes spoke; when not, I just watched.

As usual, it helped if I could see many possible goals for a given rehearsal, just in case anyone needed one. But most of the time it was a question of my being playful enough and positive enough to help generate new ideas as we worked. There is nothing new in the image of theatre as play rather than task, but the degree to which Clyde Unity's collaborative method is governed by the play spirit rather than the work ethic is what I had to notice and to adjust.

Here again, I had much to unlearn. Whether because of my serious American "Method," or having been an Equity stage manager, I tend to make distinctions between work and not work in ways that were not helpful in Clyde Unity's process. Shakespeare and Moliere teach us that real life and stage life overlap significantly all the time. Still, as a director, I tend to feel responsible for protecting the work by subtly keeping it separated from just playing around and by making sure that chit-chat doesn't eat up the schedule. Clyde Unity works in a messier and more openly casual way. Schedules are wildly approximate, and tea breaks happen anytime, often as a way to start a rehearsal. I began to see that the kettle and biscuits were kept going all day, not as an interruption of the work, but as a playful extension of it. All the jokes and small talk that I saw only as schmoozing were actually the Company's way of getting in touch and staying there. What looked to me like an evasion of purpose often turned out to be making room for a more inventive solution. Like a gathering of Quakers, Clyde Unity doesn't think that the only way for the creative spirit to manifest itself is through the relentless pursuit of a goal. Sometimes it may be more important to step back in seeming passivity and wait to see what happens. Whereas my initial impulse was to cut off the small talk to do a warm up, I began to see that small talk itself was their warm up and a cornerstone of their collaborative style: their lives and their work are one thing, and they make as few distinctions as possible between onstage and offstage, the rehearsal from what surrounds it, their lives from their art. Their life together is their work, and not just a preparation for it. What happens, happens, and its possible implications for the work at hand is taken for granted by all concerned.

From Stage to Page

At first, it was actual things we did or said that got woven into the script in slightly altered form. My description of a raucous party that startled me out of sleep my first night in Glasgow ended up in the play as the rude awakening to Scottish life that greeted the just-arrived American student in our play. Later, it was my saying that I wanted to track down my great grandfather's Scottish roots that found its way into the play as satire of American homecoming nostalgia and its cultural expression.

Maxy: So that's yir granny's highland hame.
Erin: My great, great grandmother. It's so squashed.
Basher: Don't be disappointed.
Erin: I expected more.
Maxy: Like a plaque? She probably flitted to America 'cos here was so squashed.

14   *Crossing Boundaries*

> *Basher:* Nice hillside.
> *Erin:*   I want to pick some heather for my mother. . .
>   Have you seen Brigadoon?
> *Basher:* Brigawhat?
>
>   *Accustomed to Her Face*

Beyond literal borrowing, John Binnie often used the circumstances of our work together to create the fictional circumstances of the emerging script. At an early rehearsal, for example, the actor playing Maxy, Marj Hogarth, had an abscessed tooth and couldn't work. Binnie's response to this potentially damaging event was to take positive advantage of it. After parking Marj on the sidelines with a hot water bottle, he let her situation suggest a possible event in the play that we could improvise. To make a political point, Binnie had originally conceived Maxy's character as sickly because of an on-the-job disability. Now, thanks to a bad tooth, here she was actually sick on the job, parked on the sidelines, screwing up the rehearsal in the same way she was probably screwing up Basher's chance to have some fun with Erin. A first improvisation directly exploited these rehearsal circumstances as Basher and Erin tried to make a date without Maxy overhearing and feeling left out. Having made good use of Maxy's sickness in fact and in fiction, Binnie next asked the actors to improvise the "morning-after" scene of Basher and Erin's first lovemaking, again with the added pressure of Maxy being bedded down next door.

The extraordinary productiveness of this improvisation was more than happy accident; the "given circumstances" of rehearsal were shaped by Binnie's critical choices based on his overall goal to represent truthfully ordinary Scottish life. In this sense, a common social vision is Clyde Unity's true director. The actors' first try at the morning-after scene, for example, was believeable in a general way but lacked the dangerous edge of class difference that Clyde Unity's work is always trying to define. "Youse are too middle-class," John Binnie said, "just talking about yer feelings. We need to roughen it up." First, he translated his critical response into a line for Basher by having her say to Erin: "Fuck, this is so American TV Movie o' the Week. 'Let's sit down and talk.'" Binnie then made two adjustments: first that Basher needed to be less logical and more of an "anarchist" who goes directly for what she wants without fuss. Next, he tried to get Joan to work for the "politically correct" side of Erin's character by having her hide Basher's clothes until Basher admits that making love with a woman means she's a lesbian. Binnie, who has no American "Method" scruples about naming the results he wants, says he can imagine the women actually coming to blows during the scene, and asks the actors to push Basher's character to the edge of physical violence. The improvisation that followed lasted for more than half an hour, and as Binnie predicted, it drove Basher close to an assault on Erin because she felt so shamed by the nakedness being forced upon her. Erin's character, too, was shaken by the "pushy American" edge she was developing as each woman struggled to hold to the class values underlying their respective cultural identities. When this material was improvised, we all saw it only as background and had no idea it would eventually become a defining center of the play's conflict:

Erin: C'mon lesbian, fight.
Basher: Stop it.
Erin: Fight, lesbian. You can't deck me--cos you like me.
Basher: I fuckin' love ye--or did--til' you turned into this ballbreaker.
Erin: You don't have balls. I just want you to face the real world.
Basher: Your world, no' mine.
Erin: Our world--and it's important to acknowledge what we are. (GENTLY) Lesbian.
Basher: What I am is poor, really poor. Have you ever been?
Erin: I'm a student.
Basher: And if you run oot o'dosh?
Erin: What?
Basher: Money.
Erin: My mother lends. . . .
Basher: Uhuh--I'm glad to see we share the same world. Now, my clothes please.
Erin: Not till you admit that you're a . . .
Basher: I'll think aboot being a lesbian after breakfast, OK?

Accustomed to Her Face

Up Against It

Almost two weeks after this scene was improvised, we hit a crisis: Binnie couldn't finish the play. As he had originally imagined it, the story would end with Maxy and Basher visiting Erin in America where reverse culture shock would kill the summer romance. A first draft of these American scenes had been rehearsed, but we all sensed they opened a new story, rather than bringing the old one to resolution. With less than a week before leaving for Edinburgh, everyone was getting tense about the unresolved ending--especially the actors who needed to learn lines.

Binnie called a tea break and asked me to join him in another room while the actors ran lines for the scenes that were set. Flopped on a pile of groundcloths, Binnie said he was concerned that the American scenes diminished Maxy and Basher by turning them into implausible tourists. Out of their own Scottish setting, they could only gape and be awed by the contrast between their world and the glitz of American materialism. Binnie wanted to question the impact of American values, not have them validated through Scottish gullibility. He said he kept remembering Basher's fighting spirit in that early improvisation and didn't want to betray it. Nor did he want to betray the working-class teenagers from south Glasgow whose in-your-face vigor had inspired him to create these characters in the first place.[11] What if, instead of going to the States, Erin took Maxy and Basher on a tour of the Highlands in search of Erin's Scottish roots? And what if the real Highlands, rain and all, were played off against Erin's expectations? And what if Erin and Basher actually danced to *Brigadoon* music, as if Basher were momentarily carried away by the American version of her own country? And what if Erin left Basher then, dropping her out of an American fantasy into the reality of her half-changed world? That would end the play where Binnie wanted it--on home ground where his own romance with America needed to come to resolution. Would such an ending make the play seem too anti-American? I told Binnie that I thought it might, but not mindlessly and not without representing a contrasting attraction to America in Basher's love for Erin. By the time the break was over, the decision was made and Binnie went home to write it.

(AIRPORT. ERIN WITH BAGS SINGS "ACCUSTOMED TO HER FACE")

Basher: *(SHOUTS OVER) Stop singin' yir fuckin' stupid fuckin' songs. Life is no' like a Broadway fuckin' musical--ma life isnae anyway. Ye come here and mess wi' me and fuck wi' me and then ye fuck off. Yir worse than a' those pricks fae the past--cos you leave me changed. I'm half complete and shitty scared and on ma own. Don't go.*
Erin: *I've got to. What we had . . . I'll never forget.*
Basher: *But it's over.*
Erin: *Visit me in America.*
Basher: *I will. . . . Kiss me.*
Erin: *What?*
Basher: *Fuckin' kiss me. . .*
Maxy: *She departed.*
Erin: *I departed. (TURNS UPSTAGE)*
Basher: *And so, she exited fae oor lives.*
Maxy: *Sounds like John Boy Walton.*
Basher: *I wonder if she ever 'hinks o' us?*
Maxy: *I doubt it.*
Basher: *Same here.*
Maxy: *If I get ill . . .*
Basher: *You'll no'.*
Maxy: *I don't want you to look after me.*
Basher: *Dae ye 'hink I'd waste ma life daein' that?*
Maxy: *Naw. You're gonna be a lesbian.*
Basher: *Am gonna try.*
Maxy: *Let's go--and leave her singing.*
Basher: *If only life was as simple as a song.*

Accustomed to Her Face

In Others' Shoes

The hardest part of our work together was not facing honest cultural differences, even when we disagreed. What was difficult was coming up against subtle but significant differences in our ways of working, inherent stylistic preferences that had strong emotional and aesthetic implications we only half-understood. There is no easy way to describe these things; they are too deeply embedded and invested to allow for much clarity. But subjectively, they felt like contrasts between soft and hard textures, slow and fast rhythms, personal or social focuses, naive or informed opinions, serious and comic attitudes. For me, being an American director in Scotland often meant feeling slow, soft, personal, serious, and--frankly--stupid. Perhaps one always feels slower and more stupid in another culture because nothing can be automatic and it takes time to monitor even trivial signals. And no doubt one's personal hangups stand out more clearly against an unfamiliar background. Even so, the Scots always seemed miles ahead of us in the quickness of their responses, the patterns of their speech and thinking, and their habitual rhythmic preferences, on stage or off.

Underlying this rhythmic contrast was the difference between our respective ways of expressing feelings. Joan and I had already met this contrast when we did Clyde Unity's *Killing Me Softly* in America. When John Binnie flew over to see a runthrough of that work, he was horrified at first by how slowly and subjectively we played his text, nearly doubling its Scottish playing time. At that pace, he thought we'd bore everyone to death. But when he saw our version with an American audience, he was bowled over by the emotional response we got, and he liked the production. In rehearsal on Scottish turf, however, Joan and I once again seemed embarrassingly slow with our "over-the-top" emotions, while to us the Scots often seemed dry, blunt, and evasively quick-witted. But like it or not, it was our turn to adjust to a foreign style by trying to lighten up and find out what happens when you go faster than seems normal. As Americans, we were used to "speed run" as an occasional technique and to "fast forward" as a function of tech week, but now we had to experience "get on with it" as a basic way of working and living. The inevitable results of our trying to work closer to Scottish rhythms were heightened energy--and exhaustion; emphasis on thinking clearly--and sudden brain death; emotional surprise--and affective burnout. In speeding up, technique and control seemed to take over as primary focus, while feeling necessarily followed rather than led an action.

Paradoxically, we also had to learn a different sense of "slow," based less in a subjective orientation than in taking time to expand details of social behavior to expose their gestural significance. To generalize, we tend to work through feeling toward form, whereas the Scots tend to take feeling as a given and to work instead at expressing ideas through crisp, theatrical gesture. Their way takes time, a unique sort of time focused on precise detail rather than on a broad flow of emotion. At the end of *When the World Was Young*, for example, I knew that the final goodbye between a gay boy and his female best friend should be emotionally significant and that we needed to take time to express the scene's sense of ritual bonding. But I nearly missed a detail of deep significance until Binnie tactfully pointed it out to me. The banana the boy gives to a vicar's daughter as his pledge of lasting friendship isn't just innocently sexual. It is a sign of his being poor: he has nothing else to give; he is giving all he has. Until I took time to notice and to stage the implications of this small detail, the strong emotive scene I had developed lacked the articulation of its compelling social idea.

The advantages of American slowness based in subjective feeling--here's where our "Method" label fit--were as revealing to the Scots as the quickness of their social sensibility was to us. Binnie, for example, was struck by how my directing of *When the World Was Young* focused serious attention on the gay boy's sexual identity and made it the emotional center of the play rather than a comic counterpoint to a story about class friendship. I did this intentionally by slowing down key moments of transition in his story so that what we think of as "subtext" would be clear to an audience from reflective behavior rather than from what was said. This choice downplayed quite a lot of the comedy, but it also helped pull the play's comic and serious tones together around an ongoing throughline of the boy's emotional life. I didn't invent that life; I simply helped uncover it by going more slowly.

Beyond Difference

No one can fully say how creative acts happen, or how collaborative work across cultural boundaries makes new choices possible. But the development of one remarkable scene in *Accustomed to Her Face* might serve to suggest some of the cross-referencing of backgrounds, techniques, and perspectives that came suddenly into focus and brought a unique moment of our collaboration to life. Binnie knew from the start that a key scene in the new play would be the one where Erin and Basher first realize they are mutually attracted. But he also wanted to avoid the hesitant looks and soulful confessions of stereotypical lesbian/gay fiction. Therefore he decided that Basher and Erin's first kiss should come out of nowhere and--like the improvisation that welcomed us into the Company--go for the gut before the head could figure out what happened.

Basher: *Imagine bringin' books a' this way.*
Erin: *Imagine. Don't touch. You'll soil them.*
Basher: *Hey, ma paws are clean. Looks like your mind's soiled. Check the titles. "Lesbians of Lesbos." "Up Inside Her."*
Erin: *For my dissertation--the semiology of female to female bonding.*
Basher: *Whit?*
Erin: *Forget it. You wouldn't comprehend.*
Basher: *No? Try me.*
(BASHER GRABS ERIN AND KISSES HER).
How 'wis that?

Accustomed to Her Face

After that violent start, however, Binnie knew he wanted deeper feelings to dawn on the women, using music somehow to express the power of their awakening. Binnie uses popular songs, rather than commissioned music, because he likes to exploit the emotional power of the familiar by redirecting it toward new ends. To do that, he works very closely with his actors to find out what contemporary music turns them on, and in what ways they can perform it to reveal their characters. In terms of our cast, for example, he knew that Marj Hogarth, from Leicester, England, had a magnificent singing voice and loved contemporary musicals; that Joan, the resident American, liked romantic songs and could carry a tune in a folksy sort of way; and that Mari, the authentic Scot, couldn't really sing at all but liked music with a strong beat she could dance to. From this odd mixture of skills and circumstance, Binnie began to construct the scene in which Erin and Basher's physical attraction crosses over into emotional territory. Three songs by three women, each built upon the actors' skills and cultural orientation, and each giving voice to a distinct sexual perspective, staked out a three-way conflict between love, friendship, and class during a "Kareoke Night" scene at a local pub. First, Binnie had Marj Hogarth show a surprising side to Maxy's rough character by singing a tender version of "Only for a Time" from Willy Russell's musical *Blood Brothers*. This English song, about a single-parent mother forced by poverty to sell her child, touched on Maxy's central tie to her dying "Mam," and expressed the deep feelings of class and family loyalty of her straight world. As Basher and Erin listened to Maxy, and looked at one another in disbelief, the words of her song gave voice to an underlying truth they didn't dare say:

Only for a time
I must not learn
To call you mine
. . .
You can be sure
What's gone before
Will be concealed
Friends will never learn
That once we were on easy terms.

Accustomed to Her Face

Next, to break the spell and to cover-up Basher's embarrassed sexual confusion, Binnie had Basher howl a music hall sing-a-long number--"Thank You For the Music"--while Maxy accompanied her with taunts of "Shit, shit, shit, shit," thus providing an ironic comment on Basher's evasion, and the cultural poverty of her kitschy world. Finally, Maxy and Basher trick Erin into singing, hoping to embarrass "the American."

Basher: Sing.
Erin: Me? No--I couldn't.
Maxy: Don't fuckin' let us down.
Basher: Haven't you any balls?
Erin: No, I have a vagina. What should I sing?
Maxy: (LAUGHING). "Country Road, Take Me Home?"
Basher: (LAUGHING). Or howabout "I'm Leaving On a Jet Plane?"
Erin: I prefer this.

Accustomed to Her Face

Joan Jubett, who in fact is embarrassed to sing in public, then stood up to sing "Accustomed to Her Face." As she did so, her actual struggle to perform the song infused her character Erin's struggle as a lesbian to make her feelings stick in public with Basher. Culturally, too, Erin's openly emotional American song, delivered slowly and with strong subjective emphasis, cut through Basher's macho Scottish defenses and touched feelings that Basher's fast-tempo singing was meant to hide. The real terms of our respective cultural experiences, our native skills, emotional habits, preferred rhythms, and favored personas were extracted and shaped by John Binnie's imagination into a highly theatrical moment of stage life. All of our experiences together, including our differences, came together in this moment to focus the play's dramatic purpose, and yet each cultural perspective remained distinctive and perceptible.

This scene about the transformative power of popular art to break down barriers and to reveal unexpected truths comes as close as I can to describing the experience of working in Scotland with Clyde Unity Theatre. Our cross-cultural work taught us many things: we were changed in practical ways by exploring new rhythms, by letting go of fixed roles, by questioning the social dimensions of what we do, and by trying sometimes not to take ourselves too seriously. But perhaps we changed most by simply becoming more aware of who we are, the values we stand for, or those we need to learn from one another. Like the characters of our two plays, we were willing to cross boundaries by joining hands in friendship and saying: "Am gonna try."

Notes

1. This term was coined by Julie Morrice, "Pride of the Clyde: Clyde Unity Theatre in Profile," *Theatre Scotland*, II 8 (Winter, 1994), 34-38.
2. John Binnie, letter to author, 26 December 1993.
3. Ibid.
4. Clyde Unity Theatre program for *Accustomed to Her Face* at the Theatre Workshop, Edinburgh International Festival (August, 1993).
5. Colin Chambers, *The Story of Unity Theatre* (New York: St. Martin's P., 1989) 282.
6. *MacWizard Fae Oz* is a Scottish parody of *The Wizard of Oz*, as *Wee'uns in the Wid* is of *Babes in the Woods*.
7. John Binnie, letter to author, 26 December 1993.
8. In the summer of 1994, Aileen Ritchie did finally decide to end her active role with Clyde Unity to go more fully into filmmaking. Her role as co-artistic director of the Company has increasingly been taken on by Mari Binnie, Clyde Unity's leading actor. Although many factors influenced Ritchie's decision, the 1993 guest-artist experiment helped to pave the way.
9. All citations of John Binnie's plays are to their unpublished manuscripts, copyright John Binnie (August, 1993). All inquiries about these texts and their production rights may be made to: Gary Carter and Roger Hancock. 4 Water Lane, London, NW 1 BNZ England.
10. My experience as a silent witness reminded me of the "maternal gaze" aspect of directing, as described in detail by Susan Letzler Cole, *Directors in Rehearsal; A Hidden World*. (New York & London: Routledge, 1992).
11. Matthew Hudson, "A Lesbian Highland Fling: An Interview with John Binnie," *Capital Gay* 4 February 1994, n.p.

Belgian/American Theatre Exchanges: Reflections and Bridges
by Suzanne Burgoyne

Just one foreign-play production a year at each of our theatres could make a difference in the world.

Felicia Londré, *American Theatre*

Introduction

Although contemporary American plays are performed in Europe, few non-British foreign plays appear on American stages. In "Exposing the Translation Gap," a 1988 article in *American Theatre*, Felicia Londré points out that "America seems to have raised some kind of mental 'protective tariff' against foreign plays in English translation" (48). Surveying regional theatre seasons from 1981-87, Londré found that only one in forty-four plays produced was by a still-living foreign author. Londré rails against American provincialism: "Do we not even care what subjects are being explored, what techniques are being tried, by our colleagues in theatre elsewhere on this shrinking planet?" (49).

Some of us care. While on a sabbatical leave, I ventured into the terra incognita of cross-cultural theatrical production. Having previously studied at the Belgian theatre conservatory, L'Institut National Supérieur des Arts du Spectacle et Techniques de Diffusion, I returned as a visiting professor in 1986/87 to work with my former teacher, Paul Anrieu, and the INSAS directing students on two of Arthur Miller's plays. I also continued my research on Belgian playwright Paul Willems and, on my return to the States, directed my own students in Willems's *It's Raining in My House*.

My model for intercultural theatrical work was artistic rather than ethnographic: *Salesman in Beijing*, Miller's rehearsal journal for the production of *Death of a Salesman* he directed in China. At the first rehearsal, Miller told his Chinese cast:

The way to make this play most American is to make it most Chinese . . . this play cannot work at all--it can easily be a disaster--if it is approached in a spirit of cultural mimicry. I can tell you now that one of my main motives in coming here is to try to show you that there is only one humanity. That our cultures and languages set up confusing sets of signals and these prevent us from communicating and sharing one another's thoughts and sensations, but that at the deeper level where this play lives, we are joined in a unity that is perhaps biological. I am not an anthropologist and I can't predict what we will prove through this production; but nothing at all will come of it unless you are emotionally true to your characters and the story. If you are, I am betting that the cultural surface will somehow take care of itself, although I can't be sure at this point what it will appear to be. (Miller 5)

Salesman in Beijing details the analogies Miller and his cast found between American and Chinese experience to create a production that transcended cultural boundaries--without resorting to the traditional Chinese device of imposing Western-style wigs on Chinese actors. While I did encounter cultural differences in working on the Miller project in Belgium and the Willems project in America, I found Miller's search for a common humanity inspiring and his analogical method effective.

Arthur Miller in Belgium

The INSAS directing section, headed at the time by Paul Anrieu, was a four-year program. Annually, second-year students studied an author in depth and directed each other in scenes from that author's plays, which were performed publicly. My responsibilities included providing dramaturgical support and assisting Anrieu in supervising rehearsals.

The first barrier I encountered was linguistic. Although I had armed myself with dramaturgical materials dealing with *Death of a Salesman* and *The Crucible*, few of these sources proved available in French translation. Fortunately, most of the eleven students read some English.

The second barrier was stylistic. Psychological realism, still the mainstay of American dramaturgy, now seems passé to Europeans. I spent hours in the archives of the Théâtre National de Belgique, which had premiered both *Salesman* and *Crucible* for the French-speaking world, perusing reviews to get an overview of European reactions to U.S. playwrights.[1] While the critics of the fifties could praise Miller's *Salesman* for its "naturalism," by the eighties the term "naturalistic" had become an epithet applied by scornful Parisian critics to American plays.[2] My research helped to prepare me for the INSAS students' initial response to the Miller project: resistance. In my first meeting with them, I discovered they considered Miller a hopelessly outmoded realist. Our dramaturgical sessions thus included heated discussions of Miller's significance as a playwright and the contemporary relevance of *Salesman* and *Crucible*.

The students found reason to emphathize with Miller when we considered Boyer and Nissenbaum's *Salem Possessed*, in which the authors argue that the Salem witch hunt phenomenon arose from conservative forces' attempts to maintain power in a period of socio-economic transformation (178-80). In light of futurists' suggestions that late twentieth-century Western civilization is changing from an industrial to an information-based society, an era which engenders similar dangers, the students could draw analogies between *Crucible* and the current rise of fanatical right-wing movements in Europe and America. Miller's analogical method worked.

The third barrier appeared when we began to scrutinize the available translations of our plays. Literary translation always poses challenges, but in the case of *The Crucible*, we discovered a cultural problem. Abigail, leader of the girls "crying out" against the so-called witches, has had an affair with the protagonist, John Proctor. The French adaptor, Marcel Aymé, argues that "the sympathy of the American spectator belongs to the seducer" because Proctor, as an "eminent forefather," arouses patriotic sentiments, while Abigail seems "a little slut come to sully the glorious dawn of the U.S.A." Aymé proclaims that Gallic chivalry would propel a French audience, on the contrary, to sympathize with Abigail:

> This Puritan petticoat-rumpler . . . can't fail to look bad to us, and our sympathy quite naturally will go first to the seduced girl--an orphan into the bargain, I forgot to say. It seemed to me necessary to bring the pair of lovers back into balance, that is, to blacken the victim and give her a Machiavellianism that

she does not have in the Arthur Miller play. ("I Want to Be Hanged" 240-41)

Thus, for instance, in Act One, Aymé invents a sequence in which Abigail surreptitiously spits on a cross and presents the fresh saliva on the holy icon as evidence of witchcraft (*Les Sorcières* 412). After discussing the cultural implications of Aymé's adaptation, the students decided Belgian audiences would probably not share the same viewpoint on adultery as the worldly Parisians and that we should remain faithful to Miller's vision of Abigail. We used the Belgian translation by Herman Closson as a base, modifying it whenever we could find a solution closer to Miller's meaning and style.

During rehearsals, our focus turned more towards artistic than cultural concerns. In one early rehearsal, however, a significant cultural issue arose. In the scene in which Biff tells Willy he's flunked math, the actor playing Biff asked why Biff says, "*Papa, je t'ai trahi*" (in Miller's text, "Dad--I let you down"). Anrieu pointed out to the director that extreme parental pressure to "succeed" is more an American than a European phenomenon; thus a European actor might not automatically identify with the anguish suffered by a child telling a parent he's failed a subject in school.

More cultural issues arose as we moved into technical rehearsals. I suffered mild culture shock when the Loman family refrigerator appeared--an obviously European model--and when Linda put bread boards rather than plates on the table and served Willy bread and jam for breakfast instead of bacon and eggs. However, remembering Miller's struggle to keep the Beijing Loman family Chinese, I decided not to insist on cultural authenticity. I could not restrain myself from objecting, however, when Willy's friend Charley wore his hat throughout the entire scene in Charley's office. This led to a useful discussion, with the student director insisting that Europeans picture American businessmen as wearing hats, and Anrieu pointing out that Frenchmen resent being stereotyped as wearing berets and carrying a loaf of French bread under one arm.

Following the week of performances in February 1987, the INSAS faculty participated in a detailed critique of each scene. Again, these discussions focused on artistic rather than cultural issues; however, it became clear that the most successful scenes were those in which student directors remained faithful to the primarily realistic style of

Miller's plays and did not overburden the text with directorial "concept." The directors who, like Miller with his Chinese actors, had concentrated on telling the story with simplicity and emotional honesty had not found cultural differences insurmountable barriers.

Paul Willems in Belgium

> *Are you exhausted from driving your locomotive? .... --come to Grand'Rosière, the most expensive luxury country inn in the land. At last! No bathroom, no electricity, no telephone, no television! At last! A tree in the living room ...*
>
> It's Raining

Concurrently with the Miller project, I continued my ongoing research on Belgian playwright Paul Willems. I first encountered Willems's work while studying Belgian theatre at INSAS as a Fulbright fellow in 1968/69. My translation of his play *La Ville à voile* (*The Sailing City*) subsequently served as my M.A. thesis and received its American premiere at the University of North Carolina/Chapel Hill. During the year prior to my sabbatical, professional staged readings of *Sailing City* were given at Ubu Repertory Theatre in New York and the Williamstown Theatre Festival. I had not, however, seen any of Willems's plays performed in Belgium.

That opportunity came when, during the fall of 1986, the Rideau de Bruxelles produced the seventh revival of Willems's 1962 play *Il pleut dans ma maison* (*It's Raining in My House*), staged by the original director, Pierre Laroche. Since I had gained insights into Miller's work that I could share with the INSAS students from directing my own production of *Crucible* in America, I attended about half of the *Il pleut* rehearsals to learn how a Belgian director would approach Willems's work. The two playwrights' styles contrast greatly, Miller's plays based in American realism and Willems's plays influenced by Belgian symbolism and surrealism. Just as some INSAS students struggled with Miller's realism, American actors often seemed uncertain how to embody Willems's poetic fantasy.

It's Raining in My House also has a particular resonance for Belgian audiences in that it refers, although metaphorically, to the difficulty of living in a dual-language nation. Willems is especially sensitive to the language issue since, as a Fleming writing in French, he has "always lived between two tongues" (Emond, Ronse, van de Kerckhove 13).

The dual-language problem derives from Belgium's history: the country which is now Belgium was dominated by various empires and only created as a separate nation by an international conference of major powers in 1830. As Jacques De Decker explains,

> Resistance to the occupying Dutch had elevated the usage of French to the language of power, and throughout the land which would become Belgium, the dominating classes expressed themselves in the language of Voltaire . . . and Napoleon. The first century of Belgium's history is . . . marked by a struggle of the Flemish population to obtain recognition of its identity. (2)

The French-speaking Walloon culture was initially economically dominant, with French the language of the elite, thus of educated and literary discourse. Two of the three "giants" of Belgian drama, Maurice Maeterlinck and Fernand Crommelynck, were Flemings who created their literary oeuvres in French, while Walloon Michel de Ghelderode was strongly influenced by the Flemish spirit.

However, during the sixties, economic superiority shifted to the Flemish side. The Belgians abandoned the Congo; and the failure of the coal mines, the source of Walloon wealth, led to social unrest. Concurrently, the Flemings staged a cultural revolt, not only agitating for political power but proclaiming their linguistic and literary independence. Art and literature became weapons in the cultural battle. The country eventually split into two linguistic "communities," the Flemish and Walloon, who developed separate governmental institutions under the central monarchy. It became "politically incorrect" for Flemish Belgians to write in French.

This linguistic political shift affected Paul Willems's work. Born in 1912, of Flemish ethnic stock, Willems spent his childhood at Missembourg, the family estate near Antwerp. Like his mother, novelist Marie Gevers, Willems was educated in French, which became his native language and means of literary expression. As the Fleming/Walloon battles heated up, however, Willems found himself in something of a cultural no-man's land, ostracized by the Flemish and only marginally tolerated by the Walloons.

Willems has written seventeen plays, several of which bear the imprint of the chateau Missembourg with its legendary ghost and gardens. Influenced by Romanticism, Willems celebrates nature as the source of intense sensory experiences which can open a passage to "lost paradise." Paradise, for Willems's, resembles an Edenic garden of childhood innocence, unsullied by modern civilization and man's inhumanity to man. Given Willems' cultural situation, it's quite understandable that his Romantic obsession with dualities interweaves with ambiguity towards the power of language--and frustration at the failure of human communication.

When a word has its habits, those habits don't change.

It's Raining

It's Raining portrays a "fallen" world fragmented into quarrelling polar opposites: man and woman, city dweller and country dweller, the old and the young, the living and the dead. The play is set in Grand'Rosière, an old country house, with a tree growing in the living room as an image of lost Eden. Fifty years ago, the tree was Aunt Madeleine's engagement tree, but when her fiancé George supposedly committed suicide after a lover's quarrel, she retreated to the city, leaving the estate to the benign neglect of the gardener, Bulle. The split between the archetypal male/female couple represents the "fall," and Grand'Rosière remains as the memory of paradise. But as the play begins, the heiress, young Madeleine, arrives to sell the estate so she can buy a condo in town. The action involves the efforts of those who love the old house to save it--including the ghost of George, unreconciled to his early death and determined to experience everything he missed in life, including womanly "warmth."

In the fallen world, language echoes the Tower of Babel, all the opposites speaking different languages. The country dwellers are stupefied by Madeleine's city argot of money, investments, and percentages. She, in return, is outraged by the fanciful speech of this "pack of impractical dreamers" who call a car a locomotive. Bulle's granddaughter Toune tortures her lover Thomas with "words that mean something other than what they mean," and the old gardener, knowing "a raven is not a raven," attempts to translate between lovers.

The fragmented world is restored to wholeness by a ritual of "everyday things," the reconciliation of the ghost couple George and

Aunt Madeleine. The healing on the archetypal level of the original male/female split is reflected on the mundane level: all the opposites are reconciled and the garden returned to its rightful owners. The play closes with Bulle's ode to the ephemeral, the ever-changing cycles of life, love, and death--and the reflections that allow us to see ourselves and thus to grow.

Reflections! The key to things! . . . Reflections that come and go and come again, that grow and fade, that dry out and get wet. Reflections that shimmer. And we, the living, need them even more than we need warmth.

It's Raining

I arrived at the Rideau's rehearsal room in the Palais des Beaux Arts eager to discover how Pierre Laroche, who knew this play so well, would guide the actors into the enchanted world of Paul Willems. I was also feeling concerned about how to play my observer role unobtrusively and, as always, timid about speaking French with strangers.

Pierre and Paul Willems began by reminiscing about the original production, and Paul explained how he got the idea for the play. During the war, a bomb fell, jarring Missembourg. That night, when Paul and his wife were in bed, it started to rain--in their bedroom. They hurriedly placed pots and pans to catch the drips. But then they heard the wonderful "music" of the rain, each drip a different tone according to the size and shape of the pan it struck. When Paul later wrote the play, he didn't set it during the war, but the music of rain in the house suggests the shift of viewpoint the play evokes.

Pierre told us he had encountered Zen for the first time this summer--the play is Zen! It has to do with being there, in the present moment, open to things. The "crazy" inhabitants of Grand'Rosière gradually "seduce" those competitive people who enter their world to a different view of life. "One can say this is a dream world," Pierre commented, "but in today's world of the computer, don't we need that dream?"

Everyone always forgets. The balance of things on things. A bird leans on its wings, its wings lean on the air, the air leans on the ground, and that's how beauty flies . . .

It's Raining

From the first read-through, I found myself captivated with the play, and when Paul Willems invited me to do the American adaptation, I accepted with delight.³ I attended as many rehearsals as my schedule at INSAS would allow, learning how each moment in the text could work in the theatre.

For instance, Pierre pointed out that the practical businesswoman, Madeleine, is the audience's entry point into the world of Grand'Rosière. The actress began by playing Madeleine too sympathetically; Pierre explained that she had to have "resistance" at the beginning, be "hard" and almost unlikeable. The audience starts out like her, saying "this isn't real, life isn't like this," and as she is gradually "seduced," so is the audience. So the acting must be subtle and the progression carefully managed.

In his work with the actors, Pierre emphasized rhythm and musicality. He asked the "Rosière" supporters to keep their phrases "open" at the end and Madeleine to "close" hers, pointing up the difference in character attitudes. For the "ghost supper," the reconciliation of Aunt Madeleine and George, Pierre demonstrated an otherworldly rhythm--floating and almost slow-motion. He also talked about the Flemish quality of Paul Willems's work, the quality that is sensory, sensual, visceral. Thus George's "Oh, life is . . ." required an "oh" involving the body down to the belly, whereas a French "oh" would stop with the upper chest.

Extremely precise with movement and rhythm, Pierre also proved open to actors' discoveries. He continually bounded into the scene to demonstrate business but warned the actors not to imitate him--he was just giving them a "feel" for the intention. And, in fact, he did create the atmosphere of the play with his own energy and sense of wonder.

When we moved into the theatre for technical and dress rehearsals, I discovered how Pierre integrated the audience into the production with business, originally improvised, that had become part of the play's "tradition." For instance, when rain starts falling in the house, Germaine and Toune rushed into the auditorium to hand out pots and pans to the spectators. Musician Ralph Darbo not only played his own original score on a variety of instruments but participated in fanciful business such as handing to Bulle the fabric "reflections" the old gardener fishes out of the lake.

By the time *Il pleut dans ma maison* opened on 23 December 1986, I had been transformed from a shy observer into a member of the Rideau's Grand'Rosière "family." I shared with the playwright, cast, and director the joy of watching the audience--many of whom had first seen the play as children and were now bringing *their* children--fall under Willems's magic spell. I also, at Willems's invitation, visited the model for Grand'Rosière, Missembourg. When I left Belgium for Omaha, I felt that in producing the American premiere of *It's Raining* with my own students, I would be building a personal as well as cultural bridge between my Belgian theatrical "family" and my American one.

Paul Willems in America

I discovered we've been told a lot of tall tales about the Other World. The truth is, Over There is just the reflection of Over Here.

It's Raining

Since I wanted my 1988 production of *It's Raining* to be a real cultural exchange, I arranged to bring two Belgian artists to Creighton University: Paul Anrieu and Ralph Darbo, the latter to perform with my student cast. Believing in the value of interdisciplinary as well as intercultural exchange, I also designed the project to explore ways in which theatre could assist in foreign language education. I involved our own Romance Language department and other state and local groups, as I furiously wrote grants to sponsor the guest artists.

Paul Anrieu arrived for a week's residency early in the rehearsal period. The primary focus of his visit was to provide oral proficiency workshops for French teachers, but he also sat in on *It's Raining* rehearsals. His presence brought home to the student performers that Belgium is *real*. I remember sitting onstage with Anrieu and the cast, the work lights casting shadows across our faces, as Paul talked about the dualistic Flemish sensibility, explaining that to a Fleming, the world of the spirit and of death, the "Over There" to which the ghost refers in *It's Raining*, is as true, as tangible, as the material world which the Fleming also experiences intensely.

Since Ralph Darbo's schedule--and the grant from the Belgian Ministry of Culture--didn't allow him to arrive until the week before we opened, we rehearsed feverishly. We knew many changes would occur as we integrated his Sandman character--and his music--into our performance.

Obviously influenced by Pierre Laroche's production but wanting to do my own exploration, I worked extensively with improvisation. Whereas I found the Belgian students initially resistant to realism, American students often feel uncomfortable with non-realistic styles. Darbo later commented on the differences between European and American performers, telling an interviewer that "French actors are much more intellectual. They can be brilliant but there is not always something emotional behind their action. Americans are emotionally based" (Drummond).[4] I used "realistic" Stanislavski exercises with which my actors were familiar, such as character biographies, scenes outside the play, and "inner monologue" work, to achieve believability and emotional identification. To work on style--and since "reflections" are an important symbol in the play--we made mirror exercises a staple of our rehearsal process. Thus we explored the characters' search to find their identity in the "mirror" of the Other and developed a style in which characters mirror one another's gestures, often unconsciously. The ending of the play only makes sense if the ritual of the ghost supper also heals the world of the living--if "Over There" and "Over Here" are mirror reflections--so we evolved an ensemble movement pattern whereby all characters simultaneously reflected the images in Bulle's closing speech. To concretize for us the frustration felt by the "opposites," who speak different languages, we did gibberish improvs. The combination of the Stanislavski work and the style work helped us enter a world in which characters have emotional depth but can also fish for reflections in a lake or get tossed through walls to "Over There."

Believing in the universality of the play (after all, America too has its wonderful old houses--and people who want to tear them down to build condos!), I chose not to localize the adaptation. We did, however, Americanize two of the characters: Mr. Doré, the wealthy old man who buys Grand'Rosière, became an obnoxious Texas oil man and his sexy young wife, Anaïs, a Marilyn Monroe type.

The evening of Ralph Darbo's arrival, we all took the night off from rehearsal to meet him at the airport. We greeted Ralph by blowing soap bubbles--since Bulle, in French, means "bubble"--then went out for a get-acquainted dinner.

With the arrival of Darbo, the issue of "speaking different languages" became a real one: Ralph doesn't speak English. Given that the play addresses this issue, we incorporated cross-cultural communication into the production--improvising interactions between the Sandman and other characters, sometimes in French, sometimes in English. Ralph sang one song in English and two in French; we provided translations in the program. For the student performers, working with Ralph offered a real-life experience of learning to communicate across linguistic barriers.

Ralph was our cultural ambassador, serving not only as an emissary of Belgium but of the Rideau de Bruxelles production and its traditions. Ralph's not speaking English didn't prevent him from following the action in our production or recognizing his cues, since, as he told an interviewer, he "knows the play by heart" (Delmont "Composer"). Having performed the play more than 340 times over a period of twenty-five years, Ralph embodied the very spirit of Grand'Rosière. He brought with him photographs from the latest Rideau revival, which we displayed in the lobby, and a tape recording of an earlier production. While the recording was in French, by now the actors knew the play well enough to follow along. Just as I'd tried not to impose the Belgian actors' characterizations on my American performers, I didn't encourage them to imitate the tape. However, the recording gave the cast insight into the directions I'd been giving about rhythm and style--and the importance of pace.

My intention to build a cultural bridge with this production was embodied symbolically in the set: a rustic wooden bridge at stage left led to a playing area in the auditorium. We borrowed some of the Rideau's traditional business to involve the spectators, such as handing out pots and pans when it rained, but added more direct audience address and some improvised business of our own. For instance, when our Texas oilman, Mr. Doré, went into raptures over his sexy wife, Ralph whooped a Belgian version of "yeehaw!" and waved a cowboy hat. Comparing the American to the Belgian production, Ralph told an interviewer:

> It's different, but wonderful. . . . It's funnier in English than in French. English is a more musical-sounding language. It is closer to the Flemish temperament of Willems, the playwright. French is more intellectual--but Anglo-Saxon language is earthier. (Delmont "Composer")

The cultural mix onstage was reflected in the house, as the performances attracted an inter-cultural audience. The Omaha Alliance Française sponsored a reception, and some of the French teachers who had participated in Anrieu's workshop brought students to see the play. Ralph also visited French classes in the Omaha schools, winning hearts with his charm and his guitar. I was pleased when the student newspaper's reviewer focused on the effectiveness of the cultural bridge:

> Creighton University's spring production is an invitation to cross a bridge and see what's on the other side. . . . In a play about bridges, Suzanne [Burgoyne] and her cast and crew have succeeded in bridging that one void that is the most difficult to span: an ocean. (Kokensparger)

Before our week-end run ended, we'd decided to revive the play the following fall--and to invite Paul Willems. Ralph now served as the Creighton *It's Raining* family's emissary, carrying back to Belgium photographs of our production and *It's Raining* T-shirts for Willems, Laroche, and Claude Etienne, the Rideau's artistic director. He also radiated enthusiasm for the American *It's Raining*, so with more grants from the Belgian Ministry and Nebraska sources, Ralph and Paul Willems joined us for an October 1988 revival. As we corresponded about the revival, Paul sent a letter of love and appreciation to the cast:

> Dear Friends from Grand'Rosière,
> Ralph came back from Omaha enthusiastic . . . I saw the photos, they made me want to know you . . . You have chosen a profession . . . that consists of bringing to your audience dreams, laughter, tears, and sometimes things even more precious: tenderness and love. I tried to put into *It's Raining in My House* my most cherished dreams. . . . And it has happened, when the play has been badly acted, that my dreams have been rejected. I felt then as if someone had rejected my outstretched hand. . . . I know that *you* not only communicated the theme to the audience, but that your talent, assisted by your youth, beautified your roles with a sort of joyous, happy glow.

I hope to see all of you in October in Omaha-Grand'Rosière in order to tell you that "a raven is not a raven," but you are a pack of fabulous actors, and that *"thank you is thank you."* (Willems, personal correspondence, my translation)

Paul Willems's presence made the October revival a very special occasion. Two other Willems translators flew to Omaha to join Paul and me on a Belgian theatre panel for the European Studies Conference at the University of Nebraska. We held post-performance discussions, and Ralph again visited local French classes. We were all thrilled when Paul compared the students' performances favorably with those of professional actors who'd played the roles and praised our stylistic blend of lyricism, comedy, and realism. The *Omaha World-Herald* review confirmed that Willems's poetic style could indeed work for American audiences:

> Director [Burgoyne] has fashioned a light, airy version of a play that is the purest of whimsy. The result is theatrical magic . . . Author Willems said in an interview backstage that the play was meant to touch or discover something sacred or divine for just a moment--and so it does. . . ."It's Raining in My House" is a humorous, oddly balanced tale whose whimsy carries a logic of caring for the right things in life--and in people. There is a childlike mood and a nudging, persistent suggestion that humans can live gentler lives, hear a different drummer, find music in ordinary things, discover other realities and be converted to less rigorous and selfish motives. (Delmont "Whimsy")

Conclusion

My experience as a visiting professor for the Miller project and my work with *It's Raining* both suggested that guest artists can bring a foreign culture to life for students in a personal way. *It's Raining* also demonstrated the contribution that inter-cultural theatre work can make to foreign language education. Anrieu, Darbo, and Willems received enthusiastic responses from all the teachers and students who interacted with them; and an evaluator for the Nebraska Committee for the Humanities wrote: "I am looking forward to any possible future

Suzanne Burgoyne

collaborations between the departments of Languages and Fine and Performing Arts, as this seems to me to be a very rich vein for educators to work" (Kestermeier).

Neither of my Belgian/American experiences was unadulterated delight; each had its share of catastrophes, problems--and plain hard work. Certainly, arranging residencies for guest artists can be a full-time job. Yet most of the difficulties I encountered were not cultural but the alas-too-normal problems attendant upon living in an imperfect world: actors--and directors--can get sick, fire inspectors can threaten to close your theatre, artists can disagree. Nor did I find a magical key to unlock the doors to all cultures. In fact, cultural concerns often receded into the background as we focused on artistic dimensions and the practical mechanics of getting the shows up.

What I did find was that culture seemed less a barrier than an exciting new territory to explore. As Miller suggests in *Salesman in Beijing*, there is a level of common humanity beneath cultural differences, a level which both Belgians and Americans sought in our texts and touched in each other. In the final analysis, these experiences were about *people*--artists learning from each other, inspiring each other with our love for the theatre and the joy (and sometimes the torment) we find in our work. After all, those of us who participated in these projects do share a common culture: that of the theatre itself.

Notes

1. One often finds foreign plays given their French-language premieres in Brussels rather than Paris. I asked the Théâtre National de Belgique archivist, Danielle De Boeck, the reason why, and she replied that Belgians are more "daring." Furthermore, since Belgian audiences are considered "difficult," Brussels productions serve as a European try-out for a play. Finally, Mlle. De Boeck suggested that Belgian translators tend to be more faithful to the original than their French counterparts. The Belgians, she said, are more "humble" (Personal interview). I would like to express my appreciation to Mlle. De Boeck for the research assistance she has provided, as well as to all the artists, students, and funding agencies who made both Belgian/American projects possible.

2. Thus, for instance, the Paris press interred a 1986 production of Shepard's *Buried Child*; Pierre Marcabru dismissed the play as "naturalistic peasant drama, as it was exported from Europe to New York at the beginning of the century. Since then, the Yankees have done nothing but quarry that vein" ("Drame paysan naturalist," my translation). For reviews of the Brussels premiere of *Salesman*, see, for example, *L'Unité, Le Soir, La Nation Belge*. The French and Belgian reviews I cite are collected in the TNB archives; page numbers are not available.

3. A British translation had just been published, but since British English is not the same as American English, Willems only granted the British translator rights for Great Britain. My adaptation differs considerably from the British version and benefits from the opportunity I had to observe the play in rehearsal.

4. Interviews with Darbo and reviews of *It's Raining* are collected in the archives of the Creighton Department of Fine and Performing Arts; page numbers are not available for the *Omaha World-Herald* and *Creightonian* sources cited.

Works Cited

Aymé, Marcel. "I Want to Be Hanged Like a Witch." Trans. Gerald Weales. *The Crucible: Text and Criticism*. Ed. Gerald Weales. New York: Penguin. 239-41.

---. adapt. *Les Sorcières de Salem. Arthur Miller: Théâtre*. Paris: Robert Laffont, 1959. 371-534.

Boyer, Paul, and Stephen Nissenbaum. *Salem Possessed: The Social Origins of Witchcraft*. Cambridge: Harvard UP, 1974.

Closson, Herman. "La Chasse aux Sorcières." Manuscript. Archives of the Théâtre National de Belgique, Brussels, 1954.

De Boeck, Danielle. Personal interview. 16 Aug. 1994.

De Decker, Jacques. "Belgium, a Country with Two Faces." *An Anthology of Contemporary Belgian plays, 1970-1982*. Ed. David Willinger. Troy, NY: Whitson, 1984. 1-5.

Delmont, Jim. "Composer Applauds Creighton Production." *Omaha World-Herald* 18 Apr. 1988.

---. "'It's Raining' Awash in Whimsy of Life." *Omaha World-Herald* 7 Oct. 1988.

Drummond, Sandy Bolam. "Brussels actor to perform in 'It's Raining.'" *The Creightonian* 30 Sept. 1988.

Emond, Paul, Henri Ronse, and Fabrice van de Kerckhove, eds. *Le monde de Paul Willems: textes, entretiens, études*. Brussels: Labor, 1984.

Kestermeier, Charles, S.J. NCH External Evaluator Questionnaire. 10 May 1988.

Kokensparger, Brian J. "An invitation to cross bridge." *The Creightonian* 15 Apr. 1988.

Lionel. "*La Mort d'un commis-voyageur* par Le Théâtre National." *La Nation Belge* 13 Mar. 1951.

Londré, Felicia. "Exposing the Translation Gap." *American Theatre* May 1988: 48-50.

Marcabru, Pierre. "Drame paysan naturaliste." *Le Figaro* 4 Dec. 1986.

Miller, Arthur. *Salesman in Beijing*. New York: Viking, 1983.

Paris, André. "Le Théâtre National crée *La Mort d'un commis-voyageur*." *Le Soir* 13 Mar. 1951.

"Un Commis-Voyageur." *L'Unité* 21 Mar. 1951.
Willems, Paul. *It's Raining in My House*. Adapt. Suzanne Burgoyne Dieckman. *Four Plays of Paul Willems*. Ed. Suzanne Burgoyne Dieckman. New York: Garland, 1992. 1-144.
———. Personal correspondence. Missembourg, Belgium. 20 May 1988.

Stanislavsky Meets Shepard at the Shchepkin
by Bonnie Gould

"Zdravstvuitie. Menya zavut Bonnie Gould."[1] (Hello. My name is Bonnie Gould.) This was about the only Russian I could speak, with any confidence in October 1992, so the fact that I was going to Russia to direct an American play in Russian was daunting. Russia was a Mecca for me, an actor whose training in the nineteen seventies was grounded in the Americanized Stanislavsky system. The Russian theatre tradition was a rich one, based on far more than what little I really knew of Stanislavsky, Meyerhold, the Moscow Art Theatre, and I wanted to know more. My sense of adventure was challenged.

The idea for the visit originated in March 1991, when nine representatives from the University of Tennessee-Knoxville Theatre Department faculty were invited to visit theatres and theatre training programs in St. Petersburg (then named Leningrad) and Moscow. The objective of the trip was to discover where educational exchange might be established between our institution and a Russian counterpart. Our host, the Russian arm of the International Theatre Institute (ITI), saw to it that we were graciously received by a dozen or so theatres. We were chauffeured to various theatres where we met and talked with whatever artistic staff was available. We learned of some of the problems, such as food shortages and black marketeering, which were the direct result of Mikhail Gorbachov's introduction of Glasnost and Perestroika. While these problems and policies were harbingers of the demise of the old system, for the Russian theatre they meant that the theatre was no longer fully subsidized by the state. State theatres would now have to deal with such concepts and problems of funding, sponsorship, and budgets. For example, we learned from one of the smaller theatres that during the Communist regime, they had enjoyed a full time repertory company of approximately forty actors. These actors were paid a living wage, mostly state subsidized. Now they had the same number of actors, but none could live on the salaries they received from the theatre because the government subsidy had been drastically cut. In fact, the subsidy was soon to be completely withdrawn.

Tours of the facilities revealed how resourceful these artists must be to create their art with extremely limited materials and equipment. Occasionally we sat in on a performance class or visited a shop where design or construction teaching was in progress. It was clear that these theatres had worked for a long time with less than a full complement of resources, even before the fall of the Communist regime and the loss of subsidy. At one theatre the scarcity of costume material was overcome by designing and making elaborate period costumes out of paper.

One of the last places that we visited was the Maly Theatre in Moscow, and its conservatory training organization, the Shchepkin Institute. The Maly Theatre, in spite of its name which means "small," is one of the largest and most well-established theatres in Moscow. It was originally part of the Bolshoi, which means "big," theatre. Mikhail Shchepkin was a contemporary of Stanislavsky and a well-known actor on the Russian stage. Shchepkin started the institute as a training and apprentice program of the Maly Theatre, which produced traditional Russian theatre. The Maly Theatre is situated in the center of the city, across the street from the Bolshoi. At the time of our visit the Maly was in the final phase of a major reconstruction. Caverns had recently been discovered under the foundation of the theatre and the structure was literally sinking. Once the reconstruction was completed, the Maly's gratitude and spirit were well expressed by dedicating the opening night performance to the workers and artisans who participated in the reconstruction.

The instructors of the Shchepkin Institute, most of whom were or had been employed as actors, directors or administrators in the Maly, were extremely gracious. They were proud of and committed to their theatre, theatre training program, and students. The exhibition staged for us by the third-year students was the best we had seen. The students' physical and vocal skills were highly developed. They were spontaneous and creative. Most impressive were their utter commitment, focus and naturalness, and unpretentious manners about their work. The Shchepkin students were curious about the American approach to theatre and theatre training and their questions were candid and revealing. One student asked, "Is it true that the acting student in America can choose his or her own classes and course of study?"

Another wondered, "Is it true that in America one can be an actor without any formal training?"

The competition for a place in their program is keen--more than 300 applications for each position. Once accepted they "belong" to the program. They are completely supported in the sense that they pay no tuition expenses, are given accommodations, and receive a stipend that provides for the most basic of quotidian needs. They have little choice in their curriculum, training or performance opportunities. The concept of a choice between conservatory and liberal arts training was difficult for them to understand, since the option does not exist in their country. But the idea that someone who wants to be an actor could come into a theatre or a theatre training program from another discipline, or from some years of working in another field, was simply incomprehensible. Yet despite the strictures of their system, I found these students to be the most open, curious and motivated group of young actors I had ever met. This was where I wanted to work.

Somewhere in America

The play I chose was Sam Shepard's *Curse of the Starving Class*, a play about the disintegration of an American family and its dreams. It seemed an appropriate choice: Shepard is a major American playwright; the characters are young (Ella and Weston can be in their thirties); the psychology and pace of the play is as different as possible from typical Russian drama. *Curse of the Starving Class* represents the naturalism phase of Shepard's writing, with absurd and surreal elements and explores the power—or curse—of inheritance. But more than this, through Shepard's play I wanted to explore and share with the Russian students and audiences how, for many, the American dream has gone awry. I wanted them to view this play in light of its relevance to the current economic, political and social conditions in Russia. If one sees Shepard's Tate family as a metaphor for cultural disintegration in the United States, were the parallels with Russia in 1992 valid? Would the Shchepkin students see and understand those parallels? My hope was that the Shepard text would remind us all that the disintegration of the family within both capitalism and communism is perhaps the ultimate human tragedy.

I was fortunate to discover that a Russian translation of *Curse of the Starving Class*[2] already existed. The translator, Russian born Eleni Simonov, had translated it in the nineteen seventies. She chose *Gde-te*

V Ameriki (Somewhere in America) as the Russian title, a choice I found curious. She explained that while the Russian people love their culture and their theatre, they positively devour anything having to do with the West in general, and with the United States in particular. A literal translation of the title *Curse of the Starving Class (Proklatye Goludieyisha Klase)*, Ms. Simonov explained to me, sounded too typically Russian and much too representative of the life of the Russian people. The argument made sense to me so it remained *Somewhere in America*. In fact, I discovered that this title was far more appropriate and communicative of what I wished to work on within the script than the title *Curse of the Starving Class*. That is, with all the freedom and democracy Americans have, we still are experiencing the disintegration of the family. Further, we consume more than our share of the world's resources and degrade or destroy our environment. Yet somewhere in America our undiluted and unfettered ideals and values remain untarnished. And ironically, with all that Russia is experiencing now with its "new beginning," the lessons to be learned from American mistakes are as important as those to be learned from our successes.

In the summer of 1992 I began my preparation for the Moscow production. In order to become familiar with the sounds, cadence and rhythms of the Russian text, I worked with a Russian student who read aloud the Russian script while I read along in both English and Russian. I wanted to be able to connect the specific Russian sounds and phrases to the critical moments as I understood and interpreted them in the English text. When questions arose over specific translation choices, we discussed possible reasons for those choices, which turned into lessons not only in Russian grammar and syntax, but Russian culture as well.

As a result, I had a fairly good idea of where I could anticipate at least some of the problems in the interpretation of text and character. I discovered that all of Shepard's coarseness and vulgarity, which is essential to the characters and to the story, were gone in the translation. "Pissing" became "urinating," "the curse" (menstruation) became "women's affairs," and so forth. Ms. Simonov informed me that this was partially due to the severe censorship that existed at the time the translation was done. It was also a function of the reverence the Russians have for the stage. Vulgarity was simply not appropriate. For the most part, however, the translation was fairly literal, which at first appeared to facilitate coordination between the English and Russian texts. I later discovered that the word-for-word translation presented problems for the actors in terms of contemporary accessibility and flow. After I took some rudimentary lessons in Russian grammar I was on my own.

I arrived in a cold and rainy Moscow on October 6 with our American set designer. He came for two weeks to address problems with the set and then to paint and dress it. Or so we thought. We sent sketches and a model of the set in February 1992 so that the Institute would have time to construct it and have it ready for rehearsal in October. This seemed ideal, since even in our professional theatre, the set is rarely ready and available for rehearsal at the beginning of the rehearsal process. Getting the materials to the Russians presented the first of many challenges, since the postal service was not very reliable. We learned later that even though we sent the model of the set by Federal Express, the Institute had to pay a "reception fee"--in reality, a bribe to receive the materials.

We arrived at the Institute the next day to see the performance space. This visit made me realize that my understanding of the exigencies of Russian theatre--and Russian life--was naive at best. The space was quite different from what we had understood from the hand-drawn sketches that gave some but not all dimensions. The set was designed for a larger proscenium space, which resulted in a raked platform coming out into the house nearly touching the first row of the audience. Fortunately it was workable that way, and, in fact, forced a breakdown of the fourth wall barrier which is standard in traditional Russian theatre. We did not realize that the production would be performed in repertory, which dictated an easily mounted and dismounted set. The set had been designed as permanent rather than moveable. On this day the Russian workers were trying to adapt it to a set that could more easily be mounted and struck. We also discovered that virtually nothing had been done on the set for there had been several other problems. Basic materials such as nails and hinges, were difficult to find. Additionally, Russian problem solving methods are different from those in the US. When Russian workers come up against a problem the response is to stop until someone comes in and solves it. Initiative and resourcefulness were rarely rewarded at the worker level.

The infrastructure of the daily Russian life has been quite literally crumbling for many years, and the mind-set is to expect something to be broken, or to break down, or not be available. The workers were being paid no matter what the outcome of their labors--one of the negative developments of the Russian version of the communist system. It was obvious that the designer would not be able to do any painting or set dressing. Not only was the set not constructed, but when the designer tried to describe and explain what he wanted, such as piles of dirt and farm debris around the stage, the response was, *"nie moshne"* or "not possible."

That evening I was introduced to the students: sixteen of them in their last year of training. The Shepard production was to be their diploma or final project. They performed a J. B. Priestley piece that had been directed by one of their major instructors to give me an idea of their types and talents. Though I could understand virtually none of the dialogue, the stage pictures were arresting and the honesty, commitment and believability of the actors on a kinesthetic level were impressive, reminiscent of the presentation these young actors had given us on our first visit to the Maly.

The two major instructors had cast the show but I could, of course, make any changes I wished. Their casting was nearly opposite my interpretation of the characters. I agreed with only one of their casting choices. It was obvious that their casting came out of a completely different understanding and interpretation of the characters and the text. I appreciated their concern and intention, which was to help facilitate and streamline my work. From another perspective, the instructors had a much better sense of their students' strengths and capabilities than I, so it made sense that they would try to help me. The instructors told me to come back the next day with my cast list. Since there were only nine roles and sixteen students, the instructors asked me to consider double casting some of the parts so that the entire class could be involved. When we discussed this further, however, we decided that given the time and language constraints this again would be *"nie moshne"* ("not possible").

For the most part I stuck to my instincts in spite of the instructors' concerns that I was going to have problems with some of my choices. I didn't. It was one of those rare times in life when events happen in just the right configuration, just the right people get together and things work. I was sure that the impressions I had formed of these students back in March 1991 would be substantiated. The students were excited about the prospect of this new experience. They were hungry and eager for any kind of contact with the West, so the prospect of working with an American on an American play was enticing. Their enthusiasm, training and discipline were obvious. As far as I was concerned, there was no wrong casting choice possible.

One problem I had not anticipated--that I would not have an interpreter--turned out to be resolved fortuitously. Dima, the student playing Weston (the father) was a tall, lanky twenty-year-old who spoke German about as well as I did. Katya the student playing Emma (the daughter) was a twenty-one-year-old mignon who spoke French. Another young woman for whom I created a small non-speaking role (Ellis's girlfriend) spoke English. Since I had no other interpreter, I had to make sure that at least one of the three was called at every rehearsal.

The "normal" rehearsal period in their country is more a matter of months than weeks. Since the government had supported nearly all theatres, there really was no need to rush into anything; frequently companies would rehearse for months, sometimes years, before opening a show. In addition, the Russian tradition of theatre is so strong and so well established that the public knows to check daily the kiosks, found on almost every corner throughout the city, where playbills and schedules are displayed. It was questionable to them that I would be able to mount anything resembling reality on the stage for two reasons: one, I only had seven weeks of rehearsal time; and two, I was a woman.

And thus began a wonderful, frustrating, exciting, grinding and intensive seven weeks of full and productive work. Through the play and the process of rehearsal these young actors had the opportunity of learning about, exploring and experiencing an American perspective, and through discussions and arguments, we all shared our different perspectives on the hard realities of the world. But even more importantly, throughout the whole process, we came to define our separate worlds as not so separate at all.

The Process

Rehearsal hours were left to me. I could have the students for as many hours per day as I wished, with one condition. They must attend their dance and history/literature classes. Our first full week of rehearsals was spent talking about what they thought it meant to be an American. In order to play Americans it was necessary to explore who they are, as a people and as individuals, a good bit more fully than any of these young actors had been able to do through the limited information available to them. Only one cast member, who spoke

English, had been to the States, but even her impressions were relatively superficial.

At first they were all very reticent to say anything, and when pushed only spoke of the States in the most glowing terms:

"America is the place where dreams can come true." "The United States is a country of plenty." "Things work in your country." "Everyone has at least one car." "You work all the time and make much money." "Everything that is important in the world today happens in America."

Eventually, we began to talk about the issues addressed in the play: the dissolution of the American dream, the unhealthy state of the American family and the society as a whole, the parallels of spiritual starvation in America with physical and psychological starvation in Russia. A poignant and somewhat prophetic observation came from Katya, the young woman who spoke French and played Emma. She was concerned that neither she nor any of her children would see a better life than they have at present. In many ways, she said, it may well be worse. At the end of the discussion I asked them, "If you had the choice right now of where you could live and have a better life, knowing everything you know about my country and yours, where would you choose?" Without exception they responded "Russia." There was enormous pride in the great spirit and heritage of the Russian people. They believed that the depth of the Russian soul and their understanding and appreciation of culture, art and literature was an effective counterbalance to their privation. I came to agree with them.

We began the process of putting the play on its feet, but our dialogue never stopped. Normally, I could only handle about six or seven hours of rehearsal, given the constant strain of shifting languages and the need to do so much explaining of an American response or reaction to a given moment or event, considerably different from the Russian.

One of the first and most valuable phrases I learned while working with them was *"Bis pauze"* which meant "Without pause." In most of the traditional Russian theatre I had seen, the thought process seemed to be as important as the dialogue. By that I mean it is given equal time and weight. While I am not suggesting that thought process is not important in American theatre--quite the contrary--I am suggesting, and did suggest to my young actors, that either Americans think faster or not quite so thoroughly as Russian actors. It makes sense when societal circumstances are taken into consideration. These students had spent their lives working and negotiating in a world where things were falling apart. Their lives were filled with pauses--pauses to renegotiate, to re-evaluate, to reconnoitre how to accomplish basic daily tasks. They could take nothing for granted. They could rely on very little to be the same--working or broken, open or closed, available or not--from one day to the next. Precious little came easily to them. Processing and dealing with this unpredictable lifestyle made the pace of their life slower, and, perhaps in order to survive, more internal than their American counterparts.

My teaching and coaching experience served me well. It was a challenge to teach Americanisms--physical gestures, speech inflections, carriage, tempo and rhythms. In addition to inflection differences, I discovered that many simple, or seemingly simple expressions, gestures or stances are culture-specific. Katya (Emma) found it difficult to widen her eyes as an American teenager might do, or cock her head defiantly in response to Ella or Wesley. When I asked Dima (Weston) to lower his center to create a sense of being beaten down, he found it not only uncomfortable but disrespectful to his instrument. In that same vein, in the opening scene between Ella and Wesley, I asked Gleb (Wesley) to put his feet on the table. We borrowed a red and white checked tablecloth from one of the instructors and Gleb was horrified that he should put his feet on it. I finally persuaded him to do it and immediately he put his feet back on the floor and apologized to the table and to the absent instructor. And Anya (Ella) was horrified that she would need to appear on stage in the first scene, stockingless. It was considered coarse for a woman to be on stage bare-legged.

At first it seemed incongruous that with all their physical training--dance, wushu, combat, even some Alexander work--they were far less flexible and free in their movement and their range of movement than the typical American acting student. But upon reflection, this should not be surprising when one considers the milieu in which they have lived. Freedom of expression and individuality, which we take for granted, has been suppressed. Also, their training was a product of a highly regimented system. Why shouldn't this manifest itself in terms of limited body language and less-than-open physical expression? But the task at hand was to guide them as close as possible to expression through the American perspective.

As well-trained and disciplined as these actors were, they were, nonetheless, teenagers and young adults. They had the same passions and agonies as any young American actor I have worked with. It was uncanny how their concentration seemed to come and go. On one particular day, well into the process, I was convinced their minds were somewhere in Siberia. However, frequently what I mistook for lack of focus or concentration was simply a completely different mode of working, of processing the material, of incorporating the new elements of the work into their minds and bodies. Some of the apparent lack of discipline and focus comes from the relaxation and comfort inherent in the Russian theatre, where the cast is accustomed to spending many months on one play.

Rehearsals can last anywhere from three hours to ten hours a day, six days a week, and the opening happens when the director determines the production is ready. One rehearsal, particularly frustrating for us all, was when Anya (Ella) seemed to stumble over every other word. She had been working on the text for three weeks and could not manage to speak her lines in the same order twice in a row. She excused herself, saying she had never had such a difficult time learning and memorizing lines. When we discussed it further, she decided that it was because the logic behind the words, the connective tissue between the lines, was so un-Russian. Occasionally one of the actors would say a line and the others would snicker. We stopped and discussed the joke. Inevitably, the translation was so stilted that in today's jargon, the "real" meaning was something quite different. We re-worked some of the phrases in order to provide the characters with a more colloquial context instead of literary Russian.

Encouraging the students to incorporate American inflection into their delivery created another difficulty. At one rehearsal they just giggled when I asked them to end a question with a rising inflection. They made valiant efforts at the new inflection, but they again laughed. It just sounded and felt funny, they said. It seemed contradictory that rich and well-trained voices be trapped into such a narrow range and constant downward inflection pattern.

In true American fashion, I took notes during rehearsals and at the end of each day's work I gave notes on the character and acting choices that the students had or had not made. I found it curious and somewhat disconcerting that I never once saw any of the actors writing anything down. When we came back to the same scene, I often gave the same notes again. Perhaps they were testing me to make sure that I really meant what I had said previously. Or perhaps, since they normally have such a luxuriously long rehearsal period, notes had never been necessary before this because they worked the scene or the moment in so many different ways before settling on the best choice. At one rehearsal, working on the first scene in act 2 between Weston and Wesley, I asked Dima (Weston) and Gleb (Wesley): *"Pochemu skazats?"* ("Why do you say that?") *"Pochem dielats?"* ("Why do you do that?"). Frequently, the answer came back: *"Ya niez niyou."* ("I don't know"). I responded with, "But you must know!" As the actor you must understand why you say something or do something or move somewhere. You must be able to analyze what each moment or beat is about in order to connect it to your overall journey through the given moment, beat, and scene.

It sounded perfectly Stanislavskian to me. Again the response was: *"Nie panimyiou lojeek."* ("I don't understand the logic.") That the Cyrillic alphabet derived from the ancient Greek alphabet did not mean the Russians embraced western logic derived from ancient Greece. The thought processes of these American characters in Shepard's play eluded the Russian players. This made the script difficult to memorize since they could not develop a "logical" connection between one moment and the next, between one line and the next.

It became clear fairly early in the process that many of the remaining design elements would either be my responsibility or be undertaken by the students. To underscore the text I chose music by Tracy Chapman and Bruce Springsteen, (both of whose songs were known and admired in Moscow).[3] In order to use the cassette recordings that I had brought along, it was necessary to re-record and splice the music onto a reel-to-reel tape. There were other challenges. We did not have a lighting designer, few instruments and no gels. With some assistance from the lighting technician at the Maly, I designed a basic lighting plot. I had the foresight to bring a 4-H tee-shirt with me for Emma, but what I had not considered was that she must exit to ride her horse and return in the same shirt, torn, tattered and muddy. So much for my western logic! A green tee-shirt was impossible to find, much less one with the 4-H emblem. The students were quick to respond with their own ingenuity. They immediately found some paint, a brush, and created a second 4-H shirt that even I could not tell was a copy.

Ten days before the first of three "openings" (one for the instructors, one for the Institute officials and students, and one for the public) I learned that the students would have to paint the set.

Moreover, the paint that had been procured with some difficulty from the Maly Theatre, was not the green and brown that the designer had intended (to create the illusion of weathered wood), but white, as his model had shown. When I tried to communicate this, the instructors assured me that white was a far better choice, indicating a classical look. So white it remained. The refrigerator, an essential prop in the play, was a small non-functional, rusted-out icebox, which we also painted white and rigged with a light. The non-functional stove had no burners, so Max (Ellis) brought in his hot plate and rigged it to cook the eggs and bacon.

As the opening(s) drew near the sense of excitement was palpable. The level of expectation on both sides of the footlights was high. No one had ever seen or smelled eggs and bacon cooking on stage. The refrigerator was filled with cans of American food products transported by my husband in a large, leaden suitcase. The minds of most of the faculty at the Institute were filled with doubts about anyone, much less a woman, being able to produce anything resembling life in seven short weeks of work. Teachers trained in the old school, fully convinced that no "American *Woman* director, with kind eyes" could produce anything in such a short time, were reticent to call it a success, but a success it was. The response from the audience was enthusiastic and proof that the actors had been able to create rich, multi-dimensional characters. The young cast performed with pride and confidence. They had gone through a grueling process. I am sure they found the pace unrelenting and demands upon them at times overwhelming. But there was a freedom in their bodies that was not present at the beginning of the process. Watching them perform, I could believe that they were "Americans" living an American life on stage. The absence of technical and design elements actually enhanced the performance, putting the focus completely on the actors and their world. And the fact that they were able to create such believability without the help of sophisticated costume, set and lighting elements is testimony to their physical and vocal presence of their work. Despite the difficulties these young Russians and I had all travelled together somewhere in America.

Somewhere in Russia

The Russian scene, economically and politically, was a horror story. It seemed that the life there was even worse than what was reported here. In 1992 inflation rose from 300 rubles/$1 US in October to 475 rubles/$1 US by the time I left in December. The average worker earned nearly $22 US a month with prices rising some 500 percent over the past year. Their buying power had been destroyed. I don't know how they managed to live, although the dollar is commonly used, quite openly these days. People traded almost as freely and readily in dollars as they did in rubles.

Corruption was rampant, and anyone who had any connections anywhere in the government took full advantage of them in order to survive. One day I visited the students' dance class where they were studying classical ballet. Katya (Emma) was doing her bar routine and I noticed that the only reason her ballet slippers stayed on her feet was because she had tied a string around the sole and the slipper. She explained to me later that even if she could afford a new pair, (300 rubles or $1.00 US) she could not find them to buy, except on the black market. The black marketeers (many of them young boys and girls who should have been in school) were everywhere. They hovered around exchange booths, in front of the Bolshoi, roamed the Arbat (the arts and crafts street in Moscow), selling everything from tee-shirts to communist memorabilia to matrioska dolls.

The more I learned and experienced of the typical Russian life, the more astounding it became that something as "unnecessary" or "frivolous" as theatre happened at all. As impoverished as the Russian people are in terms of material goods, consumer products and even daily essentials, they are without exception the most generous and warm people I have ever known. They are willing to share anything and everything they have. One day we had an early rehearsal. Max, the young actor from Siberia who played Ellis, asked me if he could leave rehearsal just a few minutes early. He had received a phone call from his grandmother in Siberia telling him that she had sent him a package and it would arrive at the train station that day. As he left he invited me to his room after rehearsal. When I arrived, he and other cast members had prepared a veritable feast of traditional Russian food. It was the entire contents of his grandmother's package of preserved pimentos, beet salad, potato and eggs, traditional Russian black bread and biscuits which the students had prepared on a hot plate and laid out on a six-by-eight-foot piece of plywood which all but filled Max's room. We ate and drank Russian beer, and sang Russian songs until after midnight. Never in other travels have I been so warmly received. Being welcomed into the lives of people who endure, by American standards, such difficult and uncertain times, created a relationship between us strong enough to bridge miles and years.

Notes

1. Russian language in this chapter is rendered phonetically.
2. The translation appears in *Sovremennaya Dramaturgiya*, No. 2, 1992.
3. From Springsteen I used "Mansion on the Hill," "State Trooper," "Johnny 99," and "My Father's House" from his "Nebraska" album. From Chapman I used "Talkin' 'Bout a Revolution," "She's Got Her Ticket," "Baby Can I Hold You," "If Not Now," "Across the Lines," and "Mountains of Things," from her album "Tracy Chapman."

On the Edge: Utrecht, Netherlands 1993
by Susan Vaneta Mason

In the late sixties and seventies, Augusto Boal was developing his "Theatre of the Oppressed" in Latin America. Its goal was to change the people, the spectators, into active participants in a process-oriented workshop. Participants became the playwrights, actors and directors.

At about the same time, a similar kind of theatre was introduced into communities in Asia and Africa. Eugene van Erven describes the background and current practice of some Asian versions of this kind of theatre in his book *The Playful Revolution: Theatre and Liberation in Asia* (1992). He uses the term "Theatre of Liberation" to describe process-oriented, political theatre from the developing world. He describes Theatre of Liberation in the Philippines, South Korea, India, Pakistan, Indonesia and Thailand and suggests a model of the process that, with cultural variations, is shared by the Asian countries he investigated. That model was the underlying structure of *On the Edge*, an international theatre project van Erven designed and coordinated in Utrecht, Netherlands in February and March 1993 and for which I served primarily as dramaturg. The subjects of our project were immigrants, especially third-world immigrants in the Netherlands. It was part of a larger symposium-lecture series, collectively titled "The Edge of Existence," which addressed survival strategies of people living in extreme conditions in areas outside the Netherlands.

Those of us who are dominant culture, western trained, politically active educators and theatre practitioners may want to replicate process-oriented theatre which reflects our politics, but are enticed by production both because of our indoctrination and the economic realities of our theatre practice. We usually can't get funding if a project isn't realizable as a final salable product. Furthermore, collective creation which is a basic component of Theatre of Liberation, is rarely part of our training and is even harder to attempt when the collective is a group of strangers from several different countries with different aesthetic values and without a common goal. Nevertheless, I believe what we ultimately achieved in Utrecht was a first-world effort at a process-oriented workshop as well as an inquiry into immigration and racial attitudes in the new Europe and among our participants, aesthetic values and methods in conflict and agreement, intercultural communication failures and successes, and many things we never dreamed we would be addressing. If Karl Jung was right and "it is through detours and wrong turns that we reach wholeness," then *On the Edge* was part of a journey to wholeness for all the participants.

This chapter is a description of the creation and completion of the multicultural, international project, *On the Edge,* and an evaluation of the process.

I began corresponding with Eugene van Erven early in 1992 when one of my students at California State University, Los Angeles was on an ISEP exchange at Utrecht University where van Erven teaches in the American Studies program. My student was also part of the International Theatre in Education program at the art academy, Hogeschool voor de Kunsten in Utrecht (HKU), and I was corresponding with them as well. I was subsequently awarded a Fulbright Lecture Grant for one semester (January to May) in 1993 to teach U.S. Ethnic Minority and Women's Theatre in American Studies at Utrecht University with van Erven as my host colleague. My Fulbright was also structured to include some work at the HKU with the new International Theatre in Education class.

Early in October 1992, van Erven found out from Kate Delaney, the Cultural Attache at the U.S. Embassy in The Hague who had supported my Fulbright award, that the State Department could fund bringing an American writer to the Netherlands. Van Erven recommended Elroyce Jones, an African-American playwright who had just completed a summer with Lloyd Richards at the O'Neill Playwrights Conference workshopping his play, *A Thimble of Smoke.* Van Erven had been a guest journalist at the O'Neill and had watched Jones in rehearsal. He was impressed with the strong similarities between the dialect and life in rural Mississippi in the fifties as portrayed by Jones in *Thimble of Smoke* and the Dutch Caribbean and Surinam. He also admired the speed with which Jones wrote and rewrote, and his gift as a storyteller. This and the fact that there are no full-time minority playwrights in the Netherlands were primary reasons for considering Jones an ideal playwright for the project van Erven was formulating.

Also, in the fall of 1992, the Studium Generale, a cultural division of Utrecht University, in collaboration with the Intercultural Center RASA, created "The Edge of Existence" (*"De Rand van het bestaan"*) lecture series. At the center of this symposium were eight lectures: four on traditional communities in extreme natural conditions (Amazon Indians, Inuit, Nomads of Central Asia, and the Tuaregs in Niger) and four on marginalized populations in megacities (Madras, Cairo, Sao Paulo, and Los Angeles). I was invited to give the lecture on Los Angeles and chose to focus on immigrant women, especially Latina street vendors. Films, music, lectures, and exhibits were part of this entire two-month event at RASA.

Once my Fulbright and Jones's guest visit were assured, van Erven proposed the creation of a play which would culminate in a staged reading at RASA as part of "The Edge of Existence" project. This theatre piece was to be developed using the Asian Theatre of Liberation model. The international class at the HKU was enlisted to collect stories from immigrants in the Netherlands which were workshopped in scenes, monologues, and acting exercises under van Erven's and my guidance. Jones arrived after several weeks to write the final script and I worked as dramaturg. The working script was given a staged reading at RASA with the HKU students as actors. In addition, some of van Erven's students at Utrecht University contributed their time and talents as stage manager, production assistants and composer-musicians. Furthermore, van Erven found partial funding to have the entire process video taped by Stichting Ocean Film, a professional company in Utrecht, with Cecile van Eijk as Producer, Sherman de Jesus as Executive Producer, and Hanneke Portier-Cox, a Dutch-American-Indonesian filmmaker living in Austin, Texas, as director. The completed educational video is called *The Storytellers* and focuses on the process of creating the play, *On the Edge*. Both the video and the script are primarily in English.

The Asian model described by van Erven is a three-part phased cumulative workshop: "1) a 'get-to-know-you' group interaction phase; 2) a structural analysis phase in which local stories and social problems are extracted from the participants; and 3) basic theatre training, followed by a production of a script written by the workshop participants and performed by local actors for a local audience." In addition, van Erven describes a pre-workshop phase which involves the workshop trainers "investigating the social, political, economic, and cultural conditions of a community" (20).

Our project differed from the Asian model in several significant ways. First, the larger community of our project was the immigrant community in the Netherlands, which, given the size of the country and the diversity of cultures is extremely heterogeneous. The immediate community (HKU students, production and video teams, van Erven, Jones and myself) was also disparate. When we began, I had been in the Netherlands for only three weeks. Three weeks later Jones arrived. Most of our student/participants didn't live in Utrecht and commuted from different parts of the Netherlands. They consisted of three young English women on a one-year exchange at the HKU, one Irish migrant, three Dutch women who had lived abroad (England, France and Zambia), one Dutch woman who was mixed race with a mother from the Dutch Antilles and a Dutch father, and one young black man from Curacao. Most of the production team commuted to Utrecht as well. Even our rehearsal space changed often. Creating a community under these conditions was inordinately difficult.

Another major difference in our project was that the student actors were asked to get stories from immigrants in the Netherlands, and, with a few exceptions, their own stories were not the material for the play. Furthermore, they were not actor-playwrights since an actual playwright was part of the project. So as workshop trainers, van Erven and I were coordinating two tiers of participants: student actors with a playwright and the immigrants who were in turn their subjects.

Finally, in the Asian examples described by van Erven, the participants eagerly and willingly participate in Theatre of Liberation workshops. With our project some of our student actors were neither enthusiastic nor committed to either the process or the intention of the project. This may have been because it *wasn't* their stories being told and because as students their class was *assigned* to do the project; they didn't choose it. Several of the students were also uncomfortable dealing with the potentially explosive issues of race that would inevitably play into their research as well as their acting. This became the most problematic aspect of the project. We were never really able to negotiate this obstacle satisfactorily and hence kept struggling with the students' motivation and their frustrated yearning for collective empowerment. Because of the external pressure to create a presentable product, because of the strong desire of the students to publicly manifest themselves as artists, because we did not want to use the students' stories but tales from immigrants, and because, as it turned out, Jones was unable to process the material the students had collected, frustration affected the process much more than was desirable.

Prior to the first meeting with the HKU students I began learning about the immigrant community in the Netherlands by studying Dutch at a language institute. All the students were immigrants, most from Turkey, Morocco, Iran and Iraq, and a few from Eastern Europe. Van Erven began contacting local immigrant organizations. He also arranged a meeting with Rufus Collins, the artistic director of De Nieuw Amsterdam (DNA), Holland's foremost multicultural theatre company. Although it was never realized, we originally hoped to work with both DNA and HKU student actors.

I also read several of Elroyce Jones's plays which he had sent to van Erven. My dramaturgical training and experience emphasize working *with* a playwright so I wanted to understand Jones's style of writing in order to assist him. On the other hand, I knew our project would focus on interviews with immigrants in the Netherlands and was part of a larger symposium on survival. So I saw my role primarily as dramaturg to the *project* and secondarily dramaturg to the *playwright*.

One of my biggest questions before Jones arrived was how would he use the students' research? Would he fictionalize the people and their stories or create a kind of docu-drama? My frame of reference for a theatre piece evolving out of interviews with individuals was Anna Deavere Smith's *On the Road*, a non-linear collage of personal stories around a theme or incident, with Smith enacting real people of various races and both genders. My other principal frame of reference for the kind of theatre I hoped we would create was the San Francisco Mime Troupe, especially the collaborative aspect of their working methods and non-traditional casting.

Jones's scripts were totally unlike my models. They are poetic realism. They would not lend themselves to non-traditional casting. But I understood Jones was extremely flexible and open to suggestions. He has written over a hundred plays and enjoys experimenting with style. Because of our nine actors, eight were women and seven were Caucasian, I knew we needed to address issues of race and gender as soon as we met with the students; I was committed to a production which would lend itself to non-traditional casting or we would be too limited in whose stories we could tell. Also, the directors of the theatre in education program at HKU had planned on touring the finished piece to Dutch highschools and pressed us to commit to a theme before we began. This was the first of several communication breakdowns due to language and training methods. I understood our "theme" to be about surviving under extreme conditions, but the HKU wanted a theme they could capture in one spacial image/symbol that their students could more easily "play" with in the theatrical sense. Because Jones wouldn't arrive for at least a month, and we had yet to begin the research, I tentatively suggested the theme "home." What is home? The manuscripts of Jones's I had read were sentimental, intimate, loving and domestic. I felt the theme of home would appeal to him without restricting him or us and was easily translatable into any immigrant experience. When we conferred with him in a transatlantic call he was enthusiastic about this choice. So was the HKU.

Just before we started working with the student actors, we discovered the lack of a central office, workshop and telephone was making communication between van Erven, the HKU director, Ton van Vlijmen, and myself unnecessarily complicated. None of us had answering machines. We needed a stage manager with an office who could coordinate and facilitate communications. Nico Poppes, a former student of van Erven's, volunteered and quickly became the stable center of the entire project. He is also a talented musician and accompanied the staged reading.

During the first three weeks (February 1-19) we tried to get to know one another, investigate the social and cultural conditions of the immigrant community in the Netherlands, and conduct the research. We eventually realized we should have spent more time familiarizing ourselves with one another and ideally Jones would have been with us from the first day. If we were to become a community, the whole group had to share the process.

We began with introductions and games: what home meant to each of us through collages, songs and objects. We interviewed each other and drew each other's faces. We had guest speakers from immigrant organizations: Rubina Boasman of Antillean self-help network, Bazhan Karpata, and Ina Rotsburg of the Utrecht Municipal Office for Recent Immigrants. We were given advice about interviewing by a journalist,

Ruud Buurman of *Utrechts Nieuwsblad*, a large regional daily, who had just come back from Ghana where he had interviewed prospective migrants about their vision of Holland and Europe in general as well as what migration schemes were most common for Africans wanting to find work in western Europe.

At this point several students expressed concern that the project was about race and they were not comfortable with that subject. The media had been examining racism in the new Europe from various perspectives and the subject was, they felt, explosive, exploitive and redundant. Neither van Erven nor I agreed. To our dismay we discovered several weeks into the project that the HKU had forgotten to give their students the four-page concept description created by van Erven and agreed upon by the HKU teachers. I had met the students briefly a few days before we began working with them but because of teaching commitments and the administrative chores of the project, van Erven was unable to meet the HKU students prior to the project to inform them of the details. We erroneously assumed they knew the purpose of the project. This further complicated and confused our efforts to instill enthusiasm in the students.

Furthermore, the students felt the project was not *theirs*. Their training encouraged them to create theatre pieces out of their own experience. They were also extremely concerned about protecting the individuals they interviewed so they wouldn't feel exploited. By the time we completed the project, one actor, a young woman from England who had been especially concerned about protecting the subjects, said she hadn't realized how eager people are to have their stories told, or how fertile a source of script development this could be.

Some of the students preferred doing library research on immigration in Holland and didn't want to do personal interviews. Others made telephone contacts and went into immigrant homes with tape recorders and sometimes camera crews for the video portions. All these visits were made with the permission of the immigrants being interviewed.

The HKU wanted plenary sessions once a week, led by Bodine de Walle, one of the faculty at the HKU, to review what each student had done during the previous week, to discuss problems that had arisen, and for the students to talk about how they felt about the work. I found these sessions enormously uncomfortable and counter-productive. Communication between participants in a collaborative project is obviously essential, but van Erven and I thought the purpose of our project was set at the outset whereas the students wanted to continue negotiating the focus. Levels of enthusiasm varied. Some meetings were tense. One stormy meeting, about a week before Jones arrived, revealed that the students wanted to redefine the whole project so it addressed how anyone makes a home anywhere.

The video director, who was at this meeting, had singled out three of the students to follow more than the others. Some of the remaining students were upset that they had not been chosen and began expressing disapproval about the video documentation. They noted, with intense resentment, that the video project was focused on immigrants who were people of color and they did not like that. The video director explained that her funding was based on the subjects of immigration and race. Whereas we had some flexibility in developing the theatre piece (albeit less than the students wanted), film and video are less flexible media than theatre. The demands of the video, which had become an integral part of the project by now, had an inevitable effect on the process. This was the price we paid for professional documentation, the value of which is indisputable, but if all participants do not share this conviction, it can disturb the process.

Van Erven and I reminded the students that the project was part of a larger program on surviving under extreme conditions which suggested third-world immigrants rather than first-world and therefore primarily focused on people of color. The theme of home I had suggested several weeks before was obviously too vague and allowed far too much interpretative latitude. Van Erven and I were determined to get back to the original concept. The students finally agreed after we showed them the four-page concept and project description van Erven had written in November 1992, which most of them had never seen. But some students remained resentful to the end.

The second phase (February 22-March 13) began with the arrival of Elroyce Jones from New Market, Alabama. He was caught up in a swirl of phone calls from producers and directors in the United States wanting rights to the script he had workshopped that summer at the O'Neill. He had never been produced professionally but had performed in scenes from his scripts at churches and schools in his community. He had acted in Los Angeles in the sixties, held a variety of jobs, and is a natural storyteller.

Various students took Jones with them into different immigrant communities in the Netherlands. Van Erven took him to visit an

Antillean family with van Erven's Aruban wife, Ria, as a translator. This visit eventually provided the seed for the play Jones wrote.

Although the students created monologues out of their research and we played with improvisational exercises, it became apparent that Jones was going to write his own play. He had always written by himself, in isolation, and didn't translate the exercises, which he watched, into a script. I think this was less a conscious choice not to use the research material than it was Jones's understanding of what kind of play he was expected to write and his method of writing. He had, during his first week, developed impressions of each of the student/actors and the play he wrote during his second week in Utrecht, taken from the experience of the Antillean family he visited, had specific roles written for each of the students--a play with eight female characters and one African male. Although that play, *The Threaded Sand*, could have been developed in workshops, the students, van Erven and I felt that their research had not been used and the play deviated too much from the original intention.

Van Erven and I asked Jones if he would write several scenes, in various locations, with different characters, and condense *The Threaded Sand* into one episode. Jones is a fast writer and remained enthusiastic and agreeable throughout this process. He created about eight scenes and one-acts over a four-day period of constant writing. These scenes were set in Dutch locations van Erven and I suggested.

The hardest part of this phase of the project was finding the means of translating the students' research into exercises to quickly communicate people and their stories to Jones. None of us was experienced enough in collaborative theatre making. Furthermore, when we tried to improvise scenes around people the students had interviewed, we found we immediately fell into cultural stereotypes. We were confronted with the painful awareness that even though we regarded ourselves as uncommonly knowledgeable about other cultures, translating that intercultural vocabulary into theatre is a different and difficult matter. It would have been useful to spend more time and exercises exploring our own cultural boundaries. This was potentially the most fruitful phase of the project.

When we began phase three (March 13-19) we were one week from the staged reading date at RASA. The Cultural Affairs Department at the U.S. Embassy was inviting people to the event with a reception following. During the marathon weekend before the reading, two students selected from among the HKU group, the musicians, van Erven and I camped out at van Erven's house with Jones appearing from time to time with newly written material and the camera crew coming and going to document our progress. When Jones arrived with a scene, we would read it aloud and send him away with suggestions for changes. The group became dramaturg for the weekend. Van Erven and I found a system of reading and typing the selected material into a computer, making script changes as we typed. We worked as a group all day Saturday until about 3:00 a.m. Sunday morning.

Later on Sunday I took the scripted material from the preceding day and, with the two student actors, selected and cut four long (about five to ten typed pages) scenes and a monologue written by Jones and a silent scene that had evolved out of our improvisation exercises, into a final text. The two students and I tentatively cast the scenes, nontraditionally, so each actor had one or two roles, and we cut the scenes so the format would be cross-cutting back and forth between scenes in a structure suggesting simultaneity.

The four scenes were the central scene in *The Threaded Sand* with two daughters and their immigrant mother who wants to return to the Antilles to die; *On the Scene*, composed of three different short scenes of Dutch and immigrant teenagers in a parking lot; *The Last Jam* where two male immigrant musicians fantasize about fame while smoking marijuana in a coffee shop; *Mario and Mama*, about an Italian woman at a public market with her young son sobbing over a dropped piece of pizza; a collage-monologue of a vendor at a public market (in English and Dutch); and a silent scene of a veiled woman in a laundromat being leered at by a Dutch man. A poem about migration and relocation of people and tribes in historical eras provided an epilogue to the whole piece. Karl Adams, our musician-composer, created a musical theme to identify each scene.

Although I was formally the dramaturg, I had been asked to stage the reading, so for the five days before the reading, I began thinking more visually and less thematically about the entire piece. By Tuesday, the technical rehearsal at RASA, I decided each scene should have its area on the stage, with the two musicians at the side. Lights would come up and go down to indicate the scene of focus. No props, just scripts, chairs, music, light and actors. I decided the piece would begin and end with a cluster of all the actors in slow motion as though at a stall of a public market in Holland (an image created in improvisation exercises) with one actress as a Dutch vendor hawking his or her wares.

Outdoor markets in Holland gave me the feeling of an international crossroads and I wanted the piece to begin and end with the group, then slowly dissolve into the individual stories. I decided at this point, with four days of rehearsals, that we would make few changes in the script and could work more honestly if Jones didn't attend all the rehearsals. As a realistic writer he knew every detail about the lives of the characters he had written and could explain what we needed the freedom to discover. With Jones present we would have to negotiate interpretation and there wasn't time. Also, Jones's writing is somewhat sentimental and I wanted to work against the sentiment to make the material come to life; I didn't feel comfortable doing that in his presence. Nevertheless, as a dramaturg, I felt then and now that I betrayed the playwright by grabbing the material, chopping it up, and redesigning it. I surrendered completely to performance pressure.

During this final week the work was much more performance-oriented and less collaborative, process-oriented than any of us would have liked. Because the students and their director at HKU would continue rehearsing the material for about another month after the reading prior to touring high schools, I kept emphasizing that the reading was only the end of one phase, and that the focus was to be the script. If they weren't happy with their roles or the quick choices we arrived at, there would be room to make changes after the RASA event.

Van Erven originally intended the RASA reading to be a low pressure situation, but it wasn't. It was friendly, but we were under performance pressure. The effect of stage lighting, the audience of about 200, among whom were representatives from the immigrant organizations who had talked to our group, representatives from the Cultural Affairs Department of the U.S. Embassy and several faculty members from the HKU and other Dutch universities, caused me to focus on the product. I wanted the American Embassy to feel the project was a success so they would want to support more cultural exchanges. I wanted the invited audience of immigrant organizations and immigrants interviewed, to feel their lives had been translated into art. I wanted the teachers at the HKU to feel their students had been part of a worthwhile project. I wanted Elroyce Jones to feel that, although the experience had been akin to television writing with a committee of writers and an exhausting pace, we had respected his writing and his substantial talent. And most of all I wanted to feel like we were not naive first-world people creating a theatre piece about lives and values we couldn't share or understand. The staged reading was about fifty minutes long and was followed by a discussion with Jones, van Erven and myself on stage and the actors joining the audience. When one white Dutch male suggested we had stereotyped the Antillean family, Ina Rotsburg of the Utrecht Municipal Office for Recent Immigrants, countered that she thought our *Threaded Sand* scene was a highly accurate representation of the generational conflicts she had observed in Antillean families. Most of the post-play discussion focused on the subject of immigration rather than on the subject of making theatre which suggests that the performance phase of our project was a success.

Of all the aspects of our project, our biggest failure was regarding the commitment of the student group to the project. Europe is in a period of transition. Extreme right wing parties are expanding their electoral appeal/power base by blaming people of color for the current economic recession. A new South Africa is struggling into being. Violence and riots are scarring cities in the United States. Civil wars continue in Latin America, Europe and Africa. Race, culture, ethnicity and class *are* major issues in the press daily. Self-determination is the central struggle in all hemispheres. And theatre can play a meaningful part in this struggle.

Many difficult aspects of our project--the marriage of strangers with different aesthetics, an unfamiliar country, the pressure of time-- could have been accommodated and the project could have been more effective if all the participants had shared a belief that theatre can contribute to changing the world. Only theatre, wrote Vaclav Havel in his 1994 World Theatre Day message to the International Theatre Institute, where living human beings address and speak to other human beings, "will show humankind the way toward tolerance, mutual respect, respect for the miracle of being."

Our successes in the project were manifold. We overcame cultural and gender biases among ourselves. The students believed Americans are as superficial as the characters in the television sitcoms we export. I believed I was free of cultural conditioning. Jones believed the students wanted to be film stars. I believed a group of women would "naturally" work as a collective. Still, we found a way to work together. Within the group we struggled and fought and learned about each other's aesthetics, pedagogical processes and politics. At the end of *The*

Storytellers, van Erven evaluates the project: "You can only grow if you push yourself into new challenging situations that will enable you to grow. If we use that criterion for this project, then I think every single one of the participants has grown."

Because an international, intercultural theatre project moves into unexpectedly sensitive areas that cause us to reexamine our values and adapt our ways of communicating, it can contribute to creating the global human community. It is potentially very effective, but it is slow, demanding work which is adversely affected by short cuts, such as the ones we took. But we all grew in our project, and if we learn from the mistakes we made, the next project will be better even though then, too, unexpected problems will arise. It is pioneering work for which no manuals or maps exist. We have to chart them as we go. The best way to work is as a team with complimenting skills, and with the mutual trust to check each other.

Works Cited

Boal, August. *Theatre of the Oppressed.* New York: Theatre Communications Group, 1985.

van Erven, Eugene. *The Playful Revolution: Theatre and Liberation in Asia.* Bloomington: Indiana UP, 1992.

Havel, Vaclav. Letter to the International Theatre Institute, 27 March 1994. New York: ITI/US.

The Storytellers. Videocassette. Prod. Stichting Ocean Film. Utrecht, Netherlands, 1993, 31 minutes. The video and accompanying booklet, by Eugene van Erven and Susan Mason, is available and may be ordered from the producers at Maliebaan 77, 3581 CZ Utrecht, Netherlands; fax 001-31-30-310409. *The Storytellers* was funded and sponsored with support from Audio Visual Services (C.I.M.) Faculty of Letters, Utrecht University; Hoge School "De Horst," Driebergen; Onderwijs Media Instituut, Utrecht, Netherlands; Sony Netherlands B.V.; Utrecht College of the Arts (HKU); Cultural Affairs Office, City of Utrecht; Faculty of Letters, Department of English, German & Celtic, Utrecht University; Foundation for International Film and Theatre Projects (STIFT); Netherlands Theatre Institute; Werkgroep Jeugd, Vrede en Welzijn; Alexander & Alexander BV/Chubb Insurance Co.; Cultural Affairs, Embassy of the United States in the Netherlands.

Maybe Theatre Is Born: Directing Student Theatre in Communist and Post-Communist Poland

by Kathleen Cioffi

Overview

In 1984, with very little background in Polish history, politics, language, or culture, I began a stay in Gdańsk, Poland. My husband, a Fulbright lecturer on American literature, taught in the English Institute at the University of Gdańsk, and I had some notions about investigating what was then going on in post-Grotowski Polish theatre. However, when we met the director of the English Institute, who had already heard that I was a theatre person, he greeted me with, "Well, of course we'd like you to teach English conversation for us, but what we'd *really* like is for you to direct a play." And so began what turned out to be a four-year association with the English Language Theatre Group of the University of Gdańsk, an association that taught me more about what was really going on in Polish society than almost anything else I did in Poland. Directing three plays before the fall of Communism and one play in post-Communist Poland also revealed many things about subtle and not-so-subtle effects the Communist system had on all, even the most seemingly minor, aspects of life.

The theatre group that I founded became a part of student cultural life at the University of Gdańsk. Unbeknownst to me at the time of my arrival in Poland, the institution of Polish student theatre had had a rich and turbulent history. Student cultural groups in general had been encouraged by the Communists. Even in Stalinist times, the Communist authorities, perhaps mindful of Stalin's characterization of intellectuals as "the engineers of human souls," had provided funding for a wide range of student cultural activities. One of the founders of a fifties student theatre group characterizes the flavor of Stalinist student culture:

Everyone without exception took part in the cultural movement. Each student grouping had to have some kind of cultural club and repertory. Thus we loudly and melodiously praised the last harvest; we called resoundingly for the fulfillment of the plan. (Skrzydło 104)[1]

Of course, these cultural activities, sponsored by the ideologically committed Polish Youth Union, were meant for the express purpose of glorifying Communism.

After Stalin's death in the fifties a new type of student cultural activity arose. Under the sponsorship of the less ideological Polish Students' Organization, student theatre groups flourished. Unlike student drama clubs from the prewar or immediate postwar periods, which had performed the classics of Polish and world dramatic literature, and unlike Stalinist student theatre groups, which performed works such as *The Advance of World Youth Toward Peace and Freedom for All Nations: A Montage of Revolutionary Poetry and Song*,[2] these groups established a tradition of performing theatre pieces that satirized the political foibles of the Communist regime. During periods of relative thaw, such as the mid-fifties and the early seventies, such satire was tolerated and even state-funded. In more repressive times, such as the sixties and the later seventies, the regime tried to "persuade" theatre groups to confine themselves to strictly artistic concerns. This persuasion worked well in the sixties, but by the late seventies Polish student theatre had, like the rest of Polish society, become much more militant. In fact, during the sixteen months of Solidarity's legal existence in 1980-81, student theatre groups were taken under the wing of the Independent Student Union (a branch of Solidarity), and regarded themselves as part of the independent "civil society" that Solidarity was trying to build.[3]

Because of the political content of its performances and its association with Solidarity, student theatre suffered during Martial Law (1981-83). Indeed, by the time I arrived in 1984, the student theatre movement had been decimated. Many members of student theatres had been imprisoned during Martial Law, some had emigrated, and many theatres no longer had any funding. In addition, the whole rich tradition of student culture itself had fallen apart. Students seemed demoralized, apathetic. They were forced to attend a great many hours of class per week (typically 30-45); consequently, they had very little time to do anything other than prepare for class. Gdańsk University, like most Polish universities, is primarily a commuter school, so most students were not involved in dormitory functions. It was very easy for students to retreat to their home lives, to the daily struggle "to organize" (in Polish "załatwić") food, shelter, and necessary items often in short supply, like toilet paper and sanitary napkins. In addition, students in the English Institute often were able to earn a little extra money by giving private English lessons at home ("korki"), so they had even less time than other students for extracurricular activities.

Our theatre group consisted mainly of students from the English Institute, but also included some English-speaking students from other majors such as Polish, Economics, and Scandinavian, in addition to some British and American faculty members from the English Institute. Our performances were generally nonpolitical and, in comparison with what had been created by groups in the Polish student theatre movement in the seventies, artistically much less ambitious. However, we were organized completely independently of any official student organization. The very fact that we organized ourselves at all was looked upon as an accomplishment by many, such as the former English Institute student (now an author and translator) who writes: "Those performances took place starting in 1985, in a state which, if no longer under martial law, was surely not yet completely a civil society, and when each organized group activity bordered on collaboration with the regime" (Kubińska 115). In other words, our group was regarded by many students as a sort of noble effort to restore independence to cultural life. Just by existing without official sponsorship by the then compromised Polish Student Organization (renamed in 1973 the Socialist Organization of Polish Students), our theatre group performed a kind of political function. We were--perhaps unconsciously--helping to establish the civil society for which Solidarity fought.

On my second trip (1990-91), this political function no longer existed. Poland was now officially non-Communist, and independent cultural groups were no longer subversive. In some ways this made directing much easier the second time, but in some ways it was harder. Many aspects of my work with the Polish students, from the seemingly trivial to the more important, changed because of the change in regime. I shall be discussing three productions which took place before the fall of Communism: *Cloud Nine* by Caryl Churchill (performed in 1985), *The Actor's Nightmare* by Christopher Durang (1986), and *The Varieties of Religious Experience* by William James adapted by Frank Cioffi (1987). I will contrast these productions with my post-Communist experience of directing *Return to the Forbidden Planet* by Bob Carlton (1991). I shall consider five aspects that underwent radical alteration: business and technical details, relations with the media, my own aesthetic process, choice of repertory, and student initiative.

Communism: Crafting Theatre--Contracts and Shakedowns

Under Communism, all business and technical details associated with any theatrical enterprise had to be "organized" (załatwione) in the same way that meat, light bulbs, typing paper, or any other necessary items of daily life were. In the ordinary course of events, these things were either unobtainable, or their procurement depended solely upon luck and happenstance. With the right contacts, however, virtually anything was possible. In other words, the important thing was not how much money anyone had, but rather whom they knew.

When I asked my actors how we were going to arrange a place to perform, not to mention the costumes, sets, and lights, for *Cloud Nine*, a play we had been carefully rehearsing the previous four months, they suggested that I talk to the Vice-Director of the English Institute. "Why should I talk to him?" I asked. "Oh, he knows everyone in the theatre in Gdańsk." Sure enough, he set up an appointment for me to see his friend, the dramaturg of the local professional theatre, the Teatr Wybrzeże (Coast Theatre). Nervously waiting with the student who was to serve as my translator for our appointment with the dramaturg, I thought it was surely impossible that a professional theatre would be willing to rent performance space to a student group. This was, after all, the theatre where filmmaker Andrzej Wajda had started out!

But Władisław Zawistowski, himself a well-known playwright as well as the Wybrzeże's dramaturg, reassured me and introduced me to Pani (Mrs.) Izabella, the managing director, who would arrange everything. Pani Izabella explained that for a very modest fee, and a letter from the director of the English Institute, the theatre could provide space to perform in their black box theatre, the Czarna Sala, as well as ushers and ticket collectors. The theatre could not sell tickets ahead of time since the production had not been submitted for review to the censorship office. Pani Izabella suggested that we call our tickets "invitations" and sell them ourselves to our friends. That way the performances would officially be "closed," and would not need to be submitted to censorship.

In this way I was gently introduced to the phenomenon of the "closed performance" of a theatrical work. These invitation-only performances, nominally a way for theatres to invite friends to critique a production before its opening, was one of the many ways that theatre artists had of avoiding censorship. Later in my stay in Poland I saw "closed performances" of politically sensitive plays about many subjects, such as the Russian poet Osip Mandelstam, the Martial Law experience, the Russian gulag, or the half-Polish, half-German Silesian area of Poland. Though *Cloud Nine* had perhaps one line that the censors would have objected to ("And Africa is to be Communist, I suppose"--Churchill 320), the people at the Wybrzeże seemed to think that I, as a foreigner, should not have to submit to the indignity of censorship.

Pan (Mr.) Darek, the technical director, informed me that the theatre could provide costumes, technicians, props, a minimal set, and lights. It would charge a small fee for each of these amenities and would need a letter from the director of the English Institute. And so, we were able to perform all three of our productions during the Communist period in the Czarna Sala of the Teatr Wybrzeże. Each year we had more performances, more rehearsal time in the theatre, and we paid less money to the theatre. This illustrated another law of Communist economics. Because we grew increasingly sophisticated about how to arrange details on our own, as well as because we knew more and more people who could help us, we needed to use less money.

In contrast to our cozy relations with the professional theatre, our relationship with the mass media was somewhat strained the first time I was in Poland. In fact, the media was the enemy. Since our performances were "closed," there were no reviews. We did not "invite" any reviewers to see our performances, since to do so would probably have invited the censor. In addition, all newspapers were government-controlled, and there was little in the way of arts journalism. "Reviews" in Communist era newspapers usually took the form of celebrating the achievements of "the people's" splendid artists.

Further, during Martial Law, which had just ended in 1983, the mass media had been completely compromised, to the extent that newscasters appeared on television dressed in military uniform.

Professional actors, to their credit, engaged in a boycott of television, which lasted for several years. Many people refused to buy newspapers. So, when one of my actors in *Cloud Nine* came to me to request that her cousin, who was employed by the local television station, come and film one of our rehearsals to be broadcast as part of a local program on area young people, I knew that this might have greater implications than just disrupting one rehearsal.

I put the question to the actors, saying it made no difference to me how they decided. Kuba, who had spent time in prison during Martial Law, asked to speak in Polish to the other actors. I agreed, and he launched into a long, impassioned speech, most of which I was unable to understand. However, it was evident that he did not want Polish TV to tape the rehearsal. His gestures and intonations were dramatic and moving. Everyone, including the actress whose cousin worked for the TV station, voted no.

During the three years I spent in Poland the first time, my artistic process underwent a kind of evolution. For the production of *Cloud Nine*, I spent most of the nearly five months of rehearsal running the various scenes and working on pacing. Because of various problems getting students in a commuter school together at the same time for rehearsals, I made the mistake of using an entirely different cast for Act One and Act Two (which Churchill warns against in her production notes). Unfortunately, rather than make it easier to schedule rehearsals, this "solution" multiplied problems in getting the cast together and it had the further disadvantage of making *me* feel as if I was going over the same ground with the actors again and again. Although I was able to do some improvisatory work on character with the Act One cast, the Act Two cast tended, for some reason, to get short shrift, and toward the end of the rehearsal period both casts were getting a little stale. At that point I decided to spend one rehearsal on each act where I asked the actors to translate their lines into Polish. It turned out that actresses who had been blithely mouthing obscene words for months in English had difficulty saying those same words in their native language. This exercise, however, seemed to jolt everyone out of their torpor and we went on to have successful performances. Still, despite the production's energy and hilarity in performance, I came away dissatisfied with the rehearsal process; I felt I had been less creative than I could have been as a director.

Consequently, the next year I chose *The Actor's Nightmare* by Christopher Durang because it was short, had a fairly small cast, and would definitely not need five months of rehearsal. It also seemed like an appropriate play for a group of English majors to be doing, containing as it does parodies of Shakespeare, Beckett, Noel Coward, and Robert Bolt. As it happened, we rehearsed one and a half months, and never lost our sense of momentum. We spent most of the rehearsal time improvising and going back to the source material from which Durang draws his parodies in the play. As a result, both I and those members of the cast and crew who had taken part in both productions (two actors and the assistant director) felt as if this production had a more "organic" rehearsal process than *Cloud Nine*.

Working on *The Varieties of Religious Experience,* an original script that needed lots of rewriting and fleshing out during rehearsal, forced me as director to draw on reserves of inventiveness. Prior to coming to Poland I had worked on two original plays that had in part been developed through improvisations with the actors, and I used many of the same kinds of improvs and other exercises to develop *Varieties.* I had also been studying the ways that many politically engaged student theatres had created theatre pieces. In many cases, they took works not originally meant for the stage and adapted them, usually employing similar improvisatory techniques to the ones that I was using. I felt that, with this production, our group began to have its own connection to the Polish student theatre movement and was thus somehow more than just a particularly good language learning exercise.

Our choice of repertory was affected by the political situation in Poland, at least to some extent. While it is true that my selection of plays was not always particularly well-tailored to the needs of my actors (I directed *Cloud Nine*, for example, mainly because I had wanted to direct *Cloud Nine* for several years), after I had been in Poland for a while I realized that I should be directing plays that better served the concerns of my actors and audience. At the time, many people in Poland had turned to the Catholic Church to fulfill what was a palpable longing for community. In the post-Martial Law malaise that seemed to have permeated Polish society; the Church was something of a haven. It became a sponsor of many "underground" activities previously associated with the then banned Solidarity, such as lectures, poetry readings, and art exhibitions that were free of censorship and, therefore, often took as their subject all the topics that the regime would not allow to be discussed. The Church took seriously its obligation to offer sanctuary and became a kind of "free" space where things could be discussed and meetings could be held without fear of reprisal, at least while one was actually within its walls. Many people, particularly young people, while they may have started going to church because it was an ally in the fight against Communism, began to get interested in the actual idea of religion itself. Consequently, when my husband proposed adapting William James's philosophical work *The Varieties of Religious Experience* to the stage, I was enthusiastic. It proved to be an inspired choice in that James's examination of the religious impulse in humankind touched a chord in the more thoughtful members of the cast. Also, James's uniquely American perspective on these issues gave the students another viewpoint on some of the same topics that their priests had spoken about in church.

During my first visit it seemed to be impossible for the students to initiate anything on their own. If the director of the English Institute hadn't asked me to direct a play, then there would never have been a play. Even the business and technical details had to be arranged by me, although the students did help me with translating and with acquiring or making various props. Furthermore, the Polish faculty was not very willing to help out with the productions, although most (but not all) did attend them. However, the students were quite adept at arranging parties, and we had many lovely evenings socializing with the casts of the three different plays. The participants in each play became another social support group for each other, but this didn't really translate into a cohesive group that would be able to organize itself without me.

I was sure that when I left in 1987, if the following year's Fulbright lecturer wasn't willing to direct something, then there would be no English Language Theatre Group. As it happened, I was only half right. The following year the students approached the American Fulbright lecturer's wife and asked her if she'd be willing to direct. She replied that she really knew nothing about theatre, but if they were willing to direct themselves, she'd come to some rehearsals and give them her opinion. So the students did put together a modest production of Dylan Thomas's *Under Milkwood*. The year after that the Fulbright lecturer was a theatre person and directed another Durang play, *The Marriage of Bette and Boo*. But the next year, neither the Fulbright lecturer nor his wife was interested in the theatre, and there was no production.

Post Communism: The Theatre--Maybe and Definitely

The three years between my two visits to Poland went by quickly and somewhat uneventfully for me. For Poland those years contained the climactic events that brought about the fall of Communism. Eager to see how these events had changed our adopted country, my husband persuaded his American university to initiate a private university-to-university exchange with the University of Gdańsk. We returned to Gdańsk for the 1990-91 academic year. I had no intentions of directing a play on this visit, but Beata, a student who had been involved with *The Marriage of Bette and Boo* and who became my assistant director, came to me and persuaded me to do one more show with the English Language Student Group.

The first thing that struck me about the post-Communist realities of amateur play production was that business details became more apparently "normal," although later it turned out that this seeming normality led us to make some mistakes that proved disastrous for one of our performances. This time we were doing a musical, *Return to the Forbidden Planet* by Bob Carlton, and we needed a bigger performance space than Czarna Sala. Beata, who had a part-time job working for a local arts promotion agency and who was tremendously helpful with all the business arrangements, set up a meeting for me with the artistic director of the professional puppet theatre, the Miniatura (the Miniatura had been under renovation the entire three years that I had been in Gdańsk the first time). The artistic director was happy to rent the theatre; in fact, professional theatre's government subsidies had been cut by the new, non-Communist government, so the theatre was pleased to get a little extra income from renting out their space when it wasn't being used. No letters were required. Censorship was no longer a problem, so if we liked, they could also sell tickets for us, or they could sell some of the tickets and we could sell the rest.

Partly because we could now do some publicity, partly because many more people in the Gdańsk area were now studying English, and partly (I believed) because it was good, this production proved enormously popular, so popular in fact that we sold out all performances at the Miniatura, and began to think about adding some performances. Unfortunately the Miniatura was booked up by other groups, but one of the show's musical directors, suggested that we try to book the student club, Żak (pronounced Jacques). Żak, an historic old building in downtown Gdańsk, had also been under renovation during my previous visit. As with Miniatura, Beata and I negotiated a contract with the management of Żak for a hall, sound equipment, and lights. When we arrived to set up for our first performance, however, we found no sound equipment. The sound equipment, we were told, had been lent to some group in another city, and had not been returned. Żak's sound engineer, evidently accustomed to dealing with musicians rather than theatre people, seemed unconcerned at our dismay and suggested that we cancel the production. We were unwilling to disappoint the people who had bought tickets, especially since we knew that the following night's show was sold out. We managed to borrow some amplifiers, speakers, and microphones from a band scheduled to play next door in the student nightclub, and the show went on, though with poor sound quality.

After the performance the sound man told us that he wasn't sure if the equipment would be back from the other city, but that maybe he could arrange for some other equipment, if we were willing to pay a little extra. I pointed out that this was what we Americans call a "shakedown," but said I'd pay. The next day we had all the sound equipment we could wish for. Eventually we agreed to pay what we said we would in the contract, but not a złoty more.

Later, I realized that the sound man had merely been operating by the rules of the old regime. My dealings with the Teatr Wybrzeże had gone so smoothly, because the bribery (all those small fees) had been institutionalized and expected. Everything had been decided well in advance, and there was no question of anybody's blackmailing anyone else. In several cases, I had given small cash gifts as a token of my appreciation after a theatre technician had done something for our group. In this case, however, everybody except the sound man had been operating according to a different set of rules: we had a contract which we had all agreed to, and we expected everybody to live up to their end of the agreement.

Our relations with the media went much more smoothly in the post-Communist era. For example, when Polish television wanted to tape parts of our Żak performance, everyone was excited about the opportunity. I pointed out that it would be rather disruptive to have a TV crew taping a performance, but everyone still wanted to do it. Kuba, who had been so adamant about not collaborating with Polish

TV in 1985, now took part in a group interview that the TV producers held with us after the performance. The Polish media was now a friend rather than an enemy.

In 1991 one of the local newspapers, *Gazeta Gdańska* came to review one of the Żak performances. *Gazeta Gdańska* was a privately owned newspaper, not under government control. Though its arts journalism still tended more toward reportage rather than evaluation, the reportage could be of a negative nature. For example, the paper didn't hesitate to criticize Żak for not providing us with the proper sound equipment or to criticize the singing of some of the cast.

Unfortunately, with a three-year gap between the production of *The Varieties of Religious Experience* and *Return to the Forbidden Planet*, it wasn't really possible to continue building on the ways that we had begun to create productions. However, the whole feeling of working on *Planet* was different than the first three productions. Because it was a musical, it had to be much more collaborative than the other three. The three students who shared the task of musical direction had a lot of input into the final product. Also, though there wasn't much dancing, there were two sections which needed to be choreographed. In one case, the students who were in the number choreographed it themselves; in the other, one of the students asked a friend to choreograph it. In any case, perhaps because the nature of the production demanded them to take more responsibility, the students became much more independent-- to the extent that they often felt like they could even argue with me. This had never happened during the previous productions.

During these rehearsals there came to be a kind of generation gap between those in the cast who had taken part in previous productions and those who were new to this play. Kuba, who had acted in *Cloud Nine* and *Varieties*; Irek, who had acted in *Varieties*; and Magda, who had acted in all three of the other productions, had all graduated, were working, and were either parents or about to become parents. The newcomers were all students, and though some of them worked, they had fewer family responsibilities. Jarek, the bandleader, who had acted in *Cloud Nine*, had not yet graduated or married, so in some ways he had more in common with the newcomers. The oldtimers felt resentful of the newcomers because they were so argumentative in rehearsals, and the newcomers felt resentful of the oldtimers because they kept having to skip rehearsals because of family obligations or work. The warm atmosphere of a social support group that I had felt in the earlier productions was missing.

The choice of the play was also affected by the way the atmosphere of Poland had changed. Where during my first visit it had been typical to spend hours with friends in long (sometimes vodka-soaked) discussions of deep philosophical issues late into the night, now, sadly, nobody had time for such nonsense. In any case, *Varieties* would never have touched any chords this time: the intelligentsia was much less entranced with the subject of religion than it had been during my last visit. Indeed, the Church had already begun to fritter away the enormous political capital it had accumulated during the Communist era by trying to make its own agenda the legislative agenda. Instead of letting legislators get started on the enormous task of rebuilding a shattered economy, the Church brought pressure on them to pass laws mandating prayer in the schools and restricting abortion. Where in my previous visit, people had grumbled about the "red bourgeoisie," now they were grumbling about the "black nomenklatura," that is, politicians who were under the control of the church.

The preoccupations of post-Communist Poland were very different than they had been during Communist times. Rather than longing for community or for exploration of the philosophical bases of human existence, what the students needed this time was a feeling of competence. There was a joke current about the economy at the time that said fish and water could be easily turned into fish soup, but fish soup couldn't be easily turned back into beautiful fish swimming in a tank of water. Polish people were beginning to feel like characters in American Polish jokes. So, I decided to show this particular group of Polish students that they really could do something quite difficult and do it well. They could put on a slick, polished musical.

Based on our previous success with the production of *Actor's Nightmare*, which was not only a funny play but also taught the students something about British and American theatre history, I concluded that a similar choice might be in order. Bob Carlton's *Return to the Forbidden Planet* was particularly appropriate for a group of English majors to be doing, given the quotations from various Shakespeare plays. In addition, it uses rock songs from the sixties. One of our most difficult tasks was getting down the tricky harmonizing from the Beach Boys' "Good Vibrations." *Forbidden Planet* definitely proved to have numerous technical challenges for us, but none so troublesome that we were unable to meet them, and their success in meeting those challenges made the students feel that they were capable of carrying out a complex technical task well. In addition, audiences adored the production. Perhaps they needed this type of escapist, nostalgic entertainment. Strangers hailed the actors in the streets using their characters' names. Just as the philosophically weighty *The Varieties of Religious Experience* fit its times, the philosophically lightweight and even silly production of *Return to the Forbidden Planet* fit the need of its time for competence and slick commercialism.

The most striking contrast between my Communist and post-Communist directing experiences was the degree of initiative displayed by the students themselves. Whereas during my first visit it had been the department chair who suggested I direct a play, this time a student came to me on her own with the suggestion. During rehearsals, I hadn't been so sure about how I felt about the independence of the newcomers, but after performances started, I felt that it had been wise to share power with the students. Before we finished the run, they held a meeting and decided to give themselves a name, since English Language Theatre Group had just been a spur of the moment name that I'd made up for the program and for official letters. They decided on a "Maybe Theatre." They also resolved to stay together the next year and produce at least one more production. We had taken part in a festival of English-language plays held at Warsaw University and partly funded by the British Council, but the Warsaw University English students had decided they were tired of running the festival. Maybe Theatre agreed to sponsor the festival the next year in Gdańsk.

The Maybe Theatre, still exists today, and has produced *Blood Brothers*, *Canterbury Tales*, *Alice in Wonderland*, and a Christmas pantomime to date. Moreover, the permanent faculty of the English Institute have gotten involved in directing the productions, so that the theatre hasn't had to depend on foreign lecturers who are only there for a limited period. The students themselves put together a concert of English Christmas carols to raise money one year. Despite the fact that everyone in Poland seems to have less and less time for leisure activities, the students at Gdańsk University have decided that this activity matters to them. I have a feeling that Maybe Theatre has become a permanent feature of student life at the university. Perhaps they should change their name to Definitely Theatre.

From post-Martial Law demoralization to post-Communist get-up-and-go, the participants in English language plays at Gdańsk University have undergone a remarkable transformation, just as the society they live in has undergone a transformation. They've gone from an economic world where connections were the only way to get what you wanted to one where contracts hold sway. They've gone from looking at the media as an enemy to looking at it as a friend and potential ally. They've gone from passivity and dependence on foreigners to activity and self-reliance. Unfortunately, they've also gone from a predilection for serious drama to one for commercial, lightweight fluff. Nevertheless, I'm proud to have taken part in their transformation and I look forward to watching how Maybe Theatre, as well as all of Polish society, evolves in the future.

Notes

1. All quotations from articles with Polish titles are my own translations.
2. Listed in Śliwińska 214.
3. For a more complete description in English of the history of Polish student theatre, see Cioffi, Semil, and Wójcik.

Works Cited

Churchill, Caryl. *Cloud Nine. Plays: One*. London: Methuen, 1985. 243-320.
Cioffi, Kathleen. "Alternative Theatre in Poland." *Soviet and East European Performance* 9.1 (1989): 32-37.
Kubińska, Olga. "Cioffich zabawy w teatr." *Gdański rocznik teatralny* 1991: 114-116.
Semil, Małgorzata. "Young People's Theatre in Poland Reaches for Truth." *Media Development* 35.3 (1988): 12-15.
Skrzydło, Leszek. "'Pstrąg' i 'Cytryna.'" *Teatry studenckie w Polsce*. Ed. Jerzy Koenig. Warsaw: Wydawnictwa Artystyczne i Filmowe, 1968. 103-140.
Śliwińska, Zofia. "Teatry studenckie w Łodzi 1946-1970." *Pamiętnik Teatralny* 21 (1972): 214-218.
Wójcik, Agnieszka. "Alternative Theatre." Trans. Hubert Ross. *Index on Censorship* Jan. 1985: 11-14.

The Politics of *The Professional*: Connecting the Prose with the Passion

by Dennis Barnett

In America, when we receive word of the atrocities of war in other countries our tendency is to distance ourselves. When we see the torture, the starvation, the innumerable violations of human rights; when we hear of the hate emanating globally between different factions, culturally, ethnically, ideologically; even when we view the anger of our own criminal population, we try to force such situations into simplistic terms of good and evil. We want to identify with the good, and deny all connection with the evil. We set the evil parties up as the "Other" and focus on victims, often becoming victims ourselves. Ironically, it is this distancing that creates the divisiveness behind the turmoil, and in the end, by our inability to see the conflict in human terms, we contribute to it. This is an account of the discovery and production of a play born in the heart of a shattered country, where fear of the "Other" and the resultant distancing is rampant.

In our work as theatre artists, we undergo a reversal of the distancing process. With each new project, we see the world through someone else's eyes, and, regardless of how much we might personally disagree with their perspective, the very act of trying on their point of view allows room for the acceptance of differences. Theatre has the capacity, the responsibility, to effect this reversal in our audiences as well. Where we want to separate and distance ourselves from our fellow man, it is theatre's function to join and draw us together. Where we wish to focus only on the differences, theatre can highlight the similarities. What hate wounds theatre can salve. What anger builds to the breaking point, theatre can vent.

In 1991, in Berkeley, California, a group of professional theatre artists were attempting to create work for themselves by producing a play. The group was called Upstart Stage, and the play was called *The Professional*. It was written by one of international theatre's best kept secrets--the Yugoslavian playwright, Dusan Kovacevic (Doo-shahn Kuvahshuvik). I was co-founder and the Artistic Director of Upstart. In operation since 1989, we were dedicated to the development and support of new plays and playwrights. Our energy was spent primarily on a prolific and well attended reading series.

In the summer of 1991 we received *The Professional* unsolicited. Of the eighty or so scripts on which we worked from 1989-1994, fewer than ten of them came unsolicited. The rest were generated through various efforts at networking, and, for the most part, the unsolicited scripts were marginal. *The Professional* proved to be the exception. We found it to be a profound and timely play. I knew nearly nothing about Yugoslavia at the time, nor did I understand the political reality about which Kovacevic was writing. But the political statement in the play did not unduly concern me; the play was beautifully theatrical, revealingly funny, and, most importantly, for reasons we were not yet able to voice, deeply moving. Dusan Kovacevic sparked the imaginative flint of everyone at Upstart.

While we planned a reading of Kovacevic's play, his homeland was being devastated by war. It was, thus far, primarily a conflict between Serbs and Croats. On January 1, 1992, United Nations' envoy Cyrus Vance, announced that he had won formal agreement from Serbian officials for a plan that would include a cease-fire. This would be the fifteenth truce in this six-month-long war that had killed thousands of people and driven 600,000 more from their homes. Kovacevic lived in Belgrade, where there was, understandably, much tension, as people hoped against the odds that this cease-fire would hold. The war had been a dirty one, with reports of carnage beyond our ability to fathom, on both sides.

Two weeks later, on January 16, in the tiny breakaway republic of Bosnia-Herzogovina, the Serbian minority proclaimed their autonomy. Though in the north the Croatian-Serbian truce seemed to be holding, in Sarajevo, the capitol of Bosnia-Herzogovina, a new, even more tragic conflict began. It eventually became a conflict wherein the Croats and the Serbs were not just killing each other, but together engaged in the near genocide of a third ethnic minority, the Muslims. Kovacevic is a Serb. Born in 1949 in a small village called Mrdjenovac, near the town of Sabac, Kovacevic is easily the most celebrated playwright in Yugoslavia.[1] In Belgrade alone, his plays have received over 2,000 performances, to audiences numbering more than a million. His plays had already been translated into sixteen different languages, including Chinese, Japanese, French, Greek, and German, when the first English translation found its way to Upstart Stage.

Kovacevic graduated from Belgrade University Department of Dramatic Writing in 1973. *The Professional,* written in 1990 is his twelfth play. Other works include: *Radovan III* (1973), *The Marathon Runners are Running* (1973), *What Is It That Makes Folks Drink* (1976), *Spring in January* (1977), *Space Dragon* (1977), *Village Lumination* (1978), *Meeting Place* (1982), *Balkan Spy* (1983), *Saint George Kills the Dragon* (1983), *Claustrophobic Comedy* (1987), and *Tragedie Burlesque* (1990). He has won numerous awards in Yugoslavia, as well as awards in Montreal, Switzerland, and France.

Kovacevic's work had its first English-language presentation as one of our staged readings. Before scheduling the play, we had to be certain that it met the parameters of our mission statement. We were a developmental theatre. Normally we assumed that if a play was sent to us, the writer was looking for some dramaturgical feedback. However, in this case, neither the writer nor the translator were aware that we had the manuscript; it was sent to us by a friend of the translator. If the play, or in this case, the translation was complete, and changes were not being considered, it would not meet our criteria.

When I spoke with the translator, Bob Djurdjevich, I realized the circumstances were extraordinarily favorable. He had seen a production of *The Professional* in Belgrade and was deeply moved. Djurdjevich told us of Kovacevic's popularity in Eastern Europe, and that he believed this was the first English language translation of any of his works. Djurdjevich is a Yugoslavian expatriate, who found his own experiences clearly reflected in the play and translated it as a gesture of gratitude. Though secure in his command of the English language, Djurdjevich was cognizant of his limitations and eager to hear his translation read. We felt satisfied that Upstart could assist him in shaping it, and that this project fit quite neatly into our mission.

The reading of *The Professional* took place in the fall of 1991. Ken Grantham, for years a mainstay at Berkeley Repertory Theatre, read the part of the secret policeman, Luke; and I read the role that I eventually played in the production, the writer, Teya. The reading was well attended and one of our best received. The audience, comprised of playwrights and theatre artists, was unanimous in its desire to see *The Professional* produced.

Meanwhile the conflict between Serbs and Croats intensified, and Milosevic, the Serbian president, conscripted every available male into military duty. Jasmina Bojic, a correspondent for the Belgrade paper, *Borba*, explained that most of her fellow expatriates who fled the country at this time were sickened at the thought of going to war against their fellow countrymen.[2] Serbs, Croats, Muslims, in fact members of all the ethnic minorities fled, refusing to take part in the nationalistic furor that divided their country. Among those fleeing was Dusan Kovacevic who went into hiding on the island of Cyprus. Kovacevic later applied for a visa to see our production only to be turned down by the American government. The reason for the rejection was never clear, but with the major thrust of our media in condemnation of Serbia, Kovacevic probably appeared as too great a security risk. In the eyes of our State Department, Kovacevic had become the "Other."

The Text--The Prose of Kovacevic

One might think that since *The Professional* was written before the break-up of the Yugoslavian state, it would be dated, but actually, that event served to deepen its resonance. Today, instead of one Yugoslavia hungry for change, there are six, and, among those, there are other factions hoping to break away even further. The story of *The Professional*, though specific to the reality of Yugoslavian politics, requires no knowledge of these historic details. Of course the Yugoslavian expatriates who saw our production better understood the complexities of the issues, which gave them a more personal and vital perspective. But the clamor for change in a society and the resultant disillusion when it fails to materialize is an immediate and universal experience.

The social statement that the play makes is only a small part of its universality. The questions that Kovacevic explores in *The Professional* delve deeply into the heart of all change, individual, as well as societal.

He not only asks what happens to a society struggling with change, but also what happens to the individual within that society.

Kovacevic's two main characters are ideologically, generationally, socially, and by extension, ethnically enemies. Teya, who under the communist regime of Tito was a dissident, has recently become Editor-in-Chief of a publishing house owned by the government. Tito has been dead for nine years, and the masters for whom Luke fought all his life are gone. Luke, in his late sixties and a member of Teya's father's generation, worked for most of his life as a secret policeman under Tito's administration. It was his assignment to follow Teya and record his activities and speeches. Now, Luke drives a cab. The masters have become the slaves.

The action of the play takes place in Teya's office, where, as the play begins, he sits wading through the ocean of manuscripts on his desk. Immediately Kovacevic's wonderful sense of irony becomes apparent. Teya thinks of himself as a writer. Displeased with his own meager output, he finds it particularly disgusting to read the scribbling of these "scriptomaniacs."[3] The irony extends to a playful moment of exposition, when Luke, an apparent stranger, arrives, and presents Teya with four bound volumes that Teya has unknowingly "written." These books are collections of speeches and stories, transcribed from the secret recordings that Luke made of Teya's activities over the years. At first, he doesn't recognize Luke and seems to have no recall of anything Luke tells him. Teya has shut the door on his past, and Luke's visit is written as a series of masterful pryings that eventually blow the passageway wide open. As the play unfolds, Luke breaks Teya down, one memory at time; each one diminishes Teya's faith in his pretensions, and increases the likelihood that Luke is what he says he is.

The degree to which Teya has forgotten his past proves to be a wonderful source of humor. Since the audience is one step ahead of Teya each incident in Teya's life that Luke reveals, and particularly the details surrounding Luke's involvement in that incident, increases in comic value. Learning that Luke shared a bottle of brandy with him, Teya and Luke have the following exchange:

    TEYA: You sat with us in that compartment?
    LUKE: Yes, wearing a conductor's uniform. We must have had five liters of this brandy that day. You tried to talk me into hijacking the train, so that for once,

writers would have something tangible to write about. You said "that's how Lenin got started." (16)

Later, Luke opens a large black suitcase that he has brought with him, full of items of Teya's including, "14 umbrellas, six pairs of gloves, two overcoats, 15 lighters, 11 hats" (23). Also in the suitcase are letters from his mother, his father's pocket watch, and a present Teya had bought for his son. At this point, any attempt on Teya's part to disavow the past is ludicrous, and the audience delights in the knowledge that everything Luke has said is true.

As the play evolves, we see that eighteen years of surveillance has left Luke, the "professional" oppressor, inextricably linked to his quarry. In fact, for the last two years, he has continued to follow Teya, even though it is no longer his job. The oppressor has become the protector, and it is through one of the play's most poignant constructs that we learn why.

Turning Teya's police dossier into books was an idea conceived by Luke's son Milosh, who also opposed Tito's regime. Milosh saw that this was a chance to save Serbian literature from "disappear[ing] forever in the drink and smoke" (25). Though an avid communist, Luke agreed to help his son to ease the strain caused by their political differences. When Milosh incorporated Teya's books into a class he was teaching, he and Luke lost their jobs. Weary of the struggle, Milosh left the country. Luke promised to continue his surveillance of Teya, which then became Luke's only connection with his son. When Teya's life was in danger, as it often was, Luke had to protect him in order to keep the promise he made to Milosh. It is this promise that sets the action of *The Professional* in motion.

Luke's visit to Teya is his final act before checking into a hospital for an operation he suspects he will not survive. He gives Milosh's address to Teya and asks him to contact him should he die. He asks Teya to, "tell him that we parted as decent people" (33). Against the backdrop of the Yugoslavian holocaust, his words resound dramatically. "Decency" suggests respect. It is only after dissipating the fear of the "Other" that respect for the "Other's" differences is possible. When differences cease to be threatening, humanity begins to shine through. This is what occurs between Teya and Luke. The concept of "decency" in Yugoslavia, at present, seems lost in the corridors of power. The leaders' need for power is a political reality, and an increase in their power is inextricably linked to the amount of fear they can generate in their populace. In the play, it is important to Luke that Milosh know that he kept his promise.

Kovacevic mirrors the Luke-Milosh relationship in Teya's relationship with his father, who died before they were able to reconcile the division that their political beliefs caused. This is a source of deep regret for Teya, and just as Luke has replaced, on some level, his lost son, so does Teya find his father.

To complete the dismantling of Teya's denial, Luke adds one final insight; he and Teya have essentially reversed their positions. Teya is now working for those in power, while Luke is among the oppressed. Luke shows Teya that the power to which he clings is no different from the power against which he spent his life rebelling. Of course, Kovacevic once again holds up the mirror of irony, as we are reminded that the ideas which Luke has spent his life attempting to destroy, must now be preserved by him.

Kovacevic's use of irony is multifaceted. Before departing for the hospital Luke and Teya hug. It is a moment of completion for both the characters, and the audience. The father and the son find solace in the "Other's" friendship. They have healed their own wounds, by recognizing the "Other's" humanity. Luke then points to Teya's books.

LUKE: Here are your books and here is your drama . . .
TEYA: My drama? What drama, Comrade Luke?
LUKE: Well, your first drama.
TEYA: My drama?
LUKE: Yes.
TEYA: Comrade Luke, I've written poems, stories, essays, but never a drama, please believe me. Never.
LUKE: Yes you have, Teya.
TEYA: And when, when did I write it?
LUKE: Now.

Luke then pulls out a pocket tape recorder.

LUKE: I turned it on just before I walked in. It is still recording. When I leave, all you need to do is rewind the tape, put a piece of paper in your typewriter, and transcribe everything. (32-33)

As the play ends, Teya's dream of being a professional writer has been revived and he begins transcribing the play we just witnessed. The job of preserving his thoughts is now his own.

This task of saving Teya's stories and speeches represents the main action of *The Professional*. It is what our director Peter Craze called "the passing of the baton." The "baton" in this case is the preservation of Teya's ideas. As the play begins, the baton has already been "passed" from Milosh to Luke. Now Luke, because of his imminent death and promise to Milosh, must "pass" it to Teya. The achievement of this task depends on reuniting Teya with his past, and destroying the pretensions of his new persona. Luke and Teya forge a symbiotic bond, wherein Luke makes Teya whole by keeping his promise to Milosh, and Teya gives Luke the completion he seeks by taking up the "baton" himself. Now these two enemies see each other more clearly. The "Other" has become the "Familiar."

This conciliation is not planned. It is a by-product of the characters' new perspectives which the circumstances have given them. From his new perspective, which grew from his agreement with Milosh, Luke could no longer view Teya as someone who should be "run over like a dog" (12). Teya and his ideas became important to Luke for personal reasons. His perspective changed again when he lost his job, recognizing how the system had broken both Teya and himself, seeing Teya as a fellow victim. This brings him into Teya's office with his part of the conciliation completed. Now, nearing the end of his life, Luke, the "professional," in keeping his promise to Milosh, must finish what he began. To do this, he must take Teya on a journey, which will bring Teya the new perspective he needs to join in the conciliation.

To understand Teya's journey, we must first look at where he is at the start of the play. Since Tito's death, Teya has slowly moved with his "crowd" into the circles of government. His past was a painful time, a time when his commitment to a cause meant alienating his father, breaking his mother's heart, and becoming estranged from his wife and son. He experienced all the negatives connected with the life of a dissident, but made none of the contributions. Because he was narcissistic, undisciplined and alcoholic, he failed to write anything, and the respect and recognition afforded dissidents in other countries escaped him. Luke quotes a speech of Teya's in which Teya spoke of Vaclav Havel. It ends: "After Havel's plays, plush curtains don't drop. Instead, the iron cell gates do. He is a Czech writer of world descent!"

(16). Teya praised Havel for the very things in which his life has been lacking. Luke's choice of this speech is a purposeful stab at Teya's facade. Now, to finally gain respect, Teya has had to take on a new persona, in which there is no room for the painful mistakes or the radical nature of his past. For Teya, when Luke enters his office, there is no past.

The awakening of Teya's memory is beautifully physicalized by the slow disintegration of Teya's appearance. As each new memory is placed before him, and Teya's resolve to disbelieve everything Luke says weakens, he becomes more disoriented. His secretary, Martha, whose own husband has recently gone mad and committed suicide in the hospital, and with whom Teya has begun an affair, reflects Teya's changing appearance as her concern for his well-being grows with each of her entrances. By the end of the play Teya has removed his jacket and tie, drunk brandy, missed a luncheon appointment, raged at the noises from an adjoining office, and been brought to tears. He wears a fur hat, winter gloves, and a pair of binoculars, all of which he finds in Luke's suitcase. In short, he is literally wearing his past. He struggles to hold various items, also from the suitcase: a pipe, a pair of women's shoes, a stuffed dog, a bicycle pump, and his father's pocket watch. When Martha sees him in this state, she breaks into tears, certain that she is watching another man's mental demise. At the same time, Kovacevic's audience is laughing, noting how extreme Martha's misunderstanding has become, though Martha's reaction is perfectly plausible.

Being faced with his unfulfilled potential as a writer is not enough to motivate Teya's transformation. His journey isn't complete until Luke confronts him with his failure as a person. This tears away the pretensions of Teya's new persona. By recognizing who he had been, Teya is finally able to see who he has become. This new perspective allows him to see that he and Luke have been beaten down with opposite ends of the same stick.

The tone of *The Professional* is hard to categorize. Given that the playwright is from Eastern Europe, where the roots of absurdity run deep, one would expect the influence of Havel or Mrozek to be strong. There is a tinge of absurdity present, but more in form than content. As the content is slowly revealed, we learn that what initially seemed absurd (Teya's lack of memory is utterly existential) has, by the end, been supported by steadfast realistic motivations. In addition, though it is often broadly comic, as it ends, we are stunned by the depth of its seriousness.

This seriousness is most evident in the cynicism of Kovacevic's political point of view. Given what his country has endured, this cynicism is understandable. He poses the ultimate question of political deconstructionism. Beneath all the proselytizing and campaigning, behind the democratic rebellions and the socialist agendas, no matter what system is currently in place, or how one expresses their political stance, don't we all share a primal urge toward totalitarianism, as long as we are the ones in power? Kovacevic suggests that all governments automatically dehumanize and oppress the individual, that all struggles for change essentially amount to the same thing--the oppressed longing for power. But at the same time, Kovacevic offers us a hopeful note. He shows us how humanity can break through the thin shell of politics with a new perspective; one that joins us together in our similarities, instead of separating us with our differences.

The Process--Realizing the Passion

Most of our developmental energy focused on determining how to approach what Bob Djurdjevich called the "didascalias." The Oxford English Dictionary has no entry for *didascalia*. It does, however, have *didascalic*, meaning "pertaining to a teacher" and *didascaly* and its plural *didascalies*, meaning "a document that is intended to teach."[4] The didascalias are Teya's voice, coming from some future time, describing the actions of the play in memory. Often they are nothing more than a stage direction, describing in first person, precisely what is happening on stage. Though we learned a great deal from struggling with them, without Kovacevic's involvement in the rehearsal process, we never satisfactorily deciphered his intentions. Bob was in communication with Kovacevic, but since he was still in hiding in Cyprus, it was brief and infrequent.

Bob Djurdjevich translated the didascalias as a character named--"Narrator." Certainly, traditional narration can be thought of as a character, and in some aspects the didascalias do act as narration. Tom in *The Glass Menagerie* or Salieri in *Amadeus* step out of the action and deliver the narration, as if the characters were speaking from the afterlife, or some nebulous theatrical miasma. However, in *The Professional*, the didascalias are frequent and often brief, and disrupt the action more than further it. Kovacevic's narration does not work in the same manner as that of Williams or Shaffer. Instead of demarcating transitions in the play, this narration serves more as a counterpoint to the action which continues beneath it.

In our staged reading of the play and in our full production, we tried two different approaches in our use of the didascalias. In the reading, while I played Teya, a different actor, David Winter, played the Narrator. For the production, the director, Peter Craze preferred to have me record the narration. These two approaches left very different impressions. In the reading, the Narrator was Teya, while I was Teya's memory of the action. The audience understood clearly the relationship between the two. Teya was sitting, remembering what had happened, while I performed it. In the production, I played Teya, while the recorded narration served as the memory. In this approach the action in which Teya was involved was immediate. The audience was asked to suspend its need to understand the relationship between the narration and the action until the very end. The didascalias still spoke of the action as a memory, but because Teya's voice was disembodied, the audience members felt that they were seeing the action as it occurred. The voice recalled the action simultaneously with the audience's observation of it, not just in transition or summary. This approach worked better, placing more emphasis on the action itself and less on its relationship with the didascalias. However, in the reading, when Teya (the didascalic voice) interrupted the action to describe it, it was a source of humor. As we began to rehearse for the production, when Teya (the disembodied voice) interrupted the action, it literally interrupted the action. It wasn't the character choosing to interrupt, it was a technical cue. We decided that it was necessary to edit the didascalias.

We discussed the possibility of doing without them as well. Still, there were enough clues in the text to suggest that the didascalias played an important part in Kovacevic's intention. At times, the narration provided a sweet obbligato, over and above the action, informing it with humor, pathos, and irony. It gave the audience members a second perspective that provided an immediate antithesis to what they were viewing. The didascalias are the final evidence of Teya's transformation, and in the end hover mysteriously over the action.

> LUKE: For once, you will have to be a professional. Just like I was all my life. My Milosh is not here, so you'll

have to type it all yourself, and insert those . . . those
. . . what do you call those descriptions in the
dialogue?

TEYA: Didascalias.
LUKE: That's right, didascalias.

And then a moment later:

LUKE: With these didascalias, it could even be played in a
theatre. You, I, Martha and that Lunatic. Wonderful company,
wonderful destinies. (33)

The didascalias serve as the voice of Teya recalling Luke's visit as he transcribes the dialogue. The action shows us the events that transform him into a "professional," who can now be the writer he has always imagined himself to be. The didascalias are the results of the transformation happening in some other place, as we observe the action. But we don't know this until the action is complete. It is another one of Kovacevic's surprises. His layering of these didascalias are crucial to the theatricality he has so skillfully created. Our production eventually left most of the didascalias intact. We cut the most disruptive ones, and attempted to place the rest neatly into motivated pauses within the action. This was successful most of the time.[5]

An added complication was the translator's own political agenda. At the beginning of our process, we felt privileged that Djurdjevich had such an immediate perspective on what was occurring in Yugoslavia. He had grown up there and had, since the end of the cold war, returned on a regular basis for business purposes. He spoke to us as someone who had the ear of Milosevic, Yeltsin, and Cyrus Vance, having made specific recommendations to Milosevic concerning the Croatian conflict. However, we soon learned that his perspective on the political situation was highly biased so that everything he told us needed to be filtered through that knowledge.

Originally what Djurdjevich sent us was a sincere translation of Kovacevic's work, devoid of propaganda. It was a statement about humanity that, though it takes place in a totalitarian state, reverberates far beyond the boundaries of any political ideology. We became suspect when Djurdjevich sent us rewrites in which Teya gives a speech condemning George Bush and his policy toward the Balkan states. Though his initial impulse in translating *The Professional* was honorable, Djurdjevich wasn't beyond altering the playwright's vision to include a few well honed barbs of his own. This cast a shadow of doubt over the veracity of the translation itself; a lack of confidence that to this day is still extant.

In our production I played Teya. Luke was played by Joe Bellan, a legend in Bay Area theatre. To direct, I brought Peter Craze from England, with whom I had worked at the London/Berkeley Drama Studio. He later directed the London production of the play. The presence of Joe Bellan was a special part of *The Professional*. With his rubbery Jack Gilford-like face, Joe Bellan is the ultimate "professional." His portrayal highlighted the play's humor and brought its humanity to the surface. We could see in his portrayal all facets of this marvelous character--the policeman, the father, the joker, the teacher, and the man struggling to keep his dignity in the face of death.

My natural tendency as an actor gives the characters I play a certain affability. It was clear, early on, that this was not going to work for Teya. Peter Craze directed me to be more cold and untouchable, which created greater contrasts in a number of areas. First, it contrasted the two characters. It also created a contrast between Teya and his past. This was important. The audience, early in the play, must wonder whether to believe Luke or not. If the Teya he is talking about and the one the audience is seeing seem sufficiently different, the tension surrounding that question can be sustained longer. In addition, this provided an important contrast with the Teya that would eventually appear at the play's end. Luke chips steadily away at Teya's bureaucratic persona, and the eventual unveiling of the true Teya, must be put off as long as possible. Luke draws Teya's humanity to the surface. To make this work, Teya must be withdrawn, tense, and officious at the beginning.

From the start, everyone involved seemed aware that *The Professional* was a special project. Introducing Kovacevic to an American audience was part of it, but it also allowed us a connection with a timely, international event. Our playwright was in hiding, many of our audience members had relatives in danger, and our translator had his car vandalized, due to his political standing. Yet our message was one of conciliation. We took on the guise of the "Other" and found an immediate empathy. As professionals, we know how to disguise the routine nature of our work, but performing the same role eight times a week for months at a time often becomes just another job. In *The Professional*, there was a difference, and I'm not talking about our way of working, or our approaches to the roles. It was a difference in spirit. We were reminded of the reason we were drawn to the theatre in the first place, that rare experience when we can believe in the play in which we are performing and what it says; when we recognize that the characters we are playing and ourselves are connected. It is only when such a connection is made between the performers and the material, that the potential of theatre is realized. It is a connection much like that which occurs between Luke and Teya, when they begin to experience the "Other" as themselves.

Though *The Professional* is ultimately concerned with Teya's self-discovery, and how both characters are served by it; it is important to see that Kovacevic makes this possible only through Luke and Teya's conciliation. In this play, we see that in allowing a division between ourselves and our fellow inhabitants on this earth, we also endure a division within ourselves. Our wholeness as individuals is inextricably connected to our wholeness as a species. When the reparation is complete in *The Professional*, the healing begins to take place within each character, as well as between the characters.

Kovacevic shows us the curative quality of this perspective, even as we experience it ourselves. Watching Teya and Luke, so much of what we used to define ourselves falls away. We become the Father and the Son, the Mother and the Daughter. We become the Communist and the Capitalist, the Democrat and the Republican. For theatre artists, what makes *The Professional* ultimately enduring, is that what it communicates is the very thing we practice when we perform. Zelda Fichandler in her address to the Theatre Communications Group National Conference in 1994 said it best:

> [The artist] is always observing, always formulating, always searching out the world through new angles of viewing . . . to find some hints, some clues, some truths by walking in the shoes of The Other. And, then, bringing these truths forward in a form that is elegant and precise so that they may be received and apprehended by the rest of us. [6]

Dusan Kovacevic has created the form. It is time for us to receive and apprehend.

I do not suggest that performances of *The Professional* throughout Yugoslavia will bring peace. Nor do I believe that theatre by itself can provide a panacea for the world's troubles. I do know, however, that consciousness cannot be legislated, and when laws force people to "behave" against their will, separation and divisiveness are inevitable. The only way a significant change in consciousness can be entertained is through offering new perspectives. And these new perspectives will not be accepted and integrated into a community of people overnight. Their adoption will take place slowly, in one person at a time. This is what theatre like *The Professional* can do.

These days, the world seems small. International theatre knows no boundaries. Dusan Kovacevic has spoken to his fellow countrymen, and has been heard most resoundingly, thousands of miles away.

Notes

1. All references to Dusan Kovacevic's previous writings as well as his biography, are from Dusan Kovacevic, *Drame* (Belgrade: Bigz, 1983) 271.
2. Jasmina Bojic, telephone interview, 22 September 1994.
3. All quotations are from Dusan Kovacevic, trans. Bob Djurdjevich (Unpublished. 1992).
4. In Greek, there is the word "*didaskalia*" which has two meanings. The first is "teaching: education, learning." The second, however, I found intriguing: "the rehearsing of a drama." See George Henry Liddell and Robert Scott, eds., *A Lexicon* (Oxford: Clarendon P, 1979) 169.
5. Peter Craze, our director, in preparing for the New York production spoke to Kovacevic directly. The didascalias apparently were intended to be spoken by the actor playing Teya while in the midst of the action, as if confiding in the audience. This option occurred to us but seemed likely to be even more disruptive than the recording. For the New York production there are plans to have Kovacevic involved from the beginning, so hopefully this mystery will be addressed and ultimately resolved.
6. Michele Pearce, "A Community of Difference," *American Theatre* (September 1994): 28.

Vestiges of Control: Censorship and Society in Contemporary Egyptian Theatre
by Kenneth Robbins

In his essay, "The Effervescent Egyptian Theatre," published in 1964, Irving Brown provides a clear and comprehensive overview of the state of Egyptian theatre and drama thirty years ago. He discovered in Cairo and Alexandria a vital and forward-moving theatrical scene that led him to conclude that:

> There is no reason why the Egyptian Theatre cannot be, before the end of the century, the major cultural enterprise of the United Arab Republic, the principal outlet for its young writers, and a nationally-characterized artistic endeavor worthy of international attention. (68)

His conclusions were based on a theatrical energy that included the opening of a second national theatrical troupe in Cairo (The Pocket Theatre, 1962). He also found that drama training programs in the public school system were on the increase and that effective dramatic instruction was taking place on the college level. He noted the expansion of the National Theatre and the Puppet Theatre and the maturation of the Pocket, all of which were fulfilling the goal of developing Egyptian playwrights. He viewed foreign influences as having a continuing and positive impact on play production processes, especially the top flight foreign theatre groups just beginning to discover Egypt and its hungry theatrical audience. In addition, study abroad opportunities for Egyptian theatrical artists were viewed by Brown as an important step forward in that country's theatrical development. Finally, he recognized an apparent enthusiasm and dedication among Egyptian theatre artists, educators, and administrators and anticipated its continuation.

However, Brown did not offer his conclusions of future excellence without a number of qualifiers. The Egyptian theatre, according to Brown, would achieve its place of pre-eminence within the Arabic artistic world:

> if compensation for theatre personnel can continue to rise to the point where a career in this art is financially worthwhile . . . if subordinate government officials who would make the theatre an instrument of short term social or political purposes can be restrained by the broader view of the chief ministers . . . and if the theatre can be left free to fulfill its function as one of man's most effective interpretative arts. (68)

Thirty years after Brown made his forecast for the Egyptian theatre and a few short years before the turn of the century that forms the boundary for his prognostications, I visited Egypt with the idea of exploring the current theatrical scene. My experience in Egypt, six weeks in the summer of 1993 and ten additional days in September of that same year, admittedly limited both in scope and exposure, revealed a situation in Egypt far removed from Brown's overly naive prediction. Obviously, Brown's three qualifications for the Egyptian theatre's emergence as "the major cultural enterprise of the United Arab Republic" were not met. Historical developments, principally the 1967 war with Israel, the fall from grace of Nasser and the rise to power of Sadat, and the continued battle between Islamic and secular forces, could not have been predicted. Yet, these and other events have had a profound effect on the entire art scene in the Middle East.

My experience with the theatre in Egypt began when I participated as one of the twelve American scholars in the Fulbright Hayes Summer Seminar, "Islamic Civilization and Culture." Though not a theatre event, I identified as my research project for the six weeks an overview of what is happening in Egypt in the theatrical arena. As the only scholar interested in this subject, I was left to my own resources more often than not, and, being restricted by language, I found that access to the theatre was difficult. I was, however, able to pursue my interests and make contact with Egyptian individuals who shared my love for the theatre. I also discovered that theatre was located at the core of the arts movement in Cairo and that through one contact I managed another and then another and so on until I felt that in the limited time of six weeks, I was able to touch base with much that was occurring in Cairo.

Of immense help to me was Gordon Witty, a graduate student at the University of Pennsylvania spending a year in Cairo as part of a Fulbright student award. His Egyptian mentor was Dr. Fawzi Fahmi Ahmed, President of the Cairo Academy of Arts and Chairman of the Cairo International Festival for Experimental Theatre. Dr. Fawzi, a playwright in his spare time, offered me an opportunity to return to Cairo to serve the Festival as a member of the International Jury.

The theatre scene in Cairo is dominated by two theatrical forces: the public and the private sectors, with a third, the "free" theatre, struggling to secure an audience. The public or governmental supported theatre is the affordable production core for the Egyptian population with ticket prices ranging from 5 to 20 LE ($1.50-6.00 US). The governmental theatre is the primary outlet for the established and emerging Egyptian playwright, the developing actor and director, as well as the newer, less commercial work in translation. Performances are usually in small houses with runs dictated either by audience attendance or by governmental whim.

The private theatre is the commercial venue geared for the traditional Gulf tourist with ticket prices ranging from 30 to 100 LE ($10-30 US). Plays performed in this sector range from Western musical imports to Egyptian farces. The next big event rumored for Cairo was *Phantom of the Opera* in translation. Private productions are often in large houses. The public theatre has begun to offer productions more and more like those of the private sector while trying to maintain the seriousness of its original intent.

As the two principal theatres vie for the same audience, namely the moneyed Gulf tourist, there is a small yet important segment of Cairene audience, primarily the intelligentsia who are firmly aware of the outside world and who are unserved by contemporary Egyptian theatre. Thus, a third and relatively new yet politically vital theatre movement, referred to as the Free Theatre Movement, is beginning to offer opportunities for the audiences who long for more challenging entertainment, as well as training venues for new and sometimes highly talented performers and directors. In 1987, Hassan el Gretely broke with theatrical tradition, that is working for private entrepreneurs or governmental subsidy, and established Warsha, his own production company. His efforts were to the delight of numerous unsatisfied Cairenes whose interest in serious drama was not being met. This "fringe" was discovered to be of significant size in 1990 when the state sponsored Festival for Experimental Theatre was abruptly cancelled due to the Gulf Crisis. The rallying cry of the young theatre practitioners at that time was "War or no war, the show must go on!" When the Free Theatre Festival emerged from the ashes of the Gulf War, all in the Cairo arts scene were astounded by the number and names of the emerging theatrical companies: the Jugglers, the Loonies, the Visionaries, the Rebels, the Luminaries, the Protesters, the Apollonians, and many more, characterized by writer Nehad Selaiha as "like jinnis [sic] late loosed from their bottles" (12). Today in Cairo alone there are forty or more such theatre organizations, each with its own following, usually meager, and its own cadre of youthful performers of varying talents.

The movement is called "free" because its productions are staged without requiring clearance by the government censor. According to Effat Yehia, director of the Caravan Theatre Company, the current censorship law affecting theatre production in Egypt refers to those plays intended for long runs. Plays can be performed without the censor's approval so long as no more than two consecutive performances are offered. Effat bemoans the difficulty of finding an audience for a production denied continuous performances; yet the opportunity to perform "free" of censorship is an attractive one and outweighs the need, at this point in time, for audience development.

Gordon Witty discredits the Free Theatre Movement and proclaims it to be inconsequential since it does not impact a significantly broad Cairene audience. Still, it exists as a theatrical alternative to the two principal theatrical sectors and provides training and performance outlets for emerging talent, including playwrights and offers serious drama for a small but devoted clientele. In fact there was a second festival in Cairo paralleling the International Festival for Experimental Theatre and many believe that what was being seen outside the realm of the jury was more exciting and better received than official entries.

Censorship affects all forms of artistic endeavor in Egypt, and is imposed on several levels. There seems to be a particular kind of drama that Arab tourists and moneyed Egyptian audiences will pay to see. This type is one which provokes momentary laughter and moves into simplistic melodrama supported by inane and predictable farce. An example of this kind of theatrical experience is exemplified by the major film hit for the summer of 1993, *El Mensi* or *The Forgotten*. A predictable comedy, *The Forgotten* mixes moments of slapstick farce, fantasy, political satire, melodrama, and social commentary. The government actually allowed the lead actor, a famous comedian, to parody the rhetorical style of Egyptian President Hosny Mubarak. I inquired about the unusual mixture of styles and content and was informed that such was the norm in contemporary Egyptian film as well as stage productions. As long as it is funny, there seems to be little regard for unified content or aesthetic form.

To be produced with any hope for financial return, the contemporary Egyptian playwright must satisfy the perceived desires of the paying audience. In addition to society's censorship, playwrights face a more extreme situation with the government's submerged censorship. Playwright Karim Alrawi documented his difficulties in "The Still Small Voice Within Egypt." His play, *City of Peace*, from the 1990 Free Theatre Festival fell victim to the disguised implementation of censorship.

> The subject matter of the play is undeniably controversial as it is about religious censorship, with a passing reference to [Salman Rushdie's] *Satanic Verses*. Without prior warning the committee announced that our company would be performing on a day when one of our actors would not be available, in a theatre that we had specified was unsuitable, and as a matinee performance that would have denied us an audience. When we objected we were subjected to blackmail and public abuse. (25)

An attempt to produce Ibrahim Masoud's farcical comedy, *Attia The Terrorist Woman* demonstrates how the issue of censorship is often used as a guise to submerge personal agenda. Originally, the play was written for a male lead, but with the hiring of Suheir el Babli, the most popular actress on the Egyptian stage, the role was altered, not just in gender but in other ways which were against the playwright's intent. Much of what had been done to the play was supposedly conceived to be in the best interest of the star and with the support and approval of the director/producer. It is difficult to discover if the circumstances related to Masoud's experience are common or unique. There is evidence that such is the case in most plays performed in the private sector and upon occasion in the public one as well.

All plays, except those performed fewer than three consecutive times, must be submitted to the governmental censor, an individual employed within the Ministry of Culture. This censor must approve of each play. He does this by placing his stamp of approval on each page of a manuscript. A page without such a stamp cannot be performed. Playwright Mohamad Enani reported an incident wherein the censor refused to sanction his play without a final page attached as a disclaimer for the satire in the play. The playwright composed a speech to satisfy the censor, who stamped all the pages and returned it to the playwright with the caveat that if the director did not care to include the final speech, it would be fine.

In an interview with American theatre professor Mark Fearnow, playwright Karim Alrawi responded to the question, "How would you describe the current environment for writers in Egypt?":

> This may sound a little over-dramatic, but I think that we are living the death of a culture. Censorship has reached unprecedented levels and it is becoming increasingly difficult to stage a play or get a novel published, especially plays that deal with serious social issues. It is quite easy to get what are in effect vaudeville shows put on, even some quite bawdy ones, which belies the Censor's claims that his interest is in public morality. It's quite clear that his interest lies elsewhere, that his interest is closely aligned to the thinking of the religious fundamentalist movement, which is growing quite powerful in Egypt. (23)

Alrawi's comments punctuate the scope of the censorship problem.

When doubts regarding the religious subject matter are present, the government often passes the material along to the Grand Sheik of Al Azhar and leaves the work of this kind of censorship to that fundamental arm of the Islamic religion. The Islamic attitude toward art and the act of creative expression has never been a kindly one. Today it is even less kind than at any time in the religion's past. In Enani's autobiographical essay that introduces a collection of his plays, he describes a situation in Alexandria in 1985 when a theatre poster announcing a performance of one of his plays drew unexpected attention. He reports that "they scribbled on it, tore it a part, writing remarks like 'You cannot create: only God creates: be modest!'" (38). The anti-creativity notion arising from Islamic fundamentalism was reaffirmed in the *Egyptian Gazette*, which read that "Along with the terrorist wave sweeping over the region, a coinciding retrogressive trend has been growing calling for the abolition of arts and science" (5). The fundamentalist threat to the arts and specifically to the theatre is taking three forms. Perhaps the most unusual and probably least expected is the current trend for actresses of stage and screen (twenty three in the last two years) to "take the veil." "Taking the veil" is an act of chastity among women. The external symbol of veiling one's self is an indication of her choosing a lifestyle in line with that of the Prophet; once the veil has been taken, the step cannot be reversed. Thus when an actress who has created for herself a valid and respected career within the secular activity of the stage and/or screen announces that she is taking the veil, she has proclaimed to the world that she will no longer be a participant in public life. The most shattering of these recent "retirements" was that of Suheir el Babli. Her decision to veil came only twelve days before she was to open in *Attia the Terrorist Woman*.

Speculation as to what is driving professionals like El Babli to forsake their careers in favor of a life of devotion to Islam range from age--it is better to get out while the public still loves you than to hang on too long--to a lack of decent roles in contemporary drama, to talk of a conspiracy against theatre, perpetrated out of Saudi Arabia. This last idea of conspiracy was fueled when a Cairene television personality revealed that she was offered 2 million Egyptian pounds if she would take the veil, an offer she refused. This is the only evidence to support the conspiracy notion, but, for many, one example is enough. Not all in the Egyptian theatre view the "retirements" as a negative thing. Regardless, the theatrical scene in Cairo is feeling the pinch as stars vacate the stage.

Mohamad Salmawi, former managing editor of *Al Ahram Weekly*, the equivalent of *The New York Times* to the Arab speaking world, is a playwright strongly affected by the threat of Islamic censorship. His new play *The Flower and the Chain*, has been denied production by the public theatre. According to Salmawi, fear of bombings and harassment from the Islamic right has caused the denial. Salmawi reported to me during my visit that he felt his play was a dead piece. However, the play has been included in the *Theatrical Arabic Series*, published by the General Egyptian Book Organization. So perhaps this new and important play will find its way into an English translation. The subject of Salmawi's play is Islamic terrorism. A young terrorist disguised as a woman wearing a hegab invades a peaceful home. He reveals his identity and intentions: to hold the family hostage and do the bidding of his sheik. He terrorizes the entire household while waiting for the guidance of his Amir, guidance which never comes. The play ends with the death of the invader, a victim of his own fanaticism. Salmawi's play is an honest, straightforward attack on Islam, using little or no humor to make its point. In contrast, Lenin el Ramly's popular play, *In Plain Arabic*, is a delightful satire of the entire Arab world, and sidesteps any direct comment on Islam. El Ramly believes that direct address regarding fundamental religious ideas, attitudes, and practices is not to be tolerated. Ramly's play succeeds by avoiding the most compelling issue of his day; Salmawi must wait for a more tolerant day, one that may never come.

The ultimate power of the Islamic right and the Grand Sheik of Al Azhar is the fatwa, an official decree issued by an Islamic leader. Many are aware of the fatwa issued by the Ayotollah Khomeini against Indian/British novelist, Salman Rushdi, for his novel, *Satanic Verses*. Of course this fatwa comes from a completely different culture (Iran) and relates to circumstances not at all related to situations in Egypt, but the death threat was mandated since there are those who believe that Rushdi is guilty of apostasy and the Koran orders Believers to invoke capital punishment against all apostates. Egyptian thinker, academic, and journalist, Farag Foda, was also the subject of a fatwa issued by fundamentalist extremists and was murdered by several Islamic radicals in June 1993. With the ever present eyes of the government and Islam guarding the social order of Egypt, it is no wonder that playwrights and other creative artists are acutely aware of the dangers inherent in their work.

Not only is censorship controlling the Egyptian theatre, it is also affecting the theatre imported for artistic and educational purposes. The Cairo International Festival for Experimental Theatre brings the best of the world's theatre into Egypt with the intention of assisting the development of theatre artists within the host country. Yet the censorship beast will not leave the Festival alone. It became a damaging issue in regard to an exceptional dance/theatre piece entitled *Raptus*, the work of director Claudio Bernardo of Atelier Sainte Anne of Belgium.

Raptus was a stunning dance production staged in a near ideal spot, Wekalit Al-Ghoury in medieval Cairo. Wekalit Al-Ghoury is a state owned sixteenth-century hotel preserved by the Ministry of Culture as a home for cultural events; the performance space is the inner court, surrounded by a tier of five balconies, centered by a stone fountain, and a flagstone yard. The production began with two dancers making their way down an ancient twenty-foot ladder, one carrying the other on his back, reversing positions midway like two insects. They danced their lives--lives filled with pain, toil, play, sleep, and more toil--and the audience was elevated not only by the remarkable quality of their work but by the brilliantly clear night and the warm breezes that characterize Cairo in early September. Midway through the event, one of the men appeared in the garb of a beautiful woman and proceeded to disrobe while reciting a text, taken, so I was told, from the Book of Jeremiah, and suddenly the repartee of the two began to take on a new meaning, that of two homosexual lovers surviving as best they can their less-than-accepted existences. Therein lay the problem with the Belgian production: homosexuality is taboo in the Muslim world.

Our charge as festival jurors--there were eleven of us representing Spain, Germany, Britain, Poland, Morocco, France, Mexico, Argentina, Egypt, and the United States--was to select the recipients for five major awards: best actor, actress, director, technical achievement, and production. A number of us on the jury were eager to honor the work of the Belgian director. Because of the intense feelings against the subject matter, the best we could do was a special commendation for exceptional work.

Censorship had also affected the excellent Polish production of *Dr. Faustus*. In order for the play to be performed, the actress playing Helen of Troy was forced to don a costume for her brief appearance on stage. The logic behind the censorship--nudity is taboo as well--was articulated by Sanaa Fatahalla, an ultra-conservative Egyptian journalist and fellow juror; she claimed that to honor that which is not allowed would lead to the Festival's termination. Thus, using her logic, censoring parts of the Festival was a justified means of protecting the whole. Nehad Selaiha in *Egyptian Theatre, A Diary: 1990-1992*, reports similar instances of censorship in the 1989 and 1991 Festivals. My fellow jurist from Germany argued against the idea of justifiable censorship by posing the question, "Is a festival worth continuing if it must do so while based on a lie?"

Censoring the world's theatre as it plays on the Cairene stage is not the only vestige of control manifested in Egypt. Plays translated from other languages to Arabic are severely altered in the process and are indeed transformed instead of translated. Karim Alrawi writes of such in his essay, "*Course Translation*":

> In Dr. Nehad Selaiha's Arabic translation, Harold Pinter's four-scene play, *Mountain Language*, becomes a comedy of manners. The word "shit" is translated as "shut up"; "shithouse" as "dregs," "arse" as "posterior." But it is "fuck" that comes in for the most creative mistranslation. Where possible it is omitted. Where not, it is turned into what it is not. "She looks like a fucking intellectual" becomes "I believe she associated with intellectuals, sons of dogs". . . *Mountain Language* is a play of great relevance to the Middle East, which is made up of so many minority communities. It is a play that raises questions about the structure of power and authority in our societies and its relationship to language. This is precisely what the translation avoids dealing with. The use of self-censorship by translators is another means of spreading the load of censorship and making it more difficult to recognize it as such. (23)

Nehad Selaiha, object of Alrawi's ire, is fully aware of the problems facing Egypt today:

> [T]he issue of the artist's freedom became the focus of a heated debate (as a result of the International Festival). The course the debate has taken so far does not augur well for the artist; at best, it may eventually die down, leaving the issue unresolved; at worst, it may yield further restrictions and a lot of fear, making experimentation in the theatre virtually impossible. (141)

There are no indications that control over the theatre and other arts will be lessened; in fact, all indicators point to an ever tightening stranglehold on artistic endeavors. The Islamicists, through terrorist actions aimed at the fragile Egyptian economy, possess the ability to affect governmental actions and personal attitudes. The constant threat from the religious right to the secular government cannot be ignored. There are forces at work in Egypt which will not be satisfied until a theocratic form of government, similar to that found in Iran, has been installed in Cairo.

So, what is the future of the theatre scene in Egypt? Does it have a future? I believe the answer might be yes if viewed in light of the performance of *Sketches From Life*, as performed by the Caravan Theatre Company under the direction of Effat Yehia. The production reflects the dedication, the artistry, and the energy of the Free Theatre Movement. The subject of Caravan's production was the serious question surrounding the lack of human rights for women in an Islamic society. The strengths of this group are its talented young actors and the skills of its young director. Effat's abilities, perhaps due in no small part to the fact that she is one of the few women directors currently producing theatre in Egypt, have brought her offers of work within the public sector. She chooses to remain with Caravan inside the Free Theatre Movement, a movement which holds forth the greatest prospects for her continued development as a theatre artist.

Another positive sign indicating a future of health for the Egyptian theatre is the success of Lenin el Ramly's *In Plain Arabic*, a production which has proven that a play can reach a wide and enthusiastic audience without a star on the marquee. El Ramly and his director, Mohammed Sobhi, selected a cast of novices, none of whom had appeared in a professional production. The result of such casting was a high energy, fast-paced satirical romp which delighted audiences while hurling barb after barb at contemporary Arab societies. El Ramly has been approached by a production organization to have his work performed in Jordan, with the indication that the image of Jordan as presented on the stage in Cairo must be changed. El Ramly rejected the invitation refusing to make the suggested changes in his text. So yes, there might be hope.

Even with censorship impacting negatively on the Cairo International Festival for Experimental Theatre, I firmly believe that the annual event along with the Free Theatre Movement is essential to Egypt's continued theatrical development. During my first trip to Cairo, I attended a lengthy lecture presented by Egyptian scholar Sherif Katir. The topic was the future of the Egyptian National Theatre and what shape it is to take if it continues to emerge. Katir indicated that the theatre must rely on the rituals of the Pharonic past, a theatre founded on Egyptian language, its ancient ritual, and its folklore. The lecture was followed by a question and answer session where two sides were clearly drawn. There were those, usually older and more reserved, who agreed with Katir that the Egyptian National Theatre must be purely Egyptian, relying as nearly as possible on Egyptian national pride to find definition. The others, usually younger and much more passionate in articulating views, urged all concerned to turn instead to the West, that the emerging Egyptian National Theatre must be founded on Greek principles with Western development as guide posts. Judging from the energy and excitement with which the argument in favor of a Greek foundation was received, it is apparent that the annual Festival for Experimental Theatre is essential as it provides many of the current and future Egyptian theatre artists an opportunity to witness the best from the West in their own theatrical spaces.

In its unique way, the Festival is addressing the religious right in a positive fashion. The fact that the event is a product of the Egyptian Ministry of Culture indicates that the government is capable of providing assistance to the arts in a serious and important manner. The Festival and the Free Theatre Movement are the only theatrical activities in Egypt that I witnessed which might lead the nation to Irving Brown's prediction that before the end of the century, the Egyptian theatre will be "the major cultural enterprise of the United Arab Republic." Still, thirty years after his insightful evaluation, Brown's vision for a predominant and internationally recognized arts enterprise for Egypt remains only as potential, not reality. The most significant and ever-present danger to the theatre in Egypt is that of fundamentalism.

How does the theatrical situation in a country halfway around the world affect us here in America? It indicates that we have a long way to go before we reach the level of censorship felt by Egyptian artists. Though the situation surrounding the National Endowment for the Arts is a serious one, it is ultimately insignificant since the level of support meted out by the government is at best puny and rarely felt by most producing organizations. If the NEA ceased to exist tomorrow, theatre in this country would survive. Perhaps the most important lesson we can learn from Egypt is that of dealing with fundamentalism. Most of us are aware of the rise of the religious right in this country, and though it is not nearly as pervasive nor as profoundly negative toward art and creative expression as the Islamicist movement, it is nonetheless a significant force--one to be aware of at all times. Though a fatwa has yet to be issued against any of our artists, we should be aware of the fact that there are societies in today's world that can and will attack our basic rights of free expression. It is in our best interest to be forever vigilant in our attempts to protect our freedoms lest they be victimized by the good intentions of religious fundamentalism.

Works Cited

Alrawi, Karim. "The Still, Small Voice Within Egypt." *Index on Censorship* 21 February 1992: 25.

——. "Coarse Translation." *Index on Censorship* 21 February 1992: 21.

Brown, Irving. "The Effervescent Egyptian Theatre." *Theatre Annual* 21(1964): 57-68.

The Egyptian Gazette 9 July 1993:5

Enani, Mohamad. The Prisoner and the Jailor. Trans. Nayla Naguib. Cairo: General Egyptian Book Organization, 1993.

Fearnow, Mark. "Karim Alrawi on Censorship." *The Dramatist Guild Quarterly* 31 (Spring 1994): 22-30.

The Fulbrighter: Newsletter of the Fulbright Alumni Association. (Spring 1994): 4.

Selaiha, Nehad. *Egyptian Theatre, A Diary: 1990-1992.* Cairo: General Egyptian Book Organization, 1993.

Year of Improvising in the Balkans
by Vivian K. Mason

Bulgaria has emerged from totalitarian times with shaky steps. Transition is what they call the time between communist rule and a democratic styled government with an open economy. It seems simple-- millions of ideas blasting through the Iron Curtain, newly liberated citizens excitedly examining this new information, eagerly improvising new ventures in a country where legislation has not caught up with new enterprise. Many Westerners imagine a newly democratized populace casting aside communist censorship with open broadcasting, publishing, and performing. We imagine great forces of repressed expression coursing through the new neon of freedom. The truth is more complex.

In order to aid Bulgaria's transition to democracy and democratic ideals the American University in Bulgaria (AUBG), an American structured, funded, and run liberal arts institution, opened its doors in 1991. The first class of 200 students, mostly Bulgarians, had only a vague understanding of American liberal arts education. Bulgarian teens attend specialized high schools, like their West European counterparts, and must pass stringent examinations to enter universities where they study a specialized program for five years. Because instruction at AUBG is in English, a great majority of the students have graduated from their country's English language high schools. Instead of choosing a traditional European-styled Bulgarian university they gambled on an American institution.

I came to the city of Blagoevgrad in the fall of 1993 to teach as a theatre generalist--the only full-time fine arts appointment on the AUBG faculty. The theatre program itself was in transition. My predecessor introduced students to their first participation in the theatrical process, directing two plays and teaching theatre classes. He won their loyalty. Unfortunately this man suddenly died and I was to fill his position. The interview team assured me that theatre was vital to the institution, loved by all, with active involvement by a dedicated core of students. I thought my mission would be easy.

What followed was a year of discovery for me and a year of challenge for my students. All year long we scrambled and improvised. Initially standoffish, the students slowly warmed to me. With student help I concocted a theatre program out of nothing and increased the students' opportunity to perform. They acted in many different kinds of performances, ranging from fifteen-minute classroom assignments to comic improvisations to a full-blown three-act drama. They performed texts with familiar themes and strange new messages. Over the year we traveled from witch hunt to AIDS. The doubt and distrust that faced me when I arrived ended one April night in an evening of profound theatre. The students performed scenes from contemporary American plays for their final exams. One group presented scenes from *Angels in America*. At the curtain call students from eight countries--some of those countries close to war--pressed toward the stage with tears streaming down their faces, reaching to grasp hands, thanking me and congratulating each other, drained yet exhilarated. I observed first-hand how theatre can be an agent of intercultural communication.

Throughout the year I asked my students to write about their experiences in personal journals--to record, in English, their insights and discoveries about theatre production and the process of acting. Most had not had the opportunity to take a theatre class or to experience the process of putting on a play. Consequently their journals expressed a mish mash of personal feelings and naive observations about an experience unique to their lives. Excerpts from their unedited journals chart the problems we encountered and the solutions we improvised to create an effective program in educational theatre.

Shortly after I arrived I was faced with the dilemma of choosing the fall play. The selection process proved to be an interesting intercultural consideration. What new ideas would appeal to students living in a time of transition? While American film, television, and music are now widely broadcast across East Europe, much of it is indiscriminate, like releases of marginal movies, "Alf" and faddish music such as disco. Yet AUBG students attend the cinema regularly and appreciate good American film. A colleague calls the students "cinema junkies" as they can rattle off countless lists of Hollywood screenwriters, directors, and actors. They watch MTV constantly in the AUBG café. The AUBG radio station plays American rap and disco which blares from scores of Blagoevgrad street cafés. Young Bulgarians enjoy the exposure to contemporary American culture.

Their appreciation of American culture notwithstanding, it was important to know what plays the students had read or seen. What themes would resonate in Bulgaria? It has been noted elsewhere that East European students have voracious appetites for reading and are "well read in the classics of British and American literature" (Fike and Phillips 47). It became apparent in my classroom that, while AUBG students have attended the theatre regularly through their lives, they are generally unfamiliar with American and British playwrights (Shakespeare is a notable exception), particularly contemporary writers. They have a good familiarity with their native country's playwrights, yet few have heard of Tennessee Williams, Beth Henley, David Mamet, or Tony Kushner. *Our Town*, directed by my predecessor in the fall of 1992, was unknown to AUBG students, but they liked it. For the spring he chose *Rhinoceros*, a script more familiar to them. It was staged on the wide marble staircase of AUBG's Main Building--a building, the students say, is filled with ghosts from the communist past.

Indeed, AUBG's forbidding concrete monolith building had been the newly constructed Communist Party headquarters--but the Party never settled in. Now among other students Party sons and daughters were studying history, political science, and business at a U.S. government-funded college. Every now and then a mysterious locked door opened in the interior wall along a hallway of faculty offices to reveal a cavernous room. Tentative American faculty peeked inside at a few sober-faced Bulgarian custodians who sat idly within, occasionally shifting and removing files. It turned out to be the Communist Party Regional Archives. The peek inside triggered my thoughts about communism in America and guided me to--*The Crucible*.

The decision to produce *The Crucible* generated mixed reactions. It was another experience with student distrust. I was unprepared for the onslaught of demanding, critical questions about my choice. Several students aggressively interrogated me with questions. "Why did you choose this play?" "Why do you choose an American play?" Wondering if the play would ignite hidden cultural sensitivities, I became a bit defensive to avoid being culturally offensive. My usual response was that it could be simply staged, has a large cast with many roles for women, has a universal theme, and is a good American play. I argued that they were there in part to acquire knowledge of American thinking and culture. One spirited Bulgarian student, who calls herself by the American nickname "Betty," was disappointed that I had not chosen a comedy. "I do not think this is a good choice," she informed me. "Why?" I asked. "Oh, things are not so happy now in Bulgaria and people don't want to be reminded of sad things," she reluctantly responded.

My fears were lessened when I discovered some students had already read or seen the play. An enthusiastic freshman from the Former Yugoslav Republic of Macedonia wrote about the play in his class journal, reinforcing my belief that Arthur Miller's theme of political persecution and hypocrisy was meaningful to these students:

> When I first heard that the fall production for the Introduction to Theatre course will be Arthur Miller's *The Crucible*, I thought, "Yeah, right, another of those American plays!" I was wrong. I had read the play only once, when I was 16 years old. I was in for a big surprise. I originally thought that this was one of those plays where the characters just talk and that's it . . . The most important part, and the biggest surprise was: the play said that mass hysteria is worse than communism itself.
>
> (Petar Arsovski, Macedonia, assistant director, *The Crucible*)

Petar's Albanian classmate, who had seen the play, expressed his pleasure to be cast in the role of Thomas Putnam:

> I was both surprised and glad to hear that this play was *The Crucible*. I have seen this play in Albania, in Albanian, and I really liked it. Now providence makes me to act in this play. I love it, that is why I was happy to be appointed as one of the actors.
>
> (Elton Vevechka, Albania, actor, *The Crucible*)

A journalism major interviewed me for the student newspaper about the play. Her questions were sharp and intelligent, but she also spoke of Bulgarian "witch hunts" and trials. Her comments supported my opinion of the play's appropriateness.

After maneuvering through the first cultural interchange of choosing a meaningful text, I almost came to a full stop. AUBG's building has no theatre. However, the National Ministry of Culture's regional theatre sits nearby on the same wide plaza. Through an interpreter and my slowly developing Bulgarian, I made rental arrangements with the Dramatischen Theatre's artistic and technical directors. Our agreement included rental of costumes and properties. This sounds like a routine process. In fact, it was arduous.

My preconceived assumption that Bulgaria's political transition would encourage theatrical experimentation and growth encountered an opposite truth. The Dramatischen Theatre has fallen on hard times, as have all Bulgaria's theatres, due to the lack of state funding. Eighteen regional theatres closed in 1994. National economic woes resulted in devalued currency and a rapid rise in inflation. Instead of engendering new plays and theatrical forms the post-communist Blagoevgrad theatre is recycling old plays, cutting back on performances, and putting their large staff on part-time employment. The directors are looking for new sources of revenue and have been accommodating to the American University, which they accurately perceive as rich by comparison. Yet the idea of renting their space and equipment was unfamiliar to them. They are slow to learn how to manage this potential source of income because Bulgarian theatres have no experience as capital-producing businesses. It took numerous meetings and drafts of documents in both Bulgarian and English to arrange for the rental of the black box theatre. I discovered the genius of Bulgarian bureaucracy. Bulgarians are not satisfied with the legitimacy of any document or contract without official seals or ink-stamped marks at the bottom of the page. I discovered the importance of the rubber stamp.

Added to this mounting bureaucratic nightmare was the seeming impossibility of making arrangements to rent costumes and stage properties. I rented the theatre with no technical support, since AUBG could not afford to hire a full-time professional crew from the Dramatischen Theatre for the entire year. To circumvent this problem I required all of the thirty-eight students enrolled in Introduction to Theatre to participate as actors, stage managers, house managers, designers, and technical crews in the fall play, only partly realizing I was throwing them and myself to the wolves.

We made appointments to travel to the theatre's costume warehouse. The first time I showed up with a student interpreter we discovered that the wardrobe people were on tour. The second time it became apparent that they expected me to drive them to their warehouse, since their theatre has no official car. The third time, with an AUBG vehicle and driver, the Dramatischen Theatre's wardrobe supervisor, her supervisor, and her supervisor's supervisor insisted on coming along. On this trip my student and I discovered we had made an appointment with the women's wardrobe supervisor. This was fine as we were able to pull all of our women's costumes. However, the men's wardrobe supervisor was a different person. Even though the men's costumes are stored down the hall in the same warehouse we were required to make a separate appointment with the men's wardrobe supervisor. No one else, not the women's wardrobe supervisor, her supervisor, nor her supervisor's supervisor, nor even the technical director, had the key or the authority to open the men's costume storage room. As the semester dragged on I became worried. I was directing a Puritan-era costume drama and had to clothe a nervous cast of twenty-six actors.

My worries were alleviated by an outstanding student costume crew who was able to improvise in clever ways. Erion Cano, a top student from Albania, had no knowledge of sewing, but he certainly could take control and get things done. His crew transformed Bulgarian peasant dresses into Puritan garb by hiring a professional tailor to make cuffs, caps and aprons. They created hats from cardboard and borrowed wigs from the local opera company. They attempted trips and repeated trips to the Dramatischen Theatre warehouse. For several weeks my shared office became an improvised costume shop, much to the dismay of my psychology program colleague. The costume crew's efforts ultimately paid off in the last days of rehearsal:

> Dressed rehearsal. I must admit that I feel really good in [John Proctor's] clothes. Everything seems more real with clothes.
> (Denis Dollaku, Albania, actor, *The Crucible*)

> With these props and the costumes everything was real! This was the most exciting moment--to feel like a professional.
> (Tatyana Minkova, Bulgaria, stage manager/actress, *The Crucible*)

The newness and possibilities of becoming involved in the backstage world of theatre filled a gap in the students' education. With no chance to participate in a theatre program in their high schools, students who took technical jobs faced their tasks with agitation, humor and frustration:

A real ordeal for my nerves, for my patience and experience! The thought that I can ever take part in the production of a real play has never crossed my mind. I was so excited and curious about everything that I was almost trembling all the time.
(Daniela Ivanova, Bulgaria, sound designer, *The Crucible*)

I became a specialist in posting notes. I stuck rehearsal schedules and revised rehearsal schedules and changes to the revised rehearsal schedules all over the University. At first I used only the callboards, but then I started to use all the walls available.
(Julia Musha, Albania, stage manager, *The Crucible*)

I confess that I felt quite astonished when you told me that you had no idea where we must get our makeup materials from. I had never seen any makeup materials in Bulgaria and I felt that it was difficult to find them. And you displayed a sort of carelessness that is so typical for every American who is not familiar with the situation of the markets in Bulgaria. I did not have even the slightest idea about where we could find makeup colors.
(Stoyan Atanasov, Bulgaria, makeup designer, *The Crucible*)

Despite his reservations, Stoyan did a remarkably thorough job. His comments about the scarcity of theatrical makeup in Bulgaria were true. One consequence of the transition is that the National Theatre no longer imports expensive Russian and German makeup. Ever resourceful, he bribed a staff person at the National Theatre in Sofia to "sell" him some of its limited stock.

Daniela and Stoyan's journal excerpts point to an interesting revelation to me regarding "gender preferred" production jobs. East European males do not seem to perceive costumes and makeup as a female domain, nor do the females perceive technical jobs, such as sound, in the male domain. Thus, Erion chose costumes, Stoyan chose makeup and Daniela chose sound. This completely countered my American teaching experience. In his journal Stoyan explained his rationale for joining the makeup crew:

I do not know exactly why did I choose to join the makeup crew. Since I had registered in this course to learn something new, I thought it reasonable to choose some job of which I had not even the slightest idea. I thought about ... lighting effects ... and music ... but I had no idea of how the makeup is applied. The only knowledge that I had was from watching my girlfriend doing her makeup. So the decision was taken and I joined the makeup crew.

(Stoyan Atanasov, Bulgaria, makeup designer, *The Crucible*)

I noticed another interesting phenomenon relative to AUBG's role in political transition and intercultural contact. A high percentage of the students who registered for theatre classes were "international" students. During the 1993-94 academic year approximately ninety percent of AUBG students were from Bulgaria. The other ten percent were international students, primarily other East European nationals: Albanians, Macedonians, Moldovans, Poles, Romanians, Serbians. One of my students was from India and another from the Serbian province of Kosovo. It has been observed that the Bulgarian students at our university stick together and speak Bulgarian almost exclusively outside of class. I wondered if the international students were looking for an activity to help them make friends so that they would not feel isolated from the predominantly Bulgarian AUBG community. Rehearsals and meetings for the play put the burden on Bulgarian students to speak in English in a different context than in the classroom. Theatre camaraderie developed. Working together on rehearsals of *The Crucible* and sharing the joy of its successful performances at semester's end functioned as a stimulus for intercultural friendships:

> I liked the team spirit that was created among the members of the whole group. There is always something special about being a part of a joint undertaking, there is something that separates you from the others outside the group and makes you connected with the people from your group. I experienced that same feeling.
>
> (Stoyan Atanasov, Bulgaria, makeup designer, *The Crucible*)

The participating in the production crew, and especially as an actor, brought many social contacts for me. I would never

know so many persons had I not been brought so close to them by working cooperatively in the production of a play.
(Tatyana Minkova, Bulgaria, stage manager/actress, *The Crucible*)

The most important thing is that I have learned about theatre by being a part of a play production . . . I have enjoyed working as part of *The Crucible* crew and I have found a lot of new friends among the people who shared the interest in the theatre with me.
(Snezhana Zhivanovich, Serbia, stage manager/crew, *The Crucible*)

Both Daniela and Rossen were very good at their jobs and this helped me a lot. In the last two performances I was on holiday in the booth, enjoying what happened on stage.
(Julia Musha, Albania, stage manager, *The Crucible*)

After the final performance of *The Crucible* students concentrated on preparing their fifteen-minute scene assignments--scenes extracted from classical plays read for class. Occasionally during rehearsals friction developed along cultural lines. Only rarely did the students admit it. One Albanian student working on a scene from *Lysistrata* wrote about her sense of cultural isolation when the only other international student in her group was out of town:

Anna has gone to Istanbul so today we rehearsed without a director. Probably this helped me to understand that Anna is really a good director. I didn't like at all the rehearsal of today. The girls seemed as if they didn't care about the play. But there's also another reason. They tended to speak Bulgarian most of the time and I really felt myself a stranger.
(Orieta Celiku, Albania, actress, *Lysistrata*)

At times conflicts arose simply because of personalities and did not seem to be culturally based. A culturally mixed group working on a scene from *The Glass Menagerie* experienced a serious predicament with personality conflict. Although several group members were Bulgarian, their leading actress happened to be an international student. She became uncooperative, confounding her classmates:

> Now when we are starting "real" rehearsals I can see an absolutely unexpected problem--Amanda. [She] is a discouraging agent on the others . . . a conflict is rising and I do not know when it will finally arise. [Another group member] suggests to replace her with [a Bulgarian student] but I disagree because it is unethical to take her last chance.
>
> (Bulgarian student, director, *The Glass Menagerie*)
>
> She did not want to cooperate, as usual, and we were all very embarrassed by her stubbornness.
>
> (Bulgarian student, actor, *The Glass Menagerie*)
>
> [S]he refused to do her role properly again . . . [another student] told us that he spoke with the instructor about her and her spoiling our efforts, and we decided if she did it again today we're going to tell her that she's out of the performance.
>
> (Bulgarian student, costumer, *The Glass Menagerie*)

This circumstance turned out to be the worst conflict of personalities in any of my classes or rehearsals during the academic year. I found it fascinating how fair-minded the Bulgarian students were on this occasion and how willing they were to give the recalcitrant international student a chance. They never ascribed an ethnic or cultural interpretation to her behavior.

This incident demonstrates a characteristic unique to East European students: their strong communal sense in the classroom. Their stick-with-the-group, don't-stick-out attitude surely derives from years of living under communism. Galling for Western instructors when issues of academic honesty are at stake or when trying to lead meaningful classroom discussion (Fike and Phillips 50), such cooperation has a friendly and inclusive side in the theatre.

In an interesting contrast to the notion of sticking-with-the-group, students were eager to experience the exhibitionist thrill of acting. A total of sixty students, or twelve percent of AUBG's student body, experienced the process of acting over the 1993-94 academic year. The process of acting stimulated students. It seems the acting experience helps students undergo transitions on a personal level that parallels the larger transitions in their countries and their lives. They wrote about their joy of acting and their fears of falling short of their own expectations. In these matters they are very much like their American counterparts. Still, understanding and pronouncing the words--remembering what to say and how to say it--presented a differen't, interesting perspective than I had encountered with student actors in the United States. AUBG students had difficulties articulating the English language but not with memorizing their lines. Memorization, a highly developed skill of East European students, posed no problems for them. I realized during the initial off-book rehearsals that the actors were not dropping lines. Oddly, stage managers prompted and quibbled over dropped articles or prepositions, not phrases or entire speeches. I also noticed that student actors did not paraphrase, as was common with my American students. The answer is obvious--English is their second or third language (Russian was required of all Bulgarian schoolchildren through 1989). It is not easy to improvise and paraphrase dialogue in a language other than one's own. Yet students manifested a fruitful combination of memorization and creativity:

> [W]hen I didn't know my lines properly I could not act naturally because I paid too much attention to finding the words. It was like a recitation of a poem: words for themselves, me for myself. Before the play, however, I repeated my lines so many times that they became part of my mind. I could say them without thinking, like a prayer.
> (Anna Giedrys, Poland, actress, *The Crucible*)

Pronunciation and articulation loomed as hurdles, especially when trying for a regional American accent, as the group preparing a scene from *The Glass Menagerie* acknowledged:

> Hristo made a suggestion that we might train Amanda to speak with a Southern accent. Well, I think it is terrific if we can do it but we already have some foreign accent and I'm not sure that the mixing of two accents would be something good.
> (Galina Georgieva, Bulgaria, director, *The Glass Menagerie*)

> Yesterday we learned that we had to talk with a Southern accent, because that was a very important part of the concept of the play. We went to [an American professor] and he made

a great effort to twist our tongues around. I am practicing my accent but I have the feeling that it's not going to work and will only make my speech not understandable.

(Rossen Blagoev, Bulgaria, actor, *The Glass Menagerie*)

Elton told us that he checked about how does the Southern accent sound and it was a kind of slow and melodious speech. We tried that on stage but it was very difficult, since none of us is a native American speaker and it is also difficult to remember both what to say and how to say it.

(Maia Kosteva, Bulgaria, actress, *The Glass Menagerie*)

Several students developed deep attachments to their characters. Some students had difficulties transcending their own East European experience in order to open up to a character from another part of the world. Two fascinating journal excerpts specifically relate to the cultural differences between East Europeans and Americans. These frustrated student actors wrote about the difficulties of understanding an American character well enough to play the role convincingly onstage:

> Though I don't like the play, I think the author makes his message very clear . . . I think it is highly American and the only one who can play it very well are Americans. I think I just don't understand it, or to be more precise, I misunderstand some parts of it.
>
> (Nikolay Todorov, Bulgaria, actor, *Search and Destroy*)

> The difference between me, Leonid Oknyansky, and me, Henry, is that I, Leonid Oknyansky, am not a goddamn venereal doctor and do not intend to be and I don't really know how is it to be American Old Venereal doctor. And even if I try Stanislavsky's "Magic If" I'll nevertheless play my own self or, say, I'll play Henry through my perception of the world where he lives.
>
> (Leonid Oknyansky, Moldova, actor, *Angels in America*)

Understanding character and theme became a major challenge to students assigned to perform in scenes from *Angels in America*. Tony

Kushner's demanding play about the politics of AIDS was to be produced professionally in the capital city of Sofia during the spring. The cultural attaché at the American Embassy told me that the producers had dropped the project because they felt it too controversial for the Bulgarian audience. In fact, most Bulgarians are prejudiced against homosexuals. An important distinction to make here is that their hesitation is not framed as individual moral or religious judgment, as it might be in the United States. Rather it represents a societal discomfort. Homosexuality is repressed, underground and is not acknowledged in Bulgaria. Although choosing the play was a risk, I thought it was important for the young people in this part of the world to develop an awareness of AIDS. Initially students were reluctant to perform these scenes. I explained the crisis of AIDS to them in personal terms, telling them stories of friends who had died from the disease. I warned them that they should pay attention to Kushner's message so they would know ahead of time what might happen in their own country. Perturbed, they wrote about their reactions:

> Since [the play] is dealing with rather controversial topics that are not traditionally treated in Bulgarian theatre, it is quite challenging to stage it in Bulgaria. The country is still relatively intact by AIDS, and homosexuality is more or less a taboo theme. *Angels in America* introduces a profoundly new and shocking world to the Bulgarian public: homosexual families, switching of partners, drug addiction. Yet it contains universal topics dealing with human relationships.
> (Nikola Shopov, Bulgaria, actor, *Angels in America*)

> Today we did a partial read-through of *Angels in America*. Boy, this is a strange play. I wonder how Nikola and Emo are going to cooperate as homosexuals on stage. I think it will be a little embarrassing for them. I wonder how is this play to be accepted by the Bulgarian audience. First, AIDS is more or less regarded as something that is not to be found in our backyard. Second, some of the homo jargon will be incomprehensible.
> (Blagoevesta Momchedjikova, Bulgaria, actress, *Angels in America*)

The text is strongly culturally biased; the author being American, Jew, and gay is obviously subjective. The performance here will be a strong challenge, since this play was not very well accepted outside America and dealing with cultural problems of America exclusively has a double task: a good performance technically, and a good link with the audience, needed for the override of the cultural differences.

(Petar Arsovski, Macedonia, actor, *Angels in America*)

After three or four weeks of rehearsals the students developed a different attitude. They were excited to be part of something new and controversial. They felt proud to be the first actors in Bulgaria to play these roles on the stage--even if they were students performing in an acting exam.

Friends from other classes crowded the theatre for the *Angels in America* acting finals. Apprehensive, I recalled how only a few weeks before, these students were the same audience for three riotous nights of comedy improvisations developed by the acting classes and performed in the AUBG café. I feared that their cultural nervousness about homosexuality would cause them to laugh inappropriately and spoil their classmates' performance. My acting class was jittery with stage fright and embarrassment. They had worked long hours to prepare their scenes. It was final exam week at the end of a long year, but a fresh energy shot through the air.

In an improvised curtain speech I requested the students in the audience to respect their friends' courage in performing an extremely difficult play. I cautioned them about AIDS. Although it is not in Bulgaria, I told them, it inevitably will be. In the wake of transition, Bulgaria is no longer encircled by an impermeable wall. The audience grew silent. The lights dimmed to black. The actors began to play their scenes in utter stillness. The audience was marvelously concentrated. These beginning actors--total amateurs--acted like veterans. They believed in themselves, in the author's message. They forgot about being Macedonians, Moldovans, and Serbians. They forgot they didn't know anything about being American Old Venereal doctors. They communicated naively and hopefully, an important message about the politics of AIDS in a part of the world not yet invaded by the disease.

Silence was followed by furious applause after each scene. In the final scene of the evening, Betty, who had wanted to be in a comedy, crumpled up in a drugged stupor in her character's fantasy visit to Antarctica. The lights faded. Hush. Applause. Cheers. A rush for the stage. The excited acting students were smothered by their classmates in a congratulatory mobbing. As I headed toward the door someone grabbed my hand. I turned around and looked into Betty's face. Tears streamed from her eyes. "Thank you," she half-croaked, half-whispered in her Bulgarian accented English. Her body and voice trembled. "Thank you for the warning."

The satisfaction of reaching an audience with a meaningful message was only one reward. Teaching theatre in Bulgaria has given me a unique opportunity to construct bridges between distinct cultures in a time of transition. I have observed young people crossing the threshold of a changing world and watched them open up to their creative artistry, just as their part of the world has opened up to the West. Students uncovered new information which gave them practical learning, a sense of personal responsibility, and the flexibility to improvise in difficult situations. They discovered new expression in the joys and frustrations of acting and of speaking the English language. They confronted new ideas which appealed to them and some which repulsed them. They worked together and made new friends, overriding their cultural differences. Working together, they have built on their strengths, giving them the confidence to head in new directions.

> The thing that remains in my memory is the confidence that I have learned something new. [It] was one of the few courses that gave me practical knowledge.
> (Stoyan Atanasov, Bulgaria, makeup designer, *The Crucible*)

> I think that everything I did was very helpful to me. It gave me the opportunity to work with other people, and to be responsible for my actions.
> (Denis Dollaku, Albania, actor, *The Crucible*)

Work Cited

Fike, Matthew, and Robert Phillips, Jr. "Lessons Learned: Thoughts on Teaching East European Students." *International Education* 23.1 (Fall 1993): 46-51.

After the Visit, the Ruins
by Ned Bobkoff

All art is autobiographical: the pearl is the oyster's autobiography.

Federico Fellini

In Act one of Friedrich Dürrenmatt's masterpiece, *The Visit*, set in a dilapidated railroad station in Guellen, "somewhere in central Europe" in the fifties, where "Goethe spent a night" and "Brahms composed a quartet," everything is in ruins. It is immediately after the second World War; the town has no money. Whatever buildings of value remain are being lost to pay debts. The townspeople, reduced to eavesdropping on life, wait for something to happen that will turn their lives around.

"Our last remaining pleasure: watching trains go by," says Man Three, loitering on the railroad platform, "Living on the dole." "Living?" snaps Man One. "Vegetating," retorts the second man. "And rotting to death," adds Man Three again. "The entire township," sighs Man Four, with finality (11-12).[1]c

It is September 1993. We gather for our first reading of the play in a large dance studio at the Konservatuvari, the National Institute for Music and the Performing Arts, on the Anadolu University campus in Eskisehir, Turkey. "Guellen is like Eskisehir," an actor announces, "Only more so." "How do you mean?" I ask. "Go down to the railroad station," another performer remarks, half joking, "and watch the trains go by." My translator, Erhan Tuna, turns to me with a mischievous smile. It is my first challenge.

Outside the railway station in Eskisehir, dedicated by Ataturk, the founder of the Turkish republic, and built by German engineers, coal dust from burning incinerators drifts into the fall air, coating everything in sight in a gloom of gray ash.

Inside the station the mix of people astonishes: Police drift about in the crowd, poking the luggage of travelers with beeping electronic

rods, looking for bombs. A few hundred miles to the east, a war is going on for the heart of Turkey. A war that apparently won't go away. Students carrying shoulder bags, with walkmans attached to their ears, wander, as if in a dream. Businessmen, barbered with neatly clipped mustaches and wearing well worn suits, read about the war in newspapers with bold headlines. Huddled in wool caps, frazzled beards and sulking expressions, rural Anatolian men sip black tea. Their wives, dressed in ballooning pantaloons with colorful floral patterns, shuffle through a storm of children. Isolated by choice, staring unflinchingly into space, strict Moslem woman, ensconced in black from head to toe, sit in a state of future shock.

Everyone holds on to their tickets dearly. The price of a train ticket rises overnight. The Turkish lire, like coal dust, drifts into thin air. The possibility of ruin is everywhere. Ruin becomes a working metaphor for our production of Dürrenmatt's epic play. It is a decision I never regret.

Translating the play into Turkish, Erhan Tuna distributes the text scene by scene. Rehearsals truly become a jumping off place for discovery and exploration. The performers gradually absorb the play from the ground floor up, reliving the process through which the playwright created the play. By the time we work our way through the text, the casting will be complete through natural selection and gradual assimilation. How do you behave in a town that is falling apart? I ask. What do you do to keep yourself alive, knowing that there is nothing of value left that you can call your own? What price are you willing to pay for an economic miracle to take place?

The next day the performers arrive early and pile old clothes in a heap in the center of the room. Moving in and out of the mountain of costumes, they take what they need and dispense with what they don't want, arranging and rearranging effects in the mirrors. Ideas develop, discoveries take place, psychological gestures grow. Slowly, unobtrusively, meticulously, one character rises on the shoulders of another. Like a human pyramid, the humble townspeople of Guellen emerge.

Musa, as Man One, stares at himself in a mirror, evaluating the results of his efforts. Wearing a torn black sweater, his toes stick out of shoes that have seen better days. He sits down on a beat-up old bench, sighs, wiggles his toes and waits for a train to go by. Having

Ned Bobkoff

grown old in Guellen, his character lives in a state of perpetual monotony, waiting for something to happen that will turn his life around. A bell clangs.

Murat, having worked himself into the role of the Station-master, has strung up cymbals and a collection of junk instruments on a tree stand. Wearing a station master's cap, he orchestrates the play, the clanging bell a warning that Guellen will soon be turned upside down.

Musa rises from his bench and imitates the chugging sound of an approaching locomotive. The cast joins him, huffing and puffing. The train whizzes by. Everyone laughs. Hope wanders out of Musa like a stray dog. He sits down again, wearing a wry grin. After all, this is a tragi-comedy, why not make the most of it?

Emin, as Man Two, wanders into the studio, searching for stray cigarette butts. Hitching his pants up, he shuffles around, finds a butt and lights it. Through the curling cigarette smoke, the two luckless Guelleners smile at one another consolingly. This is an old game, we might as well play it. Friends that play together, survive together. The bell clangs again. Imaginary trains are coming by a mile a minute now. Guellen is coming alive.

Cuneyt enters as Man Three. Wearing a floppy wool cap on his sprawling black curls, he hops into the studio holding a pair of shoes that he spray painted gold. He dreams of wearing gold shoes. Someday he might be rich enough to buy a pair of *real* gold shoes. Meanwhile this pair will do. Anything will do in Guellen.

Delik, playing the Painter, makes a grand entrance, wearing a tatty beret and a flowing cloak. She spreads a makeshift banner across the stage: "Welcome Claire Zachanassian," then finishes lettering the sign. Man Three mutters a negative comment. She slaps his hand, and continues to paint as if he wasn't there.

Arif Pishkin, portraying the Mayor of Guellen, full of bluster and camaraderie, enters, snapping his suspenders in expectation of the arrival of Claire Zachanassian. He is followed by Enis Yildiz, who plays the Priest--quiet, self-effacing, the spiritual decline of Guellen written all over his face. The Schoolmaster, played by actress A. Nese, moves between them nervously. Hair disheveled, fumbling with paper-- having tracked down Claire Zachanassian's dusty school records--she approaches the mayor and dutifully submits the papers to him. He studies them and decides that a mixed choir of Guellen's leading citizens will sing "Amazing Grace." He will deliver a rousing speech to Claire Zachanassian about her memorable early years in Guellen. It will be a pack of lies.

"Amazing Grace" has been selected as the theme song for the production. Translated into Turkish, and rewritten by Professor Metin Belay of the Konservatuvari, the revised spiritual anthem ironically highlights Guellen's faith in economic well being and the pleasures of accumulating material possessions. Eventually it will conjugate into the swan song of Guellen's moral decline.

Arif Yavuz evolved as the best candidate for the lead male role of Alfred Ill. With his intelligent eyes and hawk like face, he bursts with the anticipation of Claire Zachanassian's arrival, pacing on the platform of the railroad station, relishing his status as the linch-pin on the wheel of fortune that is Guellen's future.

Joking and laughing, he relives the memory of his romance fifty years ago with Claire Zachanassian, the millionairess, hoping that she will remember him fondly. He wants to win her over again, pull off a financial coup, and become the next mayor of Guellen. Everything depends on how well he can talk Claire out of her money. Guellen has high hopes for his efforts. But Alfred does not mention his betrayal of Claire--a betrayal that will seal his fate and put him into a coffin.

Fifty years ago he broke his promise to marry Claire, marrying instead Matilda Blumhard for her money. Pregnant, subjugated to a kangaroo court that accused her of sexual promiscuity, Claire was humiliated and banished from Guellen, like a common prostitute. The child she bore for Alfred died. Eventually she became a prostitute and married a millionaire. Now she returns to Guellen as a fabulously rich "benefactor." Returning not for sentimental reasons, as the townspeople believe, but for revenge.

The major role of Claire Zachanassian has been double cast. Aysel Yilmaz has a commanding presence, a powerful voice, and a sure sense of style. Her counterpart, Suhelya Elbas, withdrawn, volatile, delights in coruscating wit. Both project a backbone made of steel: the bulwark of Claire Zachanassian's formidable character and the driving force of the play. Their difference of interpretation substantially changes the response of the cast to the character of Claire Zachanassian, depending on who is playing the role when. This ongoing ambivalence leads to considerable spontaneity and rapid-fire adjustments, adding spice to the believability of the production.

The Angel of Death Arrives

When the Racing Rolland pulls into Guellen, the townspeople are stunned. The express train hasn't stopped in Guellen for years. Flamboyantly dressed in dance hall red, Claire enters majestically, leaning on a cane. Wearing a large, black hat and a web of lace that camouflages her heavily made up face in shadows and intrigue, Claire suggests nothing less than a black widow ready to buy up the town and eat her former lover alive. Only Alfred recognizes her. In a gesture calculated for maximum effect, Claire lifts her veil and seductively meows at him, a sign of an old romance remembered. Alfred is still her "black panther." The townspeople gasp. This is not the quiet, shy Claire they remember.

Elated, Alfred turns to the Guelleners, as if to say: See, what did I tell you? I have the lady in the palm of my hand! He has no idea of the trap Claire has set for him. Eventually he will walk to his death strangled in the throes of Claire's bitter revenge. How Claire manipulates the town to kill him shapes the action of the play.

Her entourage follows, strolling into Guellen like a circus act-- creatures from another world. With costumes borrowed from the Turkish state theatre, their colorful dress and larger-than-life behavior contrasts with the ragged clothing and kitchen sink reactions of the down-and-out Guelleners. Two menacing "gum chewing brutes," Roby and Toby, dash into the scene, carrying Claire's red velvet sedan chair. Suited up in black and white pin stripes, wing tipped shoes and Al Capone fedoras, they snap to attention at Claire's icy commands. As honorary pallbearers at Alfred's funeral, they will surround the shopkeeper with flowers and play poker on his coffin.

Two eunuchs, Koby and Loby, enter, chattering away compulsively. Performer Ilkay Akdagli agreed to shape these characters into grotesque finger puppets--one on each hand. Slinkies, with large bulging eyes bouncing about, the puppets comment on the action and generate comic relief. Wearing white face, a large bow tie and a striped green pitch man's jacket, disguised as a puppet himself, Ilkay manipulates the gabby eunuchs, using ventriloquism, mime, wit and rapid-fire dialogue. His creativity adds satirical commentary to the action, lifting the play into the surreal realm.

Actor Suleyman Atanisev, as Husband VII, isolates himself from the crowd. Carrying fishing gear, he dreams of gills flashing in deep pools. Suddenly Claire commands him to think. Puffing his pipe, he raises his eyebrows and draws a blank. The townspeople laugh, impressed with Claire's power--a calculated step in her eventual conquest of Guellen.

The Butler, portrayed by actor Ali Haken, is formerly the judge who exiled Claire from Guellen. He is now reduced to being her mouthpiece. He sets up a kangaroo court on the spot, as he did fifty years ago. He charges Alfred to step forward, then interrogates the surprised shopkeeper about his betrayal of Claire. Haken, with spiked white hair, nattily dressed in a butler's uniform, his voice sharp, brutal, unsparing, compels the two puppets, Koby and Loby, to testify against Alfred. Weeping, they confess how they lied about Claire's promiscuity. Alfred had bribed them with a pint of brandy. Claire tracked them down with a vengeance and had them castrated and blinded. Guellen is stunned.

Having cast doubt about Alfred's integrity, Claire now makes her next move with arresting effect. "A million for Guellen," she exclaims, "if someone kills Alfred Ill" (38). After a pause the Mayor steps forward, outraged, unconscious of the absurdity and historical inaccuracy of his remarks.

> Mayor: Madam Zachanassian: you forget, this is Europe. You forget, we are not savages. In the name of all citizens of Guellen, I reject your offer; and I reject it in the name of humanity. We would rather have poverty than blood on our hands. (39)

"I'll wait," she replies.

I walk down a street in Ankara and notice the opening of a new store. There is a celebration going on, crowds of people, a band playing, singing. The store is garlanded with flowers. Wreaths of gladiola and orchids, tied with satin bows and festooned with good wishes, are spread out on the sidewalk. Every nook and cranny is covered with colorful blossoms. There is hardly room to move. The flowers are given away. People pick them freely. They are wrapped into bouquets for loved ones and taken home.

Lambs lie on the sidewalk, legs tied together, waiting for their throats to be cut. They stare in silence and blink. A bearded man in a wool cap rests on one knee, holding a knife, taking a break. Blood runs in spurts out of the slashed throats of the lambs into the cracks in the sidewalk and then down into a freshly dug pit. A feast follows the celebration. Everyone enjoys the eating spree. But the crowd watching the slaughter is silent.

I summarize the remaining action for the performers: Claire will orchestrate a free market economy, based on easy credit. Economic revival will become the order of the day. Guellen will slowly but surely succumb to her largess. Life in Guellen will develop into a crusade of acquisition and newfound status. Alfred will be sacrificed to the miracle of "Amazing Grace" and the townspeople will rationalize his murder as a necessary and just revenge. His killing is just a matter of time. We decide to focus on the core scenes of the play, exploring the process of community sanctioned murder; concentrating on the sensual undercurrents of the drama.

Konrad's Wood

Claire and Alfred sit on an old rotting bench in Konrad's Wood. Fifty years ago in this peaceful sanctuary, surrounded by the breathing of the trees and the chamber music of bird calls, their romance bloomed. Claire recalls the innocence of her youth. Alfred speaks of his children and how hard it is for parents to instill a sense of moral responsibility today. Claire agrees, and turns to him smiling, but her eyes have the cold look of revenge. In the shadows of leaves the townspeople sway like trees in the wind, sighing--waiting for the kill. Inside their entwined limbs they hold a nest of death sealed with bird calls. Alfred will heed their calls and they know it.

Alfred lays a hand on Claire's knee; it is wooden and unforgiving. She tells him that she lost her leg in an automobile accident. He leans over and kisses her white gloved hand, as heavy as ivory. "Clara, are you all artificial?" he asks. "I am unkillable," she replies (31). He flinches, touches his throat and swallows. Blood runs in the veins of his eyes. The bird calls grow silent.

Passion Play

In the rectory of the church, Alfred rests on his knees, praying. Outside in the streets a guitar softly strums "Amazing Grace." It is a lovely day. Everyone in town has started eating chocolate and wearing gold shoes. Laughter drifts into the rectory.

Alfred confides to the priest that the Guelleners are hunting him down like a wild animal. "Because you once betrayed a young girl for money," the Priest replies, mollifying him, "do you believe the people will betray you for money?" (37). The Priest wears a gun around his neck like a cross, black and metallic. He tells Alfred not to be "surprised" by the weapon. Claire's pet panther escaped its cage and is "on the prowl." Even now the townspeople are tracking down the wild animal. Suddenly three men appear, holding high wooden crosses, like penitents in a passion play. Placing the short end of the crosses into the crook of their shoulders, they turn and point the long end toward Alfred--rifles. Bells ring in the church carillon. Guelleners surrounding the stage rise from their prayers, ready to do business. "Flee!" the Priest urges, pushing Alfred away from him. Alfred stands in the train station. Holding on to a train ticket, he is surrounded by a nightmare. With smiles, whispers, encouragement, the townspeople urge him to escape. No one keeps Alfred in Guellen but himself, they say, laying wooden crosses on his shoulders. Alfred finally realizes that he has been pressed into the lead role of a passion play beyond his control.

The two eunuchs, Koby and Loby, burst out of the crowd. Gripping a fishing rod, they whip a line out over the river of people surrounding Alfred. Alfred's head snaps back, hooked like a fish. He falls to his knees, legs kicked out from beneath him. Crosses tumble to the ground. The train flies by. Alfred watches his last chance to escape disappear down the tracks.

Next to him sits a pair of gold shoes and an empty bird cage with its door flung open. His wife stands over him holding his luggage-- evaluating him for what he is worth. In the distance the townspeople can be heard singing "Amazing Grace." A bell clangs mournfully. Alfred Ill has sentenced himself to death. There is no way out.

Once a Bride

Sitting in Petersens's barn, Claire wears a white bridal gown. She holds a bouquet of flowers in her white gloved hand and stares into space, dreaming of her youth and remembering her wound. A gangster sits on Alfred's coffin and strums a romantic tune on his guitar; another one plays cards.

The Schoolmaster and the town doctor have come to plead for the salvation of Guellen and the life of Alfred Ill. The Schoolmaster suggests a "business proposition" that will help restore Guellen to its former economic glory. If Claire will buy the Foundry on Sunshine Square and the Wagner Factory, Guellen can take its rightful place as a prosperous and respected community. Claire tells them that she now owns everything in Guellen, so why bother with a business proposition? Besides, she adds, their lives have been a "useless waste" (66).

> Schoolmaster. Madam Zachanassian! You're a woman whose love has been wounded. You make me think of a heroine from antiquity: of Medea. We feel for you deeply; we understand; but because we do, we are inspired to prove you further: cast away those evil thoughts of revenge, don't try us till we break. Help these poor, weak yet worthy people lead a slightly more dignified life. Let your feeling for humanity prevail! (66-67)

Enraged, Claire pulls off her bridal veil and tosses the bouquet to the Schoolmaster. The dream is over. "The world turned me into a whore," she exclaims. "I shall turn the world into a brothel" (67). The two gangsters raise her in the sedan chair and leave, tracking mud behind them.

Staring at the bridal bouquet, the flowers intoxicating with their decay, actress A. Nese, the Schoolmaster, breaks her concentration and turns to me. "It is terrible what Alfred did to Claire Zachanassian. I know how she feels. Her pain is something awful." Suddenly she realizes that the Schoolmaster may be more like Claire than she cares to admit. She bursts into tears. A. Nese has discovered why the Schoolmaster will succumb to community pressure, the power of money and Claire's indomitable will: the Schoolmaster cannot bear to be isolated. This shattering discovery moves the production forward with increasing velocity.

The Final Ride to Konrad's Wood

Alfred takes a ride in the new family automobile bought on credit. His son drives the car. They wave at townspeople and talk about the wonderful changes taking place in Guellen. Everyone is actively pursuing economic revival. A miracle is taking place.

Guelleners circle the car. Imitating the sounds of a gunned automobile, they weave in, out, and around the family, sitting in straight backed chairs, swaying from side to side on a roller coaster ride to Alfred's death. Wind blows through Alfred's hair; he wears a smile on his face. Life has never seemed so beautiful. The valley outside of town, the clouds in the sky, the wonderful castles in the twilight. His son, enlivened by his newfound status, maneuvers the car around the curves at high speed. Dressed pridefully in a Persian lamb coat, his wife clings to Alfred's arm. His daughter chatters away joyfully. Perhaps the family will find the time to enjoy the pleasures of life after Alfred is gone? When they arrive at Konrad's Wood, the family leaves Alfred to his fate with a fond wave and an *au revoir*. Life can be so pleasant if you give it half a chance.

Claire arrives and sits next to Alfred on an old rotting bench surrounded by mushrooms. She talks quietly about the child she bore for Alfred fifty years ago; how it was taken away from her and died of meningitis. Suddenly a deer leaps out of the forest. One of the townspeople, transformed into a deer, listens with big eyes to the muted conversation. Alfred recalls how he once found Claire waiting for him in Petersens's barn, in an old carriage "with nothing on but a blouse and a long straw between your lips" (88). Claire smiles. The guitar now breaks into a foot tapping medley of rhythmic tunes. The townspeople, hidden in the shadows of leaves, rise to the occasion with a faint whiff of blood lust and a lively snapping of fingers. Alfred turns to Claire:

> Ill: Thank you for the wreaths, and for the chrysanthemums and roses. They'll look fine on the coffin in the Golden Apostle. Distinguished. They fill two rooms already. Now the time has come. It is the last time we shall sit in our old wood and hear the cuckoo calling and the sound of the wind. They are meeting this evening. They will sentence me to death, and one of them will kill me. I don't know who it will be, and I don't know where it will happen, I only know my meaningless life will end. (88)

> It is market day in Ayvalik, a small fishing town on the Aegean sea. Mercedes Benz compete for available space with horse drawn carts carrying families piled on top. Men walk the streets with a necklace of squawking chickens hanging upside down from a ring around their necks. A spastic beggar twists on the ground holding her baby wrapped in a shawl, extending her hand for money. Passersby drop coins in her palm and move on quickly, fearing the contamination of poverty. The call for prayer, broadcast on loudspeakers in mosques throughout the

town, competes with the roar of Turkish jets flying east overhead. The war goes on as usual.

At the market a man with a bloody face is led away by a policeman through a silent crowd holding their fists tight. He has been caught stealing from one of the farmers and has been pummeled to the ground. With frightened eyes, he passes through the crowd. Blood is wiped off the green and yellow and red vegetables. The vegetables are carefully put back on the rack in neat columns piled one on top of the other. The price of survival grows higher every day.

At the Hotel Apostle in Guellen, restored to its former glory, a radio commentator describes the climax of Claire Zachanassian's visit as one of the "greatest social experiments of the age" (90). The mayor announces that Claire Zachanassian will make a donation of one million pounds: five hundred thousand to Guellen and five hundred thousand to be shared among all citizens. The crowd cheers. The Schoolmaster denounces Alfred's perfidy toward Claire, betraying him and putting the final nail in his coffin:

> When individual persons slight the ideal of brotherly love, disobey the commandment to succor the weak, spur the marriage vow, deceive the courts and plunge young mothers into misery, then Freedom is at stake. (*Cat-calls*) Now, in God's name, we must take our ideals seriously, even unto death. (*Huge Applause*) (91-92)

The Mayor asks Alfred if he will accept or refuse the Claire Zachanassian "endowment." He answers quietly, "I shall respect it" (93). Then he breaks into laughter. A Guellener darts out of the crowd and grabs Alfred by the throat. A policeman pulls the angry citizen out of camera range. Bursts of violence will not be tolerated; this is a civilized meeting. The mayor takes up a vote. "All those pure of heart who want justice done, raise their hands" (93). The vote against Alfred is unanimous; the pure of heart win.

Doors slam in the theatre. Lights go out. The coffin is highlighted. The women of Guellen are asked to leave. Alfred rejects the offer of a prayer from the priest, but he does take a cigarette, passing it on to someone in the audience. "No smoking allowed," he ad libs.

The coffin is festooned with flowers. The men reverently sing "Amazing Grace" in the shadows and raise sharpened kitchen forks into the light surrounding the coffin. Alfred falls to his knees, staring straight ahead--a penitent, the perfect sacrificial lamb. The men thrust their forks into him and then wipe the utensils clean. Alfred falls to the floor unblinking and is covered with a table cloth, declared dead by the Doctor. The banquet is over.

Claire hands the Mayor a check. Ecstatically the Guelleners chant the praises of the good life: their newfound economic status, their growing sense of community, and the overwhelming generosity of Claire Zachanassian. They spread out their hands in supplication, their palms covered with blood. Suddenly Claire raises her cane and cuts the chanting short. One by one the Guelleners drop to the ground, piling up like a monument to Alfred's death.

I visit the 500 year old Cemberlitas bath in Istanbul. Here, the heat from the fire below warms the heart stone, and the stone warms me. I throw down a towel and lie on the stone sweating, listening to the conversation of men echoing in the central chamber and the sound of cool water splashing from tin scoop dishes in the next room.

I am near the end of my Turkish journey. The social and political realities of Turkey now seem no different from those of the United States, or any other nation for that matter. The language and customs may differ, but the compromises are the same. Lambs are always available for the slaughter and scapegoats are too.

After a long and drowsy silence, the light from the dome above drifting in the mist, I rise and take a deep breath. The attendant wipes the sweat off the stone with a mop, leaving no lasting impression.

When I arrive home, after many hours in flight, I hang up in my living room, a beautiful silver Turkish lamp. It glows mysteriously through small, colorful windows. It is then that I think about the gifted young performers in Turkey, their dedication, passion, intelligence and honesty. The lamp becomes electric with memory. I turn the wattage up knowing the glow will flicker and die if I don't keep an eye on it. Sometimes I leave the lamp on all night, like a candle.

Notes

1. All quotes are from Patrick Bowles, trans., *The Visit*, by Friedrich Dürrenmatt (New York: Grove, 1963).

East Meets West Meets Hamlet: Get Thee to a Noh Master

by Jonah Salz

A History of Noho

When I first arrived in Japan in 1981, determined to examine the theatrical culture so distinct from the Western tradition in order to discover universals of performance, my lack of linguistic competence drew me to the fourteenth century noh and kyogen theatre. Noh is a kind of "medieval musical," fusing complex lyric poetry, chant, percussive music, refined dance, subtle masks, and gorgeous costumes into a unified ritual, expressing nuanced monodramas of romantic loss and martial bravery. Kyogen is the cosmopolitan noh's comic country cousin. Performed on the same stage, kyogen's actor-centered theatre mocks lazy servants and fatuous lords, cowardly husbands and shrewish wives, haughty priests, quack doctors, fallen gods, and clueless bridegrooms. I was captivated by the "total theatre" of noh, and the commedia-like slapstick and earthiness of kyogen.[1]

I co-founded the Noho Theatre Group with kyogen actor Akira Shigeyama, with whom I'd spent many evenings in a jazz club discussing theatre east and west. Noho means, "Noh Opened" which implies an openness to the possibilities of fusion with Western texts. Noho's goal is to utilize the techniques and spirit of traditional Japanese theatre to interpret Western texts.

Noho debuted in Kyoto, Japan, in September 1981 with the pantomimes *Act Without Words I* and *II* by Samuel Beckett. Since then, Noho has performed twenty-five plays at noh theatres and studio theatres, in collaboration with fifty artists from ten countries. Tours abroad have included the Edinburgh fringe (1982), Hong Kong (1988), Avignon (1994), and six times to the United States. Plays are frequently revived, with new casts, directors, languages, and performance spaces; each new production solves some problems but creates new ones, which in turn stimulates the next venture.

Noh and kyogen actors and musicians comprise Noho's core membership, with kyogen master Akira Shigeyama and myself as co-artistic directors. Guest artists join for particular production projects, influencing how close, and how far from their respective traditions the performers must bend. Japanese noh and kyogen actors and musicians joined non-Japanese (primarily American) actors and dancers, trained in noh, kyogen and nihonbuyo. Akira Matsui, a noh master of the Kita School, who has taught and directed abroad for twenty years, was a frequent participant. Over the years Noho's productions have included Yeats's *At the Hawk's Well* (1981, revived in 1982, 1985, and 1990) ten of Samuel Beckett's short plays, Woody Allen's *Death Knocks* and various English kyogen plays. It was not a coincidence that the first playwrights we attempted to produce were those influenced, directly or indirectly, by Japanese theatre--Yeats, J.M. Synge, Thornton Wilder, and Beckett. Reappropriating these texts with forms which Western playwrights had originally seized was a kind of "return home"--a trajectory the Japanese call a "U-turn."

As we continue to translate, create, revive, tour, and train, Noho faces the challenge of how to overcome three difficult barriers: First there are the aesthetic differences between the theatrical languages of Japanese noh-kyogen and modern Western theatre. Next, there is the obvious communication barrier between the English and Japanese language. Finally, there is the concern regarding the communication with audiences possessing varying degrees of expertise, interest, and tolerance for classical theatre and experimentation.

Overcoming these barriers in order to create a truly unified fusion required much effort.[2] Transformations take time, especially rehearsal time, and Noho rarely penetrated beyond the early stages; when we did it was by having Japanese actors already "fluent" in their own traditions stepping out and away from them. Without adequate rehearsal time, traditional actors, self-conscious and defensive, naturally fell back onto what they knew best. Attempts at "fusion," creating energy from putting two diverse traditions together, turned into "fission" decontextualizing existing forms. Actors and dancers departed little from their respective traditions, making the task of directing less the playful recombination of a bricoleur, and closer to a Machiavellian strategic manipulation of pieces with predetermined moves on a chessboard. The results were frequently unsatisfying.

Noho struggled with how to make a meaningful collaboration between native speakers of Japanese and English without being forced into either a confusing babel, or silent mime. One solution was to present two versions of the same play, such as Beckett's *Rockabye*, one straightforward in English, as Beckett wrote it; and one in Japanese, in a stylized form with an empty chair rocking next to a kneeling, masked noh actor, who stood to dance her final torment.

Another solution to the problem of languages was to have everyone speak in their mother-tongue, to perform bi- or even trilingually. Within the repertoire of the Shigeyama kyogen family was the "new kyogen" *Susugigawa* (*The Henpecked Husband*), based on the medieval French farce *Le Cuvier*, featuring a lazy American husband scolded by a shrewish wife and her mother. A bilingual version of *The Henpecked Husband* reconstituted as an international marriage was a great success, repeated dozens of times at speech contests, international expositions and conferences, and even at my own wedding. However, although bilingualism might be effective when portraying a squabbling couple, where the humorous disjunction only fanned the comedy, it remained to be seen whether a bilingual production which *ignored* the significance of the actor's nationality or the characters being portrayed could work.

The central challenge of how we could attract and move audiences who were ignorant of the works of Beckett and Yeats, and/or the conventions of noh-kyogen continues to be a pivotal concern. Noh and kyogen depend on connoisseurs thoroughly familiar with the repertoire, responding to slight nuances of interpretation. How could Noho reach an international audience, both in Japan and abroad, without resorting to exoticism as a lowest common denominator? We determined to perform widely, for Kyoto and Tokyo audiences who were a mix of fans of traditional and modern theatre and to display what we had created abroad, touring annually, hoping to develop our international aesthetic.

Audience reactions were mixed. Some came away with a new understanding of Japanese theatre, and of Beckett. Some felt that our interpretations "denatured" the plays so that by transposing them from their original contexts and styles somehow "killed their essence."[3] Others found that the fusion pieces lacked the depth of the traditional plays on the same program. Some young Japanese came away with a newfound respect for the musty traditions of noh and kyogen--another type of "U-turn."

Noho's *Ophelia*--Creating the Text

Noh, Japan's 600-year-old classical dance-drama, has attracted Western fascination for more than a century, but in recent decades there has been a surge in such intercultural activities.[4] This has created a loose community of insiders and outsiders experimenting with integrations between Asian and Euro-American cultures. Some call this new movement "interculturalism."[5] I prefer to call it the "entre-garde": a form between dance and theatre, between East and West, between tradition and experiment. W.B. Yeats, one of the first to recognize the importance of intercultural experimentation replied to those critical of the Irish Literary Movement's eclectic emulation of English and European authors: "We are gardeners, trying to grow various kinds of trees and flowers peculiar to our soil and climate; but we have to go for the art of gardening to men who grow very different flowers and trees in very different soils and climates."[6] The contemporary entre-garde similarly grows out of the mutual influence of second and third generation experimenters, removed from the original traditions and from each other, discovering new solutions to common problems in a multitude of situations. The process of discovery and creation revealed by the *Ophelia* production exposes some of the perils and pleasures of the entre-garde.

Noho's 1987 *Ophelia* project served as a test case in our desire to overcome the barriers of performance style, language, and audience understanding. By creating a new text with particular actors in mind and rehearsing regularly for six months, stylistic gaps among the performers could be closed. By employing bilingualism, the talents of the Japanese and non-Japanese actors were fully exploited. And by basing the selection of a play on Shakespeare's *Hamlet*, one of the most frequently produced Western plays in Japan, audience familiarity was assured.

Cross-fertilization in the entre-garde depends on a knowledgeable global community of experimenters, feeding off each other through an understanding of innovative practice, whether through witnessing productions or through reviews, photographs, and videotapes. There were many direct and indirect influences on the genesis of Noho's *Ophelia*: Robert Wilson's direction of Heiner Muller's *Hamletmachine*;

Emily's ghost's reliving of her past in Act 1 of Thornton Wilder's *Our Town*; and John Dexter's bare-stage, audience-surrounding direction of Peter Shaffer's *Equus*. Perhaps central to the structuring of the play were Beckett's looping narratives in *Come and Go*, *Play* and *Krapp's Last Tape*. And finally, Tadashi Suzuki's SCOT production of *Clytemnestra*, which made powerful use of bilingualism to appeal to an international audience, Orestes spoke in English while Electra communicated in Japanese.

Noh texts are rarely wholly new creations, but based on widely known myths, legends, and historic incident. Zeami, the master playwright, theorist and performer instrumental in creating the refined noh style in the fourteenth century, suggests that aspiring playwrights seek sources for their plays in classics such as the warrior epic *Tale of the Heike* or romantic adventures of *Tale of Genji*.[7] With Noh texts, audiences familiar with the characters, setting, and general outlines of the plot depend on the playwright for a unique perspective--a new twist on an old problem. *Hamlet* was one of the first plays imported to Japan in the late nineteenth century, and has been continually performed by Japanese and visiting troupes in a wide variety of interpretations.[8] Just as noh playwrights depended upon their audience's familiarity with the great epics of love and war to fashion their particular "takes" on a single story, I assumed general knowledge of the *Hamlet* plot to construct *Ophelia*. With some minor shuffling of lines, and changing of personal pronouns, I utilized Shakespeare's text exclusively to tell Ophelia's story.

The play begins with the central image which had first inspired me to write *Ophelia*. Ophelia's Ghost, unwittingly caught up in the intrigues at Elsinore, is incapable of a quiet afterlife until she has discovered the truth about the strange goings on in her lifetime. She returns to the church graveyard where she was buried, and last had contact with the principal players in her life. Gazing into the mirror (memory, water, time), she sees the living Ophelia, surrounded by those who manipulated her in her lifetime. The light from the candle (metaphorically, the inquiring gaze) hits the mirror and fragments onto the stage, revealing five actors on low boxes, facing front, eyes closed. As the light touches them the seated actors begin to murmur softly, like smoldering embers fanned to flame. Rising from her stool, the Ghost turns and is revealed as a masked noh actor, dressed in a gold-brocaded robe. Sliding forward in a slow intense glide, with candle in hand, she lifts the candle to each seated actor's face. As the flame lights them eerily from below, their voices rise in intensity, slowly gaining coherence while exuding violence: "Get thee to a nunnery," "Sweets for the sweet," "Mad for thy love?" "My dear sister," "Shards, flints, and pebbles should be thrown at her." Their words and costumes reveal the spirits as Hamlet, Gertrude, Polonius, Laertes, the Priest, respectively. They rise to attack the living Ophelia, who backs away, toward the audience, repeating, "I do not know what I should think." The Ghost, unable to withstand the onslaught, faces her attackers, chanting, "To die, to sleep--no more." The play that follows portrays the dreams that disturb Ophelia's "sleep of death."

    The Ghost watches in the mirror at the back of the stage the living Ophelia reenacting scenes from her life. The scenes follow chronologically: Laertes warns Ophelia that Hamlet may be merely playing with her; Polonius forbids her seeing him again. When Hamlet confronts her in her closet, Ophelia runs to her father for comfort. Instead, Polonius drags her before the court, and exposes their correspondence. Ophelia is sent as bait to the "mousetrap" set for Hamlet, as the Queen places her hopes for Hamlet's cure in Ophelia, while she and Polonius spy. Following Hamlet's "Get thee to a nunnery" tantrum, Ophelia "unravels" into her final "distraction" with the Queen and Laertes. The Ghost, finally unable to control her own bitter memories of this frenzy, rises in a violent pas de deux with the living Ophelia, while a newly created character, Doubt, creates a beckoning whirlpool with a spiraling dance. We discovered that a stage assistant was needed to move boxes and handle properties, and solutions from both noh (expressionless, "invisible" stage assistants) and Western conventions (blackouts) were considered. Finally, a new character "Doubt" emerged--a sinister shadow who echoed and twisted others' lines, and whose importance increased with each subsequent production.

    Ophelia gazes at herself in the back mirror before "leaping" to her death. At the moment of suicide, the Ghost and the living Ophelia face each other calmly, before passing down the rampway together into death. After the Gravedigger cynically recounts Ophelia's demise in a more colloquial manner, he matches wits with Hamlet, before making way for the funeral procession of the Priest, Laertes, the Queen, and both the Ghost and Ophelia's "corpse." The Queen's eulogy, originally spoken to comfort Laertes, now becomes an unconvincing gloss on the suicide. The Ghost rises to dance a protest: the death was not an accidental fall, but an intentional escape from the horrors of living, and the surrounding selfish manipulators. As all the characters chant "to die, to sleep," the Ghost sits diagonally across from her original position, where a second mirror is hung. The characters return to their original places, but now in reversed positions. The Ghost, observing the scene from a new perspective, rises with the candle and the play begins again.

The play departs most clearly from noh where normally the long suffering ghost of an unrequited lover or defeated warrior appears to a stranger to tell his/her tale, seeking to be blessed and exorcised from the cruel memory that keeps him/her attached to the earth and incapable of attaining the peace of Buddhist salvation. The unwritten subplot of Ophelia within *Hamlet* is similar to the third category of *mugen* noh plays, which often features women driven mad through loss or jealousy. One Zeami play has a strikingly similar plot. In *Uneme*, a lady-in-waiting, having been loved and left by a prince, drowns herself in a pond, then reappears in a diaphanous seaweed-drenched robe to dance her grief. However, I saw the Ghost as only a future incarnation of the tormented living Ophelia, each groping toward knowledge of her demise, and the subsequent peace that the truth might bring.

If Ophelia was the equivalent of the noh *shite* or "doer" lead, the other leading characters had become *waki* "sidemen" on stage only to illuminate Ophelia's story. Shakespeare's play was seen filtered through the intensity of Ophelia's gaze. The Gravedigger was an especially kyogen-like figure, breaking the tension and recapitulating Ophelia's tale with candor and wit. To appeal to multilingual audiences, *Ophelia* had to be evenly balanced bilingually. Hamlet, the Gravedigger, and the Ghost spoke Japanese; Ophelia, the Queen, Polonius, and Laertes spoke English. The accompanying music was also "bilingual." The usual noh ensemble of two drums and a flute was supplemented with a cello, the living Ophelia's mournful counterpart.

Ophelia--An Intercultural Production

Ophelia premiered in 1987 at the Nashinoki Shrine stage in Japan, was revived later that same year and again in 1989 at the Kawamura Noh Stage in Kyoto, and the Ohtsuki Noh Theatre in Osaka. In the premiere at Nashinoki Shrine, an ancient Shinto shrine appropriately abutting the Imperial Palace in Kyoto, the audience sat on cushions placed in tombstone-like rows. They surrounded the stage "graveyard," lit primarily by candles, with dead flowers arranged at the front of the stage. While many in the 200-person audience each night indicated that they had found it to be an intensely moving performance, some noted jarring gaps in styles, which we sought to rectify in subsequent productions. Confusing transitions between scenes were smoothed by a newly written Gravedigger's narrative, played by kyogen actor Yasushi Maruishi. When he revisits the gravesite that he dug twenty years earlier, he is disturbed by the Ghost's nightly walks. He borrows his lines from Hamlet: "Sit you down--you shall not budge . . . till I set you up a glass where you may see the inmost part of you." The one character not found in Shakespeare nor in noh was that of Doubt, who germinated out of the tension between aesthetic and practical needs, as mentioned earlier. The addition of these two narrators: the Japanese speaking Gravedigger "freezing" the action to explain or elaborate on the plot; and the English speaking Doubt echoing and twisting important lines, provided a better understanding for audience members with diverse backgrounds and varying linguistic competencies.

Balancing the intercultural aesthetic proved a constant challenge. One actor had to be constantly reminded to unclench his hands, held firmly in the kyogen basic posture. Meanwhile the English-speaking members of the cast (American, Canadian, British, and Australian) had no firm stylistic foundation upon which to fall back, only years of training in a wide variety of styles, including Stanislavsky. Their task was to stylize and tighten their work to achieve parity, while the Japanese actors in turn had to soften and lighten their acute formalization. Each revival helped to fuse the divergent styles and energies. By adjusting to the varieties of casts, spaces, and audiences over numerous "generations" of the play, *Ophelia* began to achieve coherence as fusion theatre. Working in art forms which have been perfecting themselves for half a millennium required patience and humility. Different aspects of the production (dance, costumes, and acting) developed at different paces; the inevitable inconsistencies caused consternation, from both actors and audience. The production took a giant leap forward in 1992 when *Ophelia* was presented in a collaboration between the Noho Theatre Group and Pittsburgh's Three Rivers Shakespeare Festival's Young Company at the University of Pittsburgh's studio theatre, The Pit.

The co-production with the Three Rivers Shakespeare Festival (TRSF) came about as a part of artistic director Attilio Favorini's intercultural project, funded in part by Toshiba and The Japan

Foundation, whose purpose was to bring Japanese theatrical activities to the Pittsburgh area. TRSF, in its 13th summer performed Shakespeare and offshoots at a large theatre, and experimental works at The Pit. Three members of the original cast of *Ophelia* came from Japan: myself as director, noh actor Matsui (the Ghost), and shoulder drummer, Shunichiro Hisada. Actors were MFA and PhD students in the Theatre Program at the University of Pittsburgh, most of whom had no background in Japanese traditional theatre. There were truly "three rivers" carrying *Ophelia* along on powerful currents: the Shakespearean tradition, the noh tradition, and the experimental energy of the Young Company.

Stage designer Ellen Seeling, who had worked with Matsui a decade earlier, designed a quasi-noh theatre, albeit a small one, with a long bridgeway to the upstage right-hand side. "Tombstone" boxes were built which served as the characters' home base throughout the play. Spectators sat on three sides of the intimate church "graveyard." Three weeks of rehearsals preceded a week of previews, before a three-week run. After years of directing in Kyoto, and working around busy performers' teaching and performance schedules, it was a luxury to be able to rehearse from ten in the morning to nine each night with the entire cast and crew.

The American actors wanted warm-ups each day for vocal and physical energy, but this was new to Noho, which had followed the Japanese method of practicing only the performance text. A fortunate compromise was reached: we used the opening sequence as a means to warmup. This permitted the ensemble to increase gradually the volume and tempo of their words, while fostering an awareness of the special sense of space and rhythm of the world of the play. One happy result of the transfer to America was that photographs and videotapes were available from the original production. This new collective of actors could observe how movements were blocked in a traditional noho-like way, which was to break scenes down into a limited number of patterned movements (*kata*) that were repeated and elaborated upon. Revivals of *Ophelia* with different actors permitted me to transpose these established patterns, the *katafied* movements, giving the blocking a solidity and textured richness difficult to obtain with an entirely new creation.

The ease with which *Ophelia* was "reconstituted" in Pittsburgh attests to the success of the Kyoto cast in creating the foundation and incorporating existing *kata*, for example: Ophelia takes two steps backward, crouches, on the drumbeat she rises. These kinds of movements were then polished by Matsui, with a master's eye for form and rhythm. Once the actors mastered this kind of blocking they began to develop their own novel idiosyncratic interpretations. I felt that the fundamental formal structure which the imported blocking provided for *Ophelia*, much more precise and controlled than in most Western productions, enabled the actors to reach a high level of competence quickly, and then move beyond it. It was as if they had compressed the decades-long training of a traditional noh master into a few weeks.

The initial stage of the strict imitation of prefabricated form was the most perilous. In both Japan and America, actors resisted being forced into someone else's mold. Performing according to *kata* is like filling in someone else's paint-by-the-numbers picture. Some actors rebelled against this, wishing to explore the emotional flow of the moment, protecting that zone they felt to be the creative heart of the project. For my part, I felt that those who clutched after an inner reality were blocking the possibility of seeing the physical reality which they were creating. Zeami speaks of a "third eye," a few feet above and behind, the actor which allows him to observe himself performing.[9] These actors, however, desired explanation of objectives; I gave them details of form. I followed the lead of teachers and the Japanese actors in disdaining explanation. I recognized nonetheless that as a director working in America, I had to help these actors to achieve similar ends by different means. I realized in hindsight that the production's weaknesses were a result of my inability to lead some of these actors over this bridge.

There was considerable danger when applying new rules too strictly. For example, the Queen's "eulogy" for Ophelia was transposed to the melodic eight-beat structure of noh chant by Tokyo-based composer Richard Emmert. He wrote out the song in Western notation and provided a practice tape of himself singing it for the American actors. But when we sat down to group singing lessons, the actors were confused. They were disturbed by the free pitch of Japanese music, a tonal framework, rather than fixed notes, which relied on the performers to mold the melody to their own proclivities. And so, with American pragmatism, we brought in an electric piano and the cast learned the tune to a steady accompaniment. The Japanese intensity and incongruency was replaced with a uniform melody. A similar overly-strict interpretation occurred when I explained the "*jo-ha-kyu*" rhythmic nature essential to all noh movement: a slow beginning, moderate middle, and quick climax. Before they could internalize this, the actors had to count it out Western-style when they practiced entrances and exits, chanting "*johakyu-johakyu*" in increasing tempo, like a lumbering locomotive. By externalizing and rationalizing concepts which the Japanese left purposefully open-ended and intuitive, the Young Company was finally able to generate an equivalent external appearance, a smooth surface with the same polish, if not the depth of the Japanese originals.

Ironically, there was a certain freedom in the fact that these TRSF actors had no background in Japanese theatre. They managed to learn the outer forms created by actors with decades of training. Without the heavy baggage of "tradition" the American actors were able to surpass what the Japanese actors had attempted, exploring facial expression, psychological nuance, musical flow, and dramatic intensity and shape. What they may have lacked in elegance of physical form they made up for in the youthful energy of their emotion. Three full weeks of performances further enriched the play, mellowing it beyond the Kyoto original. The actors put psychological flesh on the bare skeletal structure of movement, portraying the subtle conflict between characters, while the precise movement patterns conveyed the almost mechanical sense of inevitability. Meanwhile, Matsui, secure in the cast's precision, explored a more Western approach in the dance, moving toward a level of naturalism.

Mastering the form was one test for the actors; the other was to communicate with the audience. We eventually learned that audience appreciation and understanding for this production depended on far more than mere linguistic competence. When *Ophelia* succeeded, it was often due to a kind of "intercultural punning"; comprehensible on the surface to anyone, but with a deeper significance for those with knowledge of the particular conventions of noh. The painted design at the back of the stage offered one example. Instead of depicting the pine tree traditional to the noh stage--itself a reference to the sacred Yogo Pine in Nara, where the gods were said to have possessed the first noh actors--we used the dark silhouette of a Gothic church, referring both to the church graveyard, and to the landmark Cathedral of Learning at the center of the Pittsburgh campus. Whether as church graveyard, sacred pine, or Pittsburgh building, audiences with diverse cultural lenses viewed this symbol in many different dimensions. In the scene following the Nunnery scene, the Ghost and Ophelia face each other for the first time, mirroring each other, executing an intricate series of stamps and foot turns before passing each other. To the TRSF audience, this might have appeared to illustrate Ophelia's powerful attraction to death (and the afterlife); for noh cognoscenti, it was a "*rambyoshi*" pattern, a climactic dance sequence of many "crazy women" plays, most notably *Dojoji*, where the jealous dancer makes a mesmerizing ascent of the temple stairs to the bell she is about to destroy.[10] As director, I felt it my job to insure audience members who had different cultural expertise, come away from the same scene with consistent impressions.

Judging from the comments received during the "talkback" sessions following the performances, some spectators had less tolerance for communicative "static" than others. The exotic mix of languages and styles provoked one newspaper critic to write of the confrontation of Ghost and Ophelia as a metaphor for the production: "Their puzzled encounter, in the swirling mists of memory and across a cultural gap of centuries and half the world, mirrors that of the audience, mesmerized and occasionally bewildered by Salz's demanding work."[11] He recommended it to "lovers of the uncommon."

One problem that proved insurmountable was a form of "intercultural illiteracy" with regard to Eastern acting conventions: Americans simply do not know where to look or what to look at on stage. Whether masked or not, faces in Japanese theatre are nearly devoid of explicit emotion. Instead, subtleties of shadow and light, and head angles, must be read by those thoroughly familiar with the conventions. This is partially a reflection of Japanese society where disturbing others with one's internal emotional feelings is considered bad manners (and in samurai days, could result in instant death). It also relates to the fact that noh was originally performed outdoors, sometimes to thousands of people, who had to "read" emotion into the entire body. On stage in full view almost throughout the long play, the Young Company learned to tighten their faces into masks while seated, then "melt" into animation when "in character." Their expressions were much more lively than their Japanese counterparts, developing along a wide continuum from Hamlet's "mad" excess to Laertes's naturalistic animation to Ophelia's frightened freeze. Still, American audiences often seemed at a loss as to where to focus their attention, and what the facial masks meant.

Overinterpreting an innovation as part of the authentic tradition was another form of "illiteracy." The candlelight and mirror were symbolic elements used in every production, as the Ghost and living Ophelia became, "the double mirror that reflects the heroine's plight from two directions, thereby illuminating the universal predicament of those who die without knowing why their lives were ruined, nor how they might have been healed."[12] In Pittsburgh, some spectators assumed that the stage was an exact reconstruction of a traditional noh stage. They wanted to know where the mirror and candles were usually placed on a noh stage (there are none). In fusion performance, innovations may thus be misinterpreted as faithful recreations of an unfamiliar tradition. Conversely, otherwise bothersome staging techniques may be tolerated as unknown foreign conventions. Surprisingly, the Pittsburgh audience might have been even more tolerant of confusing elements than in Kyoto, chalking them up to their own ignorance of Japanese conventions rather than the play's sloppiness, a kind of intercultural Emperor's new clothes.

Noh has been perfected over six centuries and twenty-five generations of master performers. To charge into this supple, ancient art and expect to transform it overnight is foolhardy. To study it as an amateur until one reaches mastery is a long, humbling journey, resulting all too often in an over-reverential attitude which prevents true experimentation. However, by collaborating with masters of the traditions, and bringing one's own background to bear, something slightly new can be achieved. And if this something new is permitted to grow over "generations" of performers and productions, each seeking to first follow, and then break the patterns, then the work can quickly achieve the polish and resonance of a mature work. In time perhaps, it can even become a classic. Confronted with failure, Westerners change the song; Japanese artists tune the instrument. Each struggle provides solutions for the next generation of creators. Or as my co-founder Akira Shigeyama put it: "There is no 'best,' only 'better.'"

Notes

1. For a strong discussion of comparative approaches to Japanese theatre see Peter Arnott, *The Theatres of Japan* (New York: St Martins P, 1969), and Leonard Pronko, *Theatre East and West: Perspectives Towards a Total Theatre* (Berkeley: U of California P, 1974).

2. Using a sociolinguistic model of the continuum of pidgin-creole languages, one can explore how performers move from attraction and imitation (similar to the exaggerations and oversimplifications of pidgin language), to translation, transposition, and finally transformation of the original into a "creole" a "first language" possessing complex grammatical rules and extensive vocabulary. See Salz, "Pidgin-creole Performance Experiment and the Emerging Entre-Garde," in James R. Brandon, ed. *Noh and Kyogen in the Contemporary World* (Honolulu: U of Hawaii P, 1996).

3. This same phrase was used by Martin Esslin during a question and answer session which followed Noho's production of *Rockabye* at a 1984 conference on "Translating Beckett" at the University of Texas at Austin.

4. See Jonah Salz, "The Twain Doth Meet: Noh, Kyogen and the West," *Kyoto Journal* (Summer 1988): 54-7; John Gillespie, "L'Oeil E'coute: The Impact of Traditional Japanese Theatre on Postwar Western Performance," *Modern Drama* (March 1992), 137-148.

5. See, for example Bonnie Marranca and Gautam Dasgupta, eds. *Interculturalism and Performance* (New York: PAJ, 1991).

6. See John P. Frayne, ed., *Uncollected Prose* (London: Macmillan, 1970) 269.

7. See Janice Goff's exhaustive account of Genji's importance in *Noh Drama and the Tale of Genji: the Art of Allusion in Fifteen Classical Plays* (Princeton: PUP, 1991).

8. For a summary, see Akimasa Minamitani, "*Hamlet* in Japan," *Japan Quarterly* (April-June 1990): 176-193.

9. Zeami, Motokiyo. *On the Art of the Noh Drama: the Major Treatises of Zeami*. J. Thomas Rimer and Yamazaki Masakazu, trans. (Princeton: PUP, 1984).

10. Susan Klein, "When the Moon Strikes the Bell: Desire and Enlightenment in the Noh Play *Dojoji*," *Journal of Japanese Studies* (Summer 1991): 291-322.

11. Christopher Rawson, "Ghostly, Uncommon Ophelia," *Pittsburgh Post-Gazette Stagefax* (29 July 1992): 1.
12. Dan Furst, "A Vessel Too Fragile," *American Theatre* (July/August 1992): 7-8.

Kuando 1991: A New Beginning
A Ritual Pilgrimage
by Alexandra B. Bonds

The National Institute for the Arts in Taipei, Taiwan, was founded in 1982 to provide baccalaureate level degrees in the fine and performing arts. The Institute houses four departments, Fine Arts, Music, Dance and Theatre Arts, each offering a four-year program of training toward professional careers. While these programs were supported by the government of Taiwan, the young school spent its first ten years without a permanent home. The location of the Institute was shifted every few years. Each time they were housed in a borrowed space and each move was intended to be a temporary location until a suitable permanent home could be found or constructed. In 1989, the government finally completed plans for the permanent home for the N.I.A. Land was located in Kuando, Peitou, a suburb north of Taipei and a new campus was designed by C.Y. Lee, one of the leading architects in Taiwan.

The faculty of the Institute desired an appropriate celebration to mark the auspicious occasion of the final relocation of the Institute in a home of its own. Professor Chiu K'un Liang, a cultural anthropologist in the Theatre Arts Department developed a plan for the celebration based on religious rituals and the use of theatrical performances in the traditional practice of Taiwanese Taoism. His goal for the events was to mark the new beginning of the school as well as to introduce the students to their own traditional roots by examining ritual celebration. The students would participate in the annual pilgrimage honoring the birthday of the goddess Ma Tsu, one of the largest religious festivals in Taiwan, and use that experience to design their festival for the school's dedication. The combination of the two types of activities was developed to demonstrate the ritual roots and communal participation shared by theatre and religion, and to provide the students with a living example of how the theory of theatre applied to their daily lives. The living and learning connection was enhanced as the development of the theatre performances and rituals connected to the celebration was the focus of many of the theatre courses over the year.

Background of the Project

In the fall of 1990, I began a teaching assignment at the Institute through an appointment sponsored by the Fulbright Foundation for Scholarly Exchange. At that time, the Institute was housed in an abandoned Japanese High School in Lu Chou, a suburb to the west of downtown Taipei. The layout of the buildings and grounds was suitable for the Institute as the buildings consisted of four squares of classrooms and offices around four quadrangles of grass and exotic trees, including a banana tree outside the costume shop. Each department was located in one of the quads, and there were additional buildings for the library, administration building and cafeteria. However, as this location was still considered temporary, little was done in the way of maintenance or upkeep. The once attractive buildings had unpredictable plumbing, broken windows and intermittent air conditioning, a basic necessity of life in the tropics.

As the school had not been designed with the need of an Arts Institute in mind, there were practical drawbacks as well. The Theatre Arts Department did not have a performance space on the grounds. The sets and costumes were built on campus and then transported to one of the theatres in town for the run of the productions. Classes had to be canceled during the weeks of the technical rehearsals and performances because of the distance between the school and the performance space. In spite of the adversity of the physical plant, the school thrived. The Theatre Arts Department receives hundreds of applications each Spring for the thirty-two positions in each year's class. The students are eager and talented and many of the graduates find employment in theatre or theatre-related positions when they complete their studies.

Shortly after my arrival, I was given an orientation to the department and the initial ideas for the celebration. The dedication of the new campus was arranged for May and preparatory events were scheduled for the six months prior to that time. There were plans for three productions to be performed in various venues throughout Taiwan. Two of these plays would be written by the students and would illuminate aspects of student life in the theatre department and the history of the Institute. The third was to be a production of *Zui baxian* or *Eight Drunken Immortals*, a Chinese Opera regularly performed as part of Taoist ritual.[1] In addition, the students were to plan a pilgrimage parade from the old grounds to the new campus. A principle feature of the parade was to be eight larger-than-life puppets representing members of the faculty. The use of the puppets paralleled the incorporation of puppets in religious festivals. As a member of the costume faculty, I was invited to supervise the costume needs for the scheduled activities.

The first of the ceremonies was held in the entrance courtyard of the Lu Chou campus on December 22, 1990. Using traditional Chinese celebratory elements, an orchestra of Chinese instruments played music while the crowd of students, faculty and members of the community gathered. The students constructed thirty large, colorful banners announcing to the gods that they were leaving in six months. By displaying the banners, they were thanking the gods for their hospitality and asking for their blessing upon their departure. As these banners were hoisted into the air, thousands of firecrackers were set off. The use of firecrackers evolved from the earlier custom of burning bamboo. The cracking sound was thought to scare away evil spirits. Afterwards the participants were served a traditional festival food, a soup of broth and sweet rice dumplings. The pink and white round dumplings represent fullness and unity for those who eat it together. Once the opening ceremonies were performed, the execution of the plans could begin in earnest.

Organization of the Plays

Anyone with production experience can imagine the scope of this project, mounting three productions simultaneously, including two new scripts, and constructing the puppets for the parade. While we held production meetings at regular intervals, the project was made even more challenging as the meetings were all conducted in Chinese. Sometimes I had an interpreter and sometimes not, but even an interpreter could not have fully explained to me the total scope of this event. The execution of these ambitious plans required contributions from all members of the theatre department, especially the students. A typical course load for theatre majors is approximately forty hours a week, including courses in both Chinese and Western theatrical history, styles and production, as well as classes in acting, directing, and design and technical theatre. All students are also involved in each semester's productions. The plays are cast at the beginning of each term. Students who are not cast are then assigned to crews in either the costume or scene shop. They are required to work 105 hours in the shops during the semester. Running crew hours are not included in the requirement. Because of the student's course work schedule the only time left for crew hours is nights and weekends. Where possible, class activities were designed to interface with the celebration events, alleviating some of the work load.

My assignment for the school's festivities was to costume the three productions, and to design and construct the eight larger-than-life mobile puppets. The coordination of the four projects and the division of labor was a primary concern. The topics of the student-written plays covered differing aspects of student life at the school. One play, *Da Guo Ming*, or *The Legend of a Grand Citizen*, featured the janitor for the department, who most often could be found dozing on the couch in the department office, the only room where the air conditioning worked. The students developed a history of the school as told through his eyes. The second play, *Ya Mu Wong*, or *The King of the Ducks*, focused on the embarrassment of being a national arts school without a permanent home. A rewrite of a traditional story, it was more rural in nature. The costume designs for the two plays involved a ten-year history of clothing in Taipei and a delineation between city and country clothes. In order to be able to administrate all of the costume needs of this event, I decided to assign these two plays to two junior level costume design students. They had taken my courses in costume design, pattern drafting and construction. Although they had not previously designed, this seemed like a good opportunity for a first project, as they could draw on their own experience for design ideas. As the coordinator of the overall project, I would oversee their work and guide them through the design and execution process.

For the historic based play, we relied on students' wardrobes, and some of the costume stock. Student designer, Chong Chong, collected the appropriate clothing, sized it and sorted it by character. To research the country play, student designer, Fang In, and one of her friends visited one of their grandmother's homes outside Taipei where they raided her wardrobe. They took the garments into the back yard and photographed each one to show me how rural people dressed. The clothing style was more traditional than the modern western influenced dress of the residents of Taipei. The blouses had Chinese style asymmetrical closings and were worn with mid calf length pants.

The acquisition of period and rural clothing for the costumes was complicated by the lack of second-hand stores in Taiwan. Either they don't give away old clothes or they keep wearing them until they are too worn to use. The one market where we did find used clothing was across from the Lung Shan temple, the oldest temple in Taipei and a gathering place for the retired members of the population. The clothing in the market catered to this older segment of the community and was surprisingly high priced. However, we were able to locate a few items there and in the local night markets.

When the designers were ready to hold fittings, I joined in their deliberations to advise them on timeline and characterization. I quizzed them on what they had presented, sharing with them what the image projected to me and asking them if such an image will be appropriate for that character in that scene. I asked them where they had gotten the idea for the costume, and what their reference or research was. In this way, we were able to costume the two plays. They learned about putting a pulled show together and I learned about the differences between recent clothing trends in Taiwan and America.

The third production, the Chinese Opera, was a stylistic challenge for the students. Although they had studied the history and performance characteristics, this was their first opportunity to execute an opera in this tradition. The faculty and guest artists trained both the performers and musicians so that the entire presentation was accomplished by the students. Chinese Opera costume and makeup is standardized by character and role, so that the audience can always recognize the characters. The eight immortals in this script are also often depicted in paintings and temples so the local population is quite familiar with their imagery. The costume challenge for an opera is not in developing a design concept, but rather in dressing the characters in the appropriate style. Rental was the most logical solution to the costume needs. The rental costumes came with experts to dress the students properly in the layers of garments and to apply their makeup.

Design of the Puppets

With the plays delegated to others, my principal involvement in this project became the design and construction of the eight super-puppets for the parade. The parade was to be modeled after the largest folk religious festival in Taiwan, the annual pilgrimage of followers of the goddess Ma Tsu, the protectress of fishermen and goddess of the sea. The scope and significance of the pilgrimage might be compared with re-enactments of the Passion at Easter. Large, mobile puppets are used in this pilgrimage and other Taoist celebrations to represent important mythical figures and gods from the Taoist canon. At ten feet tall, these magical puppets tower over the crowds. The operators see out of a mesh covered opening just above the waist of the puppet. The puppets' legs are the legs of the operators and their built-in arms are jointed. When they march by majestically, they are quite animated as the feet dance and the arms swing in coordinated rhythm. They are dressed in elaborately embroidered armor, long beards and lavish headdresses, a combination similar to the "Ching," or painted face characters in the Chinese Opera.[2] Our puppets were to portray prominent members of the faculty, the mythic figures in the school's history. In our parade, the puppets were to represent not only the individual professors, but also their knowledge and wisdom which was to be transferred from the old location to the new. The faculty members to be depicted were selected by Professor Chiu. He chose to represent the head of each department, the president of the school, and two of the founders of the school who were also professors in the Theatre Department. Professor Chiu's colleagues convinced him to include himself as the Grand Master of the event.

Research for this portion of the project covered many areas. I visited temples and attended temple festivals to see what the traditional puppets looked like and how they were used. The school's library contained a reasonable selection of resource material in English. I examined sources on Chinese Opera costume as well as Chinese Imperial clothing. I was also able to explore various aspects of puppets in performance ranging from Picasso's costume designs for Cocteau's ballet, *Parade*, to the Bread and Puppet Theatre in America. From this collection of sources, I decided that each puppet's body would be unique in its shape so that we could use a variety of techniques to better express the individual professors and their fields. Each puppet figure was designed to represent the professor and his or her role in the school as well as a visual reflection of traditional Chinese culture.

The president of the institute, Bao Yo Yu, was depicted as the warrior general drawn from the Chinese Opera tradition. The body of his puppet followed the traditional form of the religious figures, using wooden jointed arms and the legs of the operator. His elaborate armor pieces were worn over an academic gown thereby combining his qualities of a strong leader and an intellectual guide. The Chinese Opera costume of the warrior general has four flags mounted on the back of it, a vestige of battle when generals needed markers for their messengers to carry. The four flags on the president's back were designed so that each represented one of the four departments in the school. His headdress was a mortarboard with two Chinese style tassels hanging from it.

The puppets of the four department heads emphasized their areas of the arts. The head of the Music Department, Ma Shui Long was depicted with only a head and very long arms. In the middle of his body, instead of a chest he had a large gong. As he moved along, the operators could strike the gong with the mallets he had in his extended arms. Picasso's cubist designs for *Parade* were most influential in the depiction of the head of the Fine Arts Department, Li Je Wen. His puppet was designed as a blocky, cubist form in a Chinese Opera costume. Both the shape of the body and the pattern on the fabric were fragmented and geometric. The head of the Dance Department, Ling Hiu Min, was a prominent choreographer in Taipei and the founder of Cloud Gate Dance Company. He was depicted wearing the costume from one of his most well-known dances. His puppet was the tallest as it also had jointed legs so that it could leap and dance in the procession. Lai Sheng-chuan, the head of the Theatre Arts Department, was a leading playwright in Taiwan. His personal style of wearing a goatee, along with his writing prowess, inspired me to depict him as a Chinese version of William Shakespeare. His puppet's body was designed like the temple models, using constructed arms and the legs of the operator.

The other three puppets were additional members of the Theatre Arts Department. Professor Chiu's puppet, as the leader of the event, was designed to be riding the mythical lion from the lion dances performed for the Chinese New Year and other auspicious occasions. Wang Chi Mei and Yao Yi Wei were among the original founders of the Institute. Wang Chi Mei was an expert in Chinese traditional theatre and Opera, so she was depicted as a "Ching Yi" or young female heroine with Chinese opera makeup and costume. Her puppet was designed to float above the heads of the operators, similar to the type used by the Bread and Puppet Theatre in *Washerwoman Nativity*.[3] The body stopped at the waist and the figure was completed by a train of chiffon eight yards long. Yao Yi Wei was a distinguished senior professor who had been teaching longer than any of the other theatre faculty. He had, in fact, been the teacher for many of the faculty members. To illustrate his long career and wide influence, his puppet was designed with very long arms. Perched on top of the arms in his embrace were dozens of small puppets representing the generations of students that he had fostered.

The planning of the construction of the puppets was one of the greatest challenges of my career. I had never been involved with building puppets before, and I was faced with developing a plan to create them without a framework of references for process or materials, and I was in an unfamiliar environment, devoid of my usual resources. I decided to use techniques that were as simple as possible, both for finding materials and working with them. The heads of the puppets were carved out of Styrofoam as Taiwan is the center of the universe when it comes to plastics and artificial products. The bodies were made of wood strips which proved to be an unfortunate choice. The wood, if not properly dried becomes very brittle, and also is quite heavy for the operators to handle. In planning the construction of the puppet costumes, at least I was in more familiar territory choosing fabrics and trims. The scale of the puppets differed radically from that of humans, though. Whereas a person's period dress might use eight to ten yards of fabric, a puppet gown required twenty to twenty-five. Most fabrics are manufactured in twenty-yard lengths. The excessive amounts of fabric needed limited my choices because of both cost and availability.

Acquiring materials was exacerbated by the traffic congestion in Taipei. There are traffic jams from six in the morning to after midnight. I was limited to buses and taxis; my shop manager had a car and the cutter had a motor scooter. In order to make best use of the people in the shop, we divided up the shopping. It was not a good use of time to have more than one of us out of the shop at a time because each trip was guaranteed to be an all-day affair.

The shop manager, Ricky Lo, shepherded me to fabric stores for my initial orientation. Merchants for the same products tend to be located together in Chinese cities, so our main source was the fabric market in the center of the old part of the city. It was a huge black foreboding warehouse building with no windows and on a block by itself. It seemed to loom over the surroundings. The building was several stories tall, and each floor was jammed with tiny fabric stores the size of a small bedroom, but filled with a treasure house of fabrics. Several alleys radiated out from the warehouse, each one lined with stores carrying a certain kind of accessory. There was a ribbon street, a button alley, a lace section and so on. The choices were unlimited, and yet I ended up using primarily satins and lamés for most of the costumes because I wanted a simple, but bold statement. Once I had been given my initial introduction, the shop manager provided me with a note written in Chinese to hand to a merchant each time I wanted to make a purchase.

An interesting part of the shopping was finding products that were unfamiliar to me to incorporate into the project. The most intriguing item I found was cellophane string used to wrap packages. It is made of layers of translucent cellophane, flattened and folded, one half inch wide. I used it to make hair for the puppets as it was light and buoyant and came in several colors. Another delightful discovery was the jewel shop where they sold plastic gems in a variety of colors and unusual sizes, some large enough to suit the scale of the puppets. For the dozens of small figures on Professor Yao's arms, we purchased little plastic heads from a doll factory. Their tiny shoes were carved out of Styrofoam using an ingenious battery powered miniature hot wire cutter available in local hardware stores.

Execution of the Plays and Puppets

While the celebration events replaced the main production of that semester, the graduating seniors still needed to proceed with their thesis productions. This meant that, in addition to all of the events connected to the celebration, two other plays were being prepared in the shops at the same time: Chinese translations of *Hughie* by O'Neill and *Woyzeck* by Brŭchner. To provide construction staff for all the productions, we needed to divide the pool of student crew members. Of the students assigned to the costume crew that semester, ten were placed on the crew to prepare all the costumes for the celebration. As the student-written plays needed to be completed in time for the Ma Tsu pilgrimage in April, the first month of the semester, we used the skilled stitchers to construct the few costumes for those plays that could not be bought or pulled. Other personnel sewed alterations and prepared the simpler details for the puppet costumes, made banners and dressed the little puppets. Because of the scale and non-realistic nature of the puppets, much of the embellishment was simple patterns of geometrics and scallops. These patterns were enhanced by large ribbon trims designed to provide additional animation when the puppets were moving. With the temporary nature of the puppets, many of the decorative elements were simply cut to shape and glued or lightly stitched in place. The edges were finished by a burning process. Whereas in the States, we might use a cigarette lighter for this technique, here we used several small oil lamps in the costume shop as the heat source.

I began the process of creating the heads of the puppets by sending a student to photograph each of the teachers to be represented. As the honor of being chosen for a puppet depiction was to be kept secret until the parade, the students used a ruse of a class project to cover up their real need for the portraits. Using a front, right side and left side photo of each professor, I sketched caricatures of their likenesses. I sculpted the heads for the puppets in the scene shop, although it meant being far from the costume crew. The scene shop crew prepared blocks to my dimensions and I whittled them to size using a variety of tools, including kitchen knives and a rasp. The caricatures were sketched on graph paper to give me a reference for the size of the facial features, but the translation from sketch to sculpture was still a difficult one. My best judge of success was when someone came in the shop and recognized who I was working on.

The Ma Tsu Pilgrimage

In April, halfway through the building of the puppets for the institute's celebration, all of the theatre students traveled to Tachia, a city in central Taiwan, to perform the three plays we had prepared and to participate in the annual pilgrimage honoring the birthday of the goddess, Ma Tsu. Every Spring, during a time that the soothsayers decide is most auspicious, the followers of Ma Tsu begin their annual pilgrimage. Ma Tsu, as the goddess of the sea and protectress of fishermen, is an important goddess for an island country. Included in the Taoist canon, Ma Tsu is worshipped in southeastern China and Taiwan. Thousands of her devotees assemble in the mid-island city of Tachia to participate in this annual gathering. The carved image of Ma Tsu from the Cheng Lam Kung temple, the primary Ma Tsu temple, is taken on the journey to visit all of the other Ma Tsu temples in the region. The devotees of Ma Tsu travel from Tachia to Shenkang and back on a twenty-two-mile circular route over a ten-day period. They travel in community groups dressed in matching uniforms to represent their regions. The pilgrims all carry flags with their names on them so the gods will know who they are. They also bring along their images of Ma Tsu and other ritual figures to be a part of the parade.

The opening festivities began at midnight. The Cheng Lam Kung temple was twinkling with strings of lights shrouded in the haze of incense smoke as the marchers assembled nearby the streets. After speeches from local dignitaries and blessings from the temple shaman, a fury of firecrackers was set off creating a deafening roar and covering the streets with paper debris. Out of the seeming chaos, the groups slowly merged onto the pilgrimage route. Several different kinds of representations were included in this celebration. There were drunken immortal puppets, dragon and lion dancers, as well as trucks carrying Chinese orchestras and singers. The tall god puppets in the style that we emulated were accompanied by shorter, stumpy figures serving as comic interludes. Behind the ritual figures march the members of each community. At the end was the palanquin carrying the statue of Ma Tsu followed by another entourage of devotees. The procession took one and one half hours to pass by and then continued on into the night to the city of their first destination. I joined them for the first three days of the journey and then returned to campus to continue preparation of the puppets.

The weather in Taiwan in April is unbearably hot, so the pilgrims march at night for several hours at a time. When they reach their destination for that leg of the journey, they are welcomed into the temples of that town for rest and food. During the day, after sleep and food, the pilgrims need something to do. Entertainment is usually provided by theatrical troupes that join the pilgrimage. In this year, the students of the Institute were invited to join the ritual and present the plays for the entertainment. Performing for this religious festival was an honor for the students as well as an ideal opportunity for them to witness their heritage first hand. They performed all three of the plays in various locations in the towns along the route. In each city, the students created their performance space. They devised a portable stage that could be assembled in a variety of dimensions to suit each site. Performances that are presented as part of a religious event are offered for the gods regardless of whether or not there is a human audience, therefore the stage was always set up to face the temple. Often, there were no dressing rooms nearby and the cast applied their makeup and put on their costumes in full view of the audience. This form of theatre introduced the students to a closer interaction between the performers and the audience, as they lived with the pilgrims on the road, in the dormitories and the food halls. By participating in this event, the students better understood the interaction between people's lives, and religion and the significance of performance in liturgical ritual. They also acquired a clearer insight into the purpose of their school's ritual pilgrimage.

The Institute's Pilgrimage

At the conclusion of the Ma Tsu festivities, the theatre students traveled back to campus to finish preparations for the school's pilgrimage. The student crews returned to the shops for the completion of the puppet costumes and the final stages of preparation for the parade, while the three productions continued to perform throughout the Taipei area. As the sculpting of the puppet heads was completed, they were covered with newspaper maché and painted with latex paint. The hair and jewels were glued in place. The headdresses, made of cardboard and covered with matching materials were also glued on. When the components of the puppets were finished, we began the complex process of fitting the pieces together. We dressed the wooden frameworks and secured the heads to the bodies. As each puppet was assembled, we took it for a trial walk in the courtyard. Some lost their heads, while others performed beautifully on the first try. Gradually, we fixed most of their weaknesses or discovered ways to operate them to avoid breakage. We were no longer able to keep the secret of the puppets' identities as crowds of admirers gathered to watch our first tentative processions around the campus.

In May, two days before the pilgrimage to the new campus, we had two mini parades near the old school grounds to the local temples, Pao Ho Kung and Yung Lien Su. The parades included the puppets and a collection of the students dressed in assorted costumes along with the actors and musicians of the Chinese Opera. On each day, they went to one of the temples to show gratitude to the local deities for hosting the school in the past and to ask for good wishes in the new location. After the parade, a performance of the Chinese Opera was offered to the gods. On the last night before the main parade, there was a final performance of *The Legend of a Grand Citizen* on the grounds of the old school in the Theatre Arts courtyard.

The pilgrimage was scheduled to take place on Saturday and Sunday, May 11 and 12, 1991. On the morning of the first day, the members of the school gathered at the entrance to arrange the procession. I had no idea of the enormity of this event, and was surprised to see the large crowds that had appeared. Most of the students of the institute attended. Each department was assembled behind its respective department head's puppet. In addition to the puppet figures we had made, the local temples sent their own traditional puppet figures to join the pilgrimage and wish us well on our journey. There were several pickup trucks carrying large plaques decorated with floral messages and other vehicles with members of Chinese orchestras playing traditional instruments. We were joined by performing groups from other schools, a marching band and an alumni delegation. A large crowd of local residents joined in the celebration. The parade route was lined with saffron banners with blue and red printing announcing "Kuando 1991: A New Beginning," our destination and purpose. As the parade got underway traditional music was played and hundreds of firecrackers were set off. The street was so littered with firecracker papers that it looked like confetti from a New Year's party. The formal groups slowly emerged from the melee to create a procession that included several hundred people spanning ten blocks long.

As the marchers moved along the route, they were occasionally surprised by planned "attacks " from local school children in disguises. These interferences were representative of the challenges we needed to face in making the move and to strengthen our resolve to reach our goal. They also were another way for the community to express its support of our move to the new location. As we passed through large crowds of well wishers we marched a mile through Lu Chou. The onlookers thinned out as we reached the edge of the city. The terrain between the two schools was quite varied. We walked in less developed areas for another mile, and finally progressed on a road between fields of livestock. The weather was unusually pleasant which was fortunate as we chose to have our pilgrimage during the day instead of night. One of the highlights of the first day came when we reached the Kuando Bridge. The new campus was barely visible to us from its hilltop location on the other side. We crossed over the river into Kuando, entering a cityscape again. Our journey had taken about four hours.

Instead of marching directly to the new school, we stopped and paid our respects to the gods of our new local temple, Kuandu Kung. As we entered the temple grounds, each of the god puppets from the Lu Chou temples approached the altar at the entrance of the temple and bowed. One by one the professor puppets entered the courtyard, and bowed to the altar. The students had been quite rowdy along the parade route, but here they were transformed once they entered the temple grounds. I was moved to see the puppets that we had created become part of this ritual. At that moment the puppets transcended caricature and personified human spirit. I began to understand what Professor Chiu had wanted the students to gain from this experience. By personalizing the events and living them for several months we all were enlightened about the significance and the inherent theatricality of tradition and ritual. After the homage to the local gods, the students performed their Chinese Opera for the gods and a large crowd of onlookers who had gathered. The performance marked the end of festivities for the first day and as the crowds dispersed, we packed the puppets into pickup trucks and unceremoniously returned them to the old school. Their feeble frames had taken quite a beating from the wind and the rigors of their journey, and they needed to return to the scene shop for repairs.

The next morning we reassembled at the temple to begin the final leg of the journey. The temple was close to the new campus, so the procession reached the entrance to the school early in the day. As we walked up the hill, the still unfinished road was lined on both sides with a bugle band dressed in red and white military-style uniforms with pseudo Roman helmets. An anomalous vision amidst the Chinese tradition, they played a Western-style triumphal march. One by one the puppets made their way on to campus and walked into the new theatre building. The courtyard there was lined with "Kuando 1991" banners and a stage was set up for the continuing celebrations. The puppets were arranged around the perimeter of the courtyard so that they could preside over the events of the evening.

The Dedication Ceremonies

The other three departments presented programs of their work during the afternoon. The Music Department offered several concerts of both Western and Asian music. In the rehearsal halls of the Dance Department, the dance students presented their choreographed works. The Art Department mounted a display of student work. In the late afternoon, a lavish banquet was served to the participants and honored guests. That evening, the theatre students performed one of their plays again and then all were invited to a masquerade ball held on the rooftop lounge of the theatre department.

At midnight, the closing events began in the courtyard of the Theatre Department. Wang Chi Mei, the theatre professor who teaches Chinese Opera, presented a short scene from the opera about Chung Kuei, the patron saint of scholars. This segment is often included in Taoist rites. Then a shaman prepared the stage for a ritual blessing of the grounds and buildings. He blessed a bowl of tea leaves which was then passed around to the members of the audience. Each person took one leaf and placed it in his or her mouth. From that moment on no one was to speak until the ceremony was completed. The shaman performed a cleansing ritual by sprinkling the blood of a duck and a chicken around the altar on the stage. Blood sacrifice is not a part of Taoist ritual, so the shaman only drew a small amount of blood by biting each of them on the beak.

The shaman led us out of the courtyard to each building of the new campus. Our path was lit by torches held by the students. For the last phase of his blessing, he brought out a marionette dressed as a god and used it to perform a ritual in each of the buildings. As the consecration was completed, firecrackers were set off. The purpose of the blessing was to invite the favorable spirits to join in the life of the new campus. After the final building was blessed, we were lead back into the courtyard of the Theatre Department. An ensemble of musicians played music from the Yuan Dynasty, a time known for the development of music and theatre forms. Each participant in the activities was presented with a "Kuando 1991" banner from the parade route. We were then served sweet rice dumpling soup, the same kind of soup that had been prepared for the initial event six months earlier. This was a way of coming full circle and bringing the celebration to a close.

Reflections

The series of events was a once-in-a-lifetime experience. Though I had attended the production meetings, I realized during the days of the ceremonies that I had no concept of the full extent of this project. I felt as though I were attending a play presented by another theatre organization, it was all such a surprise for me. The events were quite magical and moving. I will always feel a bond with the National Institute of the Arts as a result of my involvement with their birth. While my specific knowledge of the specifics of Taiwanese ritual was not greatly increased, I came to understand the place of tradition in our lives and how the Taiwanese culture has developed ways of controlling the mysteries of the world around it through ritual performance. As the only way to understand what happened was to live through it, I also gained a valuable insight into the process of participating in both theatre and ritual in another culture.

The Institute moved into its new buildings for the Fall term of 1991, and the new campus is an excellent facility, considered to be one of the finest in Asia. There are two large theatres on campus, one for the Dance and one for the Theatre Department. In addition, the theatre has a black box performance area. The costume shop is on the fourth floor with plenty of windows and a lovely view of the surrounding hills and the city of Taipei in the distance. And somewhere in the basement of the building in a storage vault, I imagine eight puppets taking up more space than is available, but as they are part of the school's heritage, they are as revered as ancestors would be. And perhaps, once a year on tomb sweeping day or on the school's birthday, someone opens the storage vault for a few minutes and remembers their part in the creation of the permanent home for the National Institute of the Arts.

Notes

1. Chinese Operas are generally unattributed.
2. For further information on Chinese Opera, see Hsiu-ling Cheng, *Secrets of the Chinese Drama* (London: Harrap, 1937).
3. See Stephen Brecht, *The Bread and Puppet Theatre* vol. 2 (London: Methuen, 1988).

Israel's Rina Yerushalmi and Her Directorial Experiments in Spatial Interrelations
by Yael Nir

Dedicated to the memory of Moshe Sternfeld

Against all financial odds and an artistically degenerate local theatre scene, Director Rina Yerushalmi's experiments stand out in more than one way. Born in Israel, Yerushalmi traveled extensively, studying theatre arts in England, the United States and Japan. Eventually dividing her home between Tel Aviv and New York, teaching and directing in both, she established herself as Israel's eminent acting coach as well as innovative director. The following account is based on a two-year research which I undertook for my M.A. thesis. Since no one was allowed to observe the process, I began serving as Assistant Director, ending up as Stage Manager and eventually Executive Producer of the company. This enabled me to experience the many creative and performative facets of Yerushalmi's work. Yerushalmi has a remarkable capacity to integrate several composites of the theatrical art in a spatially based, coherent whole. Her projects on *Hamlet* and *Woyzeck*, in which two distinct aesthetic structures were used, respectively a circle and a grid serve as definitive examples to examine.

The Itim Ensemble, Yerushalmi's company, had its roots in a 1988 summer workshop on Shakespearean texts. After unprecedented critical acclaim of an ensuing production of *Hamlet* at a local theatre festival, the experiment found a permanent home in the Tel Aviv municipal theatre, The Cameri. For three consecutive seasons it was performed regularly in the tight, twenty-seven-feet-square rehearsal room. Competing with inadequate ventilation and with complete disregard for fire regulations, *Hamlet* played to exhilarated full houses. The production toured internationally including presentations at the Braunschweig Festival, The Brooklyn Academy of Music and the

Holland Festival, and closed in 1993. The second experiment, based on Georg Buchner's *Woyzeck*, began in 1990 and was performed alongside *Hamlet* for two seasons.

Yerushalmi's attitude to space and to audience required that both productions' auditorium/performance spaces be fitted especially for her experiments. Her closest collaborator in this endeavor was the designer Moshe Sternfeld, whose genius and understanding of the theatre complemented Yerushalmi's concepts, and supplied the physical leverage for her projects.

The most available models for Yerushalmi's affinities and sensibilities are Jerzy Grotowski's Poor Theatre and the environmental orientation in Richard Schechner's work. Yerushalmi questions what is essential to the art of the theatre that engenders an aesthetic experience uniquely its own. Her approach to the theatrical event is that of an *encounter* with the issues of the play which she deems relevant (the term she uses is significantly less aggressive than that of *confrontation* used by Grotowski).[1] This encounter, explored by each member of the ensemble, is then exchanged with the other members and shared later with the audience. Such an approach leads to a very open reading of the play, placing the essence of the theatrical experience, indeed as any aesthetic experience, on the audience's ultimate encounter with itself.

"What is this thing in the audience, that we need to keep vibrant," Yerushalmi asks of her actors, "so that we can go on talking *with* it, instead of talking *to* it?" Expressive of a fundamental respect of the spectator as an individual, this relationship is also a prerequisite in Yerushalmi's actor training. She believes that when actors agree to enter into a dialogue, without dictating their values or viewpoint to their partners, the audience will then tune in on these premises.

Determining the Space

The work on each experiment began with a deliberation as to the physical image of the theme (myth, in Grotowski's terms) to be encountered. The relation between the acting area and the audience seats was assumed to affect the decoding of the event by both parties, and to lead to a particular attitude.

In order to reach those decisions, Yerushalmi posed the following leading questions: What is the action/event unfolding in the play? What image would reflect this action and its place? From whose (which of the characters) viewpoint is it relevant to discuss the dilemmas of the play today? How is the audience related to the action? What does the physical design of the space signify about the relationship between the acting area and the audience seats? Once a decision was made and a shape attributed to it, in conjunction with the designer, it remained open to constant re-evaluation.

For *Hamlet*, the audience was seated in two rows lining the empty square on three sides, while a similar row of seats lined the fourth side, for use by the actors. The center of the dark wooden floor was sanded to reveal a circle of a lighter shade. The image that Yerushalmi had in mind when the work began emphasized her spatially oriented perception of the theatrical event. She wanted a circle, as if the audience and the actors were holding hands, all together in the same place. She sought a warm intimacy, in a state of equality. The tone evoked would enable the spectator to listen, to think at a pace together with the actors. Seeing the audience as Hamlet, Yerushalmi made him sit with the audience, not with the other actors. The actors understood that they had to tell the tale outward, not directly across to each other. A phrase or a gesture was like a wave, engulfing the audience on the way to be hurled at the partner. Thus, Hamlet personifying the audience, is talking to himself.

As the experiment proceeded, the image that emerged was that of the play emanating from Hamlet, as his dream. Sitting in a circle, the audience dreamt, together with Hamlet, of the events unfolding inside it.

In the case of *Woyzeck*, the theme of the encounter was the scientific, functional approach as expressed in the Doctor's attitude to Woyzeck, the subject of his (her, in Yerushalmi's version) research. Buchner's foresight as to the dangers of this attitude, combined with the scientific presumption of deciphering life's mystery, made the play relevant in a society where the moral issues raised by genetic engineering would soon be eclipsed by its abuse. The Doctor scenes, therefore, became the key to the play and the students' roles were expanded. Considerable external material was inserted in the form of lessons in genetics and human biology. The space would, accordingly, suggest a research center or a laboratory, with overtones of secrecy and military security. An auditorium would accommodate the audience, mirrored as an elite of fellow students and scientists, guests at the final stage of the experiment Woyzeck had submitted to.

With this in mind the space was designed as a white-box, shared without demarcation by both audience and acting area. Seven rows of seating were located at one of the narrow ends of the rectangular box. The same grey floor extended from the stage to the stalls. The design was abstract and bare, with a minimum of props, all functional, including slide projectors which were operated by the actors. The slides, projected onto the back wall, were black-and-white drawings taken from anatomy books depicting sections of the human body. The scientific and military themes in the play engendered, at first, two overlapping fictional environments. Gradually, the military theme receded into the background, and the khaki uniforms were replaced by dark blue suits. The martial leitmotif was, however, constantly recalled by the repeated marches and drills performed along a grid of paths, parallel to the walls.

Spatial Forms as Infrastructures

In both experiments, the structure of the space--the circle, in *Hamlet* and the grid of paths in *Woyzeck*--was also the basic spatial relationship between the actors themselves, and between them and their future audience. Having most, or in the case of *Woyzeck*, the entire cast on stage throughout the performance, it was the shifts in those relationships that transformed the abstract space in each scene.

In addition to aesthetically organizing the space and the mise-en-scene, the circle and the grid fulfilled the role of infrastructure for the creative process of each experiment. Hence, they provided a powerful link between the work process and its outcome. Yerushalmi's use of a builder's vocabulary was another facet of her architectural approach. At the end of the first week of rehearsals on *Woyzeck*, she commented after a grid session that the play was now laid out on the floor, and that all that was needed was to raise it to the ceiling. However evanescent it might seem to the spectator, the accumulated history of the process accompanied the actors and was embodied in the performance. The grid allowed encounters with characters who would otherwise have no direct contact in the play. Thus it enriched the history of the actors/characters' relations in performance, even if it turned out eventually to be different than what was initially explored.

During rehearsals, the circle and the grid structured and generated the performing techniques of the ensemble. These infrastructures also provided the creative means to infuse the actors with the play's subject matter through their respective filters and patterns, and by inversion, served as a device to draw a wealth of images from the actors' personal life experience. The director thus aimed at making the actors responsible co-authors of the work.

The Dynamics of Space in *Hamlet*

The circle and the grid, virtually opposed though they may be, each supplied in its own way, a *temenus* for the work. The term "temenus" suggested by Jung in his seminal works on symbols and their functions, offers a potent model for Yerushalmi's theatrical encounter. It relates both to the spatially based dynamics of the creative process and to those partaken by the audience in the performance. In *Psychology and Alchemy* Jung writes:

> The drawing of a spellbinding circle is an ancient magical device used by everyone who has a special or secret purpose in mind. He thereby protects himself from the "perils of the soul" that threaten him from without and attack anyone who is isolated by a secret. The same procedure has also been used since olden times to set apart as holy and inviolable . . . a protected temenus, a taboo area where he [the dreamer] will be able to meet the unconscious.[2]

This circle or temenus shelters the self from splintering. It is inside this temenus that the drama takes place.

The ritual action of the drawing of the charmed circle has the effect of leading the subjects' attention back into the inner precinct in order to rediscover the lost unity of life and consciousness. According to the Tao, says Jung, the circular movement [of the wheel] activates this work, involving all sides of the personality, all psychological opposites, for the purpose of inducing self knowledge.[3]

Suzanne Langer, who sees dance as the first religious activity engaged in by man, claims that the circle of ritual dancing symbolizes the sacred realm: "In the magic circle all demonic powers are loosed. The mundane realm is excluded, and with it, very often, the restrictions and properties that belong to it."[4]

Yerushalmi's theatre space is a realm set apart from mundane reality, where both actors and audience meet themselves. The temenus also links them together in a bond of trust in the artistic endeavor. This aspect, respective of "the willing suspension of disbelief," translates in Yerushalmi's work in a daring removal of the traditional illusionistic shield. For *Hamlet*, the play's situation was accentuated by the drawing of this "charmed circle" leading Hamlet's (and the audience's) attention back into the inner precinct.

A pertinent example is the ghost scene. As the ghost appeared and Hamlet was left alone to encounter him, the two figures proceeded into the circle. Hamlet cut into its center, imploring for the truth, and crashed to the floor. The ghost walked slowly around the sphere all the while, and finally stepped in, grabbing Hamlet as he began to speak. Their contact was passionately physical, as they twisted and shuffled in a menacingly symbiotic embrace. Meanwhile, the peripheral lights had dimmed, leaving the circle visible, as if floating, while a faint beam revealed the line of actors sitting behind it, watching, as an inner audience. The metaphorical content of this scene established the play in a conceptual "dream zone." In returning to the idea of the temenus, the circle here functioned as a protective boundary for Hamlet's psyche in danger of being shattered by the encounter.

The absence of masked stage machinery, the primary use of top lights to allow for eye contact between actor and audience, the use of the entire floor as acting area, and moving the audience to watch the players-play, were all means to achieve audience inclusion. Moreover, the setup of seating on three sides inevitably inserted the audience into the spectacle itself, as the viewers were seen, dimly lit, from every angle. The row along the fourth side, being occupied by actors, further enhanced this unity. In several instances, actors would sit, stand or simply listen and watch the action, thus functioning as an inner audience and contributing to the testimonial quality of the event. This feature was effective as one New York critic noted, writing of the performance at the Brooklyn Academy of Music:

> As the performance begins, the entire ensemble appears and stands, facing the audience in a stylized formation. For a long moment, cast and audience silently take one another in. This opening sets the tone for the entire three hour production, where characters in the play are always deliberately aware of the audience to whom they are playing. One cannot remain aloof in the face of this *Hamlet*. The performance is designed to bring the audience directly into the world of the play.[5]

This long moment of silence also served Yerushalmi as a device to plant an element of the working process into the actual performance, thus having the audience accompany the play from its initial creation, as well as reminding the actors why they were there. Every rehearsal day began with the company sitting in a circle, in total silence. Nobody was to say or do anything unless it was something of value to the partners in the circle. To describe this action a phrase was coined: "to give in the circle." It was meant to emphasize to the actors that it is an actor's responsibility to give of her/himself something that bears meaning for the others. In this way, she/he brings this understanding to the performance. It is noteworthy that prior to every performance, the ensemble would convene on the stage floor, to sit around the circle for approximately twenty minutes. The cast would first sit in silence, taking each other in and endowing each other with their characters. Gradually they would "give in the circle," recite some lines from the play, listen to the iambic meter being reborn again. This "moment of recollection," in the full meaning of the word, was also practiced before every performance of *Woyzeck*. It became the working ritual of the ensemble, re-creating the temenus of the play, projecting its aesthetics and the initial impulses that set it in motion.

The circle, as a space for the actors to give of themselves, had two complementary frameworks. In one, the actors took turns sharing material brought to the space. This material was chosen independently and was only loosely associated with the play content, if at all. The ensemble would then store it as luggage for the road. It would become a meaningful part of the history of the process, knots to be treasured in the network of ties between the participants. Some material was eventually incorporated into the performance. For example, in one of the circle-sessions, the director requested that everyone give something to the actor playing Hamlet. The actor playing Horatio rose, stood behind Hamlet, placed his hands above him and chanted a traditional Hasidic song: "Who is the man that cherishes life." This simple, poignant song was his way of offering purity of intent in the forthcoming endeavor. Both actors were the only ones to have come from orthodox Jewish families. Both had adopted secular behavior, while remaining emotionally rooted in their religious experience. For them it was a way of connecting with their common past, creating a special bond that would eventually make them Hamlet and Horatio to each other.

The other framework was a group practice that held several functions. It began with total silence, lasting at first for long periods of time, and resulting with the mastering of a technique used to focus the actors' attention on their impulses to act. The technique was based on the assumption that in the process of upbringing, the impulses, such as jumping with joy, were oppressed. The immediate translation of impulses into action was thus hampered and needed to be recovered.

The ground rules for the circle work have the actors agree to respond without reserve and to share in any impulse, both in action and in sound, offered by any actor inside the circle of improvisation. Energy generated in this fashion has a sweeping and amplifying nature, mobilizing the actors' faculties in listening to the various impulses being born, then contributing to their permutations and development. In the circle-session, the lines and the characters are free for the taking. This makes it an effective method for assembling images in an associative manner.

However, a circle is centrifugal, centered upon itself and closed to the outside. It needs the hand of a director to pick and choose the pertinent moments and place them in the *mise en scène* in a way that will not leave out the audience. The freshness and vigor of the impulses, indeed their authenticity, are carefully harnessed to the requirements of the ensuing performance.

In *Hamlet*, the action rotated on a single axis, optically centered in the circle in the middle of the floor. That was true also of the many split-focus scenes. The action unfolded either within the circle, around it, or both.

This circle was, therefore, heavily charged, all the more so because it provided, together with the four walls, the only available orientation in the space. Politically, this meant that there was no hierarchy; no point of view was favored over another. The spectators were all involved in the event on equal terms, which was rendered even more informal by the proximity to the acting area. The mere name of the space--the rehearsal room--and its backstage appearance, made them accomplices to the "foreboding secrets" of an ensemble of experimental artists, as well as those of the royal family.

The Grid of Interdependence Versus Alienation

The infrastructure for *Woyzeck* was a grid. With axes of movements parallel to the walls, the length and width of the rectangular space were emphasized. In the beginning, this endowed the entire floor with equal spatial value. But with the length being about thirty seven feet from the back wall to the audience seats, a three-zone division organically emerged, establishing a front zone, a middle and a back one. The grid concept implied that all the components existed simultaneously, as opposed to sequentially. It therefore manipulated the elements of time and of narrative, and allowed for split scenes and multiple focuses. The grid served as a pertinent structural context for the material Yerushalmi chose to encounter. The play itself is a collection of fragments with no canonized sequential order, and Yerushalmi's adaptation needed room to implant an array of anatomy lessons. The choice of a grid-based approach, therefore, implied that the universe of the play predominated the plot. The next step was to create a work process that would condition the actors and contribute to the inclusion of the audience "from square one."

The method initiated in the process of *Hamlet* evolved further in this second project, as the grid acting technique imposed another set of requirements. The content and shape of the framework established in *Hamlet* for "giving" were altered. Instead, the task became performing something one excelled in, except acting. The encircled stage situation was replaced by a frontal address, with the group sitting in a straight line. Several skills discovered in this way were incorporated into the play. Some were discarded along the way, while others reached the final version. One of them that generated an entire scene was the preparation of fresh pasta on location. The sensuous, flexible spaghetti spooled out of the pasta-maker unleashed a bestial streak in the otherwise restrained characters, leading to a grotesque commentary on human nature.

However, it was the group practice of the grid that brought up the most deeply dormant individual and collective imagery, and provided the journey on which the ensemble had originally wanted the audience to accompany it. The technique implies that the space is a virtual network of longitudes and latitudes that extends to the walls. At any point the actors are at crossroads from which they can move forward, backward or from side to side along these lines. Since it is a network, everyone in it maintains spatial relationships all round, reacting to the space and to the other actors, in action and in sound.

The ground rule this time stipulates that the actors do not initiate anything, but act in a conscious reaction to something. They should be attentive to all the activities, whether nearby or at a distance, throughout the grid. They do not stop to discuss the scene or try to lead it, dictating their interpretation. The approach should be that of an invitation. At the beginning of the session, the actions are restricted to a minimum: walking, standing, turning and running. As the grid session evolves, these restrictions drop, but the movement axes along the lines parallel to the walls persist. Peculiarly, the grid allows, on the one hand, for simultaneous, unrelated activities to be carried on throughout its space, while, on the other hand, it creates an aesthetic interdependence between those activities, which, in turn, generates a comprehensive approach toward its entirety. A general, scene-unspecified grid session enables every actor to touch upon any of the play's layers and to use any line from the text, irrespective of character. They may perform any fragment of meaning, either in aesthetic form or content that has bearing on the play. Even while working on a specific scene, the actors plant into it elements from another scene or from the entire store of luggage. Yerushalmi uses the image of an archaeological site, cutting across the play's several different archaeological layers.

One way in which the characteristics of the grid bore an acute relevance to the work process, was reflected in the actors' difficulty to deal with the military theme in the play. Belonging to a society where military service is not a mythical image but a common reality, it took the actors several days of halfhearted drills and marches until they identified their resistance. They finally consented to radicalize soldierly perfection, assuming they would thus make the audience encounter, together with them, the anguish of alienation. This factor contributed a cool-fire atmosphere to the performance which was further enhanced by the scientific them. To actualize the damage caused by medical studies, the image Yerushalmi suggested was that in every stage of the experiment, the students figuratively severed one more neuron in their nervous system.

These metaphors took their toll on the process. The work was both fascinating and excruciating. As the aesthetics became more rigid by the *mise en scène*, they put extra strain on the actors' endurance. However, the numerous military marches were both an essential and an effective feature. They swept the stage clean almost after every scene, reorganizing the space as a grid of parallel lines, ready for the next chaotic outbreak.

The work on the prayer scene sheds light on the entire process. It is the moment when Marie recites verses from the New Testament, telling of the encounter between Christ and the woman who sinned. During one of the grid sessions, there occurred a moment when Woyzeck, facing the wall with the actors huddling behind, began to utter sounds that colored the scene with the shades of a Jewish prayer. This was later referred to as "The Prayer," and was kept in the collective memory store. When work was started on Marie's verses, with the intention of involving the whole space in it, the director recalled the prayer moment and suggested that all the characters be praying for the expiation of their respective sins, in chorus. Whichever way the actors were distributed through the space, in the several grid sessions that were tried, the scene was powerfully redemptive. Performing that would have implied Marie's and everybody else's eventual salvation. However, the meaning Yerushalmi advocated was that Woyzeck alone recovered his integrity through the murder act. The prayer was therefore replaced by a marching drill performed in the background by the other characters. In other words, the grid session practice produced a warmer, more integrated environment than was appropriate, and was replaced by a formal, grid aesthetic solution. The drill continued all through the murder scene that followed, superimposed by the anatomy lesson on the human heart. It is hard to tell if the drill actually resonated with the memory of the prayer for the audience. The theory of the accumulation of the work history does point in this direction. As a participant observer, the drill to me was indeed a prayer, invigorated by the thematic inversion. In this scene, the original plot, the military and the scientific elements were all distinguished and reciprocally empowered by superimposition and all vibrated in unison.

The Dialogue between Director and Designer

Designer Moshe Sternfeld had the gift, the authority and the thorough understanding of the art to realize the nature of the intervention that would benefit Yerushalmi's experiments. A circle drawn at center stage surrounded by seats was enough to conjure up the spatial image Yerushalmi sought for *Hamlet*. A rectangular white space fronted by a long, white rectangular table, facing the small auditorium, embodied Yerushalmi's metaphor for *Woyzeck*.

Sternfeld's manipulation of the design for *Woyzeck* warrants a brief discussion. He came to the first run-through of *Woyzeck*, and the next day the space was transformed by a simple addition of a "bridge." This new element was a long, white table of a clean geometric shape, in perfect line with the grid infrastructure. It was set across the front zone, elevating it and, instead of barring the acting area from the audience, defined proximity.

The "bridge" had various functions and was moved around in all three zones during the rehearsals, transforming the spatial relationships between the physical data and the live mass of actors. Eventually, it began and ended the performance up front, with only one diagonal shift to the middle zone in the drinking scenes (originally, at the inn).

The fictional functions of the "bridge" evolved during the experiment. At first, it was established as Marie's base of operation. Marie's most intimate scenes with Woyzeck happened three feet from the first row. As the anatomy classes took shape, some of them were advanced to the front or were even performed at the "bridge." It accommodated the company in the "last supper" scene. At the play's end, it was the site of Marie's murder and later, that of Woyzeck's brain surgery.

Despite its position, the "bridge" did not obliterate the rest of the space nor cause an imbalance. On the contrary, it organized and further defined its structure by giving spatial reference. The axial relations, typical of the grid, were thus emphasized and the *mise en scène* was oriented.

Conclusion

Yerushalmi explores, together with her ensemble, the potential of the medium and its limits, toward the achievement of an essentially theatrical experience. To that end she deals with classical drama, whose quintessential subject matter can be approached and interpreted from diverse personal and social levels. This firm, broad base allows her to focus on the validation of the means, indeed the nature of the experience she seeks to foster. The assumption is that if the actors are authentically engaged in the encounter with the play, their audience will join them. The role of the director is to facilitate the audience's reading, selecting the communicative elements and placing them in a coherent structure.

Yael Nir

Yerushalmi's approach is inspiring, not only because of her ensemble's remarkable achievements but for the formulation of an original working model. The principles suggested by this model are the following: The director selects the spatial image of the event, subordinate to the theme of the play she deems relevant. This, in turn, fosters a specific relationship with the audience. While this image is translated into a fundamental aesthetic form (such as the circle and the grid), and given a physical shape by the designer, it also structures both the performing technique and the mise-en-scene, and processes the subject matter through improvisation.

As improvisation techniques, the grid and the circle practice sessions were not essentially different. Both allowed the actors not to invent the scenes but to encounter them as they emerged from their own creative faculties, which were impregnated by the plays' subject matter. Both were based on the assumption, or concept, that a character's motivation was only one driving force in the complex set of interrelations that built a play into an encounter. The understanding of the moment in which this motivation would come to fruition and manifest itself needed to be discovered, not imposed on the scene. Moreover, the support of the ensemble in the creation of a coherent world, required an atmosphere of trust and reciprocity, which the circle and the grid are apt to encourage. They were both used in one way or another in the many experimental endeavors that defined ensemble work as a significant element in the group's artistic creed. The circle's faster, sweeping and focusing quality made it more suitable to use for the discovery of impulses. The grid had a better potential for organizing the actors' multi-directional attention, one that encompassed the physical space and the simultaneous chance compositions, of which they were an integral part.

As a further evolution from the circle, in the grid practice the actors had to be aware not only of their impulses as they focused and developed in the center, but of all the impulses unfolding in space and time. The grids' additional elements were increased liberty in, as well as responsibility toward the space. The dynamics of both infrastructures fashioned the processes of assimilation and embodiment of the subject matter, producing a statement with minimal fictional means. They contributed respectively to the creation of the virtual universes of each play--universes maintained through the actors' trust in their collective endeavor.

Notes

1. See Richard Schechner, "An Interview with Grotowski," *The Drama Review* Fall 1968: 44.
2. C.G. Jung, *Psychology and Alchemy*. (London: Routledge and Kegan Paul, 1968) 54.
3. C.G. Jung, *Alchemical Studies* (New York: Princeton UP, 1963) 24-25.
4. Suzanne K. Langer, *Feeling and Form* (New York: Scribner's, 1953) 191.
5. See Shari Troy's review of *Hamlet* in *Theatre Journal* 44 (1992): 530.

Diablomundo and the Royal Hunt: The Shadow and the Sun
by Judy Lee Oliva

Between the conception and the creation
Between the emotion and the response
Falls the shadow

T.S. Eliot

Between the concept of a theatre piece and its realization on stage, serendipity merges with artistic consciousness. And somewhere between the space of actor and audience an emotional connection is made which then elicits a response. How we create art and how we evaluate its ultimate effect is often the shadowy business of theorists and rarely is it based on specific performances; more often it is discussed in terms of collective generalizations and demographic statistics. I suggest that the endeavor to define, discuss, and deconstruct the "shadow"--where, why and how the intersections of conception and creation, of emotion and response cross--might offer some insightful clues about how the theatrical event evolves and its subsequent acceptance or rejection by an audience. A collaborative production of Peter Shaffer's *The Royal Hunt of the Sun* between an American regional theatre company and an Argentina theatre troupe was an experiment not only in the creation of a cross-cultural aesthetic; but also in the implementation of a non-traditional process to realize both the text and the essence of the text. This experiment in the exploitation of content, form and style stimulated my curiosity regarding the above queries, thus my observations included in this essay are grounded in the work that evolved from this international collaboration.

On April 15, 1994, the Clarence Brown Theatre Company, in Knoxville, Tennessee, celebrated the thirtieth anniversary of Peter Shaffer's *The Royal Hunt of the Sun* by creating a revisionist production in collaboration with Argentina's Diablomundo. The presentation was a culmination of an eighteen-week residency by Diablomundo, a theatre troupe whose specialty is puppetry and movement and who reside in Lamos de Zamora, Buenos Aires. The six-member company evolved from the politicized factions of the early seventies, where an oppressive military government menaced the Argentinean populace until the early eighties. Though they draw from the traditions of South America's gauchos, and from commedia dell'arte, it is Diablomundo's work with life-size puppets that has become the company's hallmark and has established the troupe in the international arena.[1] The troupe performed in both the 1990 and the 1992 World Theatre Festivals held in Knoxville, and thus established the initial ties that brought them back for a long-term residency, substantially supported with a major grant from the Lila Wallace-Reader's Digest Arts Partners Program. As a part of the grant proposal, in addition to working on the production of *The Royal Hunt of the Sun*, Diablomundo worked on community development projects. With the East Neighborhood Center the troupe created a series of workshops and creative activities for economically challenged neighborhoods. They collaborated with Carpetbag Theatre, one of the oldest African-American companies in the United States, on a new piece for their touring repertory. And they also worked in public outreach with the Jubilee Community Arts Center, an organization dedicated to the preservation and advancement of performance arts native to the Southern Appalachian region. All of these outside projects helped the South American company to achieve a greater understanding of the politics, the people and the aesthetic of both professional and non-professional theatres in East Tennessee.

For the production of *The Royal Hunt of the Sun*, my role was listed as "Dramaturg" but in essence my role was more of a documenter, observing the process and the product, but having no aesthetic input. This can be a frustrating task, but I believe it also afforded me a kind of objectivity that I might not otherwise have had. I attended workshops, observed rehearsals and conducted weekly interviews with Diablomundo in order to understand their process--which they refuse to define, because to define implies limits and theirs' is a theatre that is process oriented--a piece is never really finished. Their goal is to establish boundaries as they explore, not the other way around.

The goal of the production was to connect the story of the 450-year-old massacre of the Incas to modern-day Peru and modern-day

America, while exposing and often exploiting volatile issues including religious ideologies, the nature of God and what men do in his name; the clash of cultures and the humanity or lack of humanity of man. For Diablomundo, working in this multi-perspective is one of its trademarks. Scenic designer for the production, Robert Cothran explained this notion quite well.[2] He stated that in North American and Western European art, we find unity in one point of view. Diablomundo communicates not one point of view, but many. They're working with another kind of theatrical reality. The spectacle is still there, but the audience is asked to understand things about what they are seeing through the way it is staged. Usually the goal of a production is to create such a unified point of view that it is like throwing a javelin at the audience. With this production, it is like creating a tidal wave to overwhelm them. Cothran likens this multi-perspective to much of American Indian art as well, where one might see a picture of an Indian warrior, superimposed with a buffalo head, and superimposed again with additional images of sky, water, earth and fire.

The goals for the project were lofty and as with any art form difficult to assess upon completion. Those involved with the production of *The Royal Hunt of the Sun* faced the challenge of working in an unfamiliar collaborative way, where there were no absolutes, save for Shaffer's text and the mandated dates of performance; no one director to provide specific answers; no comprehensive understanding or articulation of the "process"; no one "style" of acting or movement; and no traditional use of props, costumes or lights that would ordinarily establish a kind of theatrical reality and theatrical time. It was "as you wish"--the motto of the Diablomundo players and one adopted by all. Everything could be "negotiated"--the use of space, character relationships, the sound of the language--so that there was an ongoing dialogue among everyone involved and decisions were made only after exploration and negotiation.

In the beginning there was the "dream table" where ideas, concerns, issues and dreams were placed. All of Diablomundo's projects begin this way. For Diablomundo, it may take years from the time a dream is placed on the table for thought, until its final reincarnation of a theatrical piece, such as their production of *Castaways*.[3] The "play" is really a meticulously choreographed pantomime about a Man and a Woman, both artists of sorts who cannot seem to get together until Fate comes in and literally and repetitively offers them doors of Destiny. The piece contains only one spoken line and a song at the end. However, the complexity of the ideas explored, textured by the exploitation of objects which become human in order to dehumanize, and punctuated with the marriage between a surreal world where puppets seem more "real" than their human manipulators, reflects an eclectic "style" of theatre that defies specification, but reifies Diablomundo's creative ethic. This creative ethic begins at the dream table and is sustained by the troupe members' perspective that art is never finished; that it must change as the audience changes; and that there are always "dead puppets" that can come back to life. "Dead puppets" is a term applied to things--puppets or ideas - that don't work for the moment, but may, at another time or in another production. Their philosophy, so infused and ingrained in their art form, resonates as a kind of political statement regarding how art is created. The form of their art is at once their content and the freedom that it takes to allow the form to become content is ultimately their "process." So, it was with this process, this philosophy and this creative ethic that began an eighteen-week residency for Diablomundo, who were to collaborate on a production of *The Royal Hunt of the Sun* with a company of actors composed of undergraduates, graduate MFA actors, amateur community actors and equity professionals. As with the multi-perspective of the theatre piece that evolved from Shaffer's play, there are layers of issues that emerged from the production evoking responses not only about aesthetic choices, tradition, symbols and metaphor; but also about stereotype, ritual and the perception of authenticity.

The Workshop--Defining the Function

I need--more desperately than my children need me--a way of seeing in the dark.

Equus, Peter Shaffer

The workshops conducted by Diablomundo began in October 1993 and primarily involved the graduate students in the MFA acting and design programs at the University of Tennessee. Faculty, staff and others interested in the *Royal Hunt* project observed and much of the work was videotaped. Though Diablomundo conducted separate workshops in mask construction, of interest here is the workshop with

Judy Lee Oliva

the graduate students in the exploration of Shaffer's text via Diablomundo's creative approach. As discussed earlier, the Argentina troupe does not define its process, but rather shows a "way of exploring." Carlos Uriona, a founding member of the company elaborates:

> We don't explain the philosophy, we explain the function, and in a way when you explain the function you're explaining the philosophy. We give clues, and let people follow the clues and find things. Sometimes they are not the things that we found, or we learned.[4]

It should be noted, that preceding the workshops, Diablomundo members shared their extensive research conducted in South America. One member of the group, designer Santiago Elder, offered twelve hours of videotape from his visits to Peru and Ecuador. The company brought with them a number of musical instruments, photographs, books and plays which served to enlighten us about the history of the country as well as to inform us of the contemporary views of both Spanish and Incan societies. They shared songs, sounds and stories, while we shared our understanding of Shaffer's text, our Western aesthetic of creating and our Western ethic of ethnicity.

In all of Diablomundo's work, objects are central to its presentation, whether the objects are puppets or people, ropes or sticks, masks or musical instruments. The object and the approach to it, the reaction toward it, the dynamic between it and the actor, and the possible personifications of it, propel experimentation. Having identified key moments in Shaffer's text and listing them on a large cardboard sheet, the workshop members explored each moment by using objects such as long sticks and a large piece of cloth, accompanied by drum beats, wooden flute music and shell rattles. In some instances, various lines from the text were extrapolated, but rarely more than a phrase or a sentence. It was a way to deconstruct the text into action and events such as "The empire is founded" or "The Incas are massacred." Actors played various "parts" such as Pizarro or Atahuallpa, or played more generally soldiers and indians. The exploration was much like improvisation, but with one significant distinction. The goal was not to find an answer as to how the scene or moment should be played, but rather to learn what it looked like; what images, for example, might emerge during the exploration of Atahuallpa's entrance.

As the workshop members explored the various moments/actions throughout Shaffer's text, the Diablomundo members gently guided the exercises, many times answering questions with "As you wish." The workshop served to introduce a way of working. Everyone involved, including Tom Cooke, the director (along with Diablomundo) and the designers became more cognizant of sound, spatial relationships, group dynamics, and, most importantly, of the way an object can encapsulate a moment, can heighten emotion and can resonate meaning. An object can function on a literal, metaphoric, and symbolic level all at the same time; can define space; and can project several meanings at once. Workshop members learned to view an object as something that can be larger than life or smaller than it really is, depending on the way it is used. The cloth, as an object, is a good example. In the workshops the cloth was merely a piece of muslin about the size of a sheet. In performance the cloth stretched the length of the stage and was used in almost every way imaginable, functioning as a cauldron, a rope, a tent, the literal physical "burden" of supplies that the soldiers had to carry, and the symbolic "burden" of their task. It defined the "circle" of the world on a metaphoric level, while at the same time it established the circular boundaries of the physical acting space. It "grew" larger than life as it served as a stage-size rope to strangle Atahuallpa.

The exploration with objects was the single most important experiment in the workshop--the one means of experimentation that carried over into the rehearsal process and remained a vital component in performance. Using objects to explore character relationships and to serve as a bridge between language and movement provided a "way of seeing in the dark" for workshop members who were unaccustomed to a process that is open-ended and non-goal oriented. The challenge was to understand how to theatricalize the idea that a line from the text suggests, rather than how to deliver the line itself. Additionally, the investiture of ritual that evolved in the exchange and handling of objects by the actors was a way to realize the inherent energy in Shaffer's text as well as to extend the notion of ritual not fully developed in the text. For example, in the workshop, the members explored the exchange of paper, pen and rope--primarily to learn more about how characters might feel about the history of the story, their involvement in it and what it would mean today. In performance, this experiment translated into an ongoing ritualized exchange between three versions of Atahuallpa's wife: old Ocllo (included in Shaffer's text), young Ocllo, and contemporary Ocllo. The young and contemporary Ocllos were added as a means to create a universality and a timelessness to the play. They had no text but enhanced the play via movement and critical physical placements which posed them in striking visual images throughout the play. Young and old Ocllo often carried primitive looms on which they weaved and tied ropes in a ritualized fashion. Contemporary Ocllo represented modern Peru and Incan society. Like a silent narrator contemporary Ocllo was an invisible observer, seen by audience but not by characters. She picked up props, guided the audience visually and enacted rituals which were not a part of the text. An omnipotent presence, contemporary Ocllo walked through the action of the play often opening scenes with stylized rituals. Other ritualized presentations with objects heightened the Incan presence while helping to achieve a stronger balance between the portrayal of two civilizations.

There were other less pivotal, but important discoveries in the workshop that also carried over into performance. Workshop members explored how to theatricalize time, in one instance, by using their physical movement to represent the passage of time on the sun dial. Shaffer often suggests using standard conventions such as slow motion or a stylized presentation of mimed action to represent such things as the massacre of the Incas or the climbing of the Andes. Generally, what the workshop members concluded was that it was not as important to dramatize the passage of time as to dramatize the effect of that passage and the effect of the events that occurred. One other discovery that remained prevalent throughout the rehearsals and into performance had to do with the distinction between kinds of movement. What emerged was a heightened awareness of an actor's individual movement or blocking; movement or blocking en masse; and stationary movement that often served as ritualized enactments of events. Consequently, movement patterns emerged which were sometimes extremely successful in portraying an idea or establishing a kind of energy or mood, most notably with the soldiers. However, these three distinct types of movement patterns also created a redundancy in staging in places. Additionally, these movement patterns were not employed equally between the soldiers and the indians and what resulted was an unclear view of the Incas, which was detrimental to the production as whole, given that the intent was to dramatize two equally powerful civilizations.

The Concept and the Text--Discussing the Fiction

We were both ordinary men, he and I. Yet from the ordinary he created Legends--and I from the Legends created only the ordinary.

Amadeus, Peter Shaffer

In the early discussion stages of the project, the goal was to create an original piece with Diablomundo, including members' performance in it. However, it was decided that the lack of time would be detrimental to that kind of a project and thus the idea emerged to do *The Royal Hunt of the Sun*, albeit with a contemporary South American consciousness. Tom Cooke elaborated on the importance of the social and cultural awareness to the piece: "The key to our production and our whole approach to the play has been guided by our reactions to the way the story of the conquest of the Incas by the Spaniards is retold today in Peru."[5] As explained by Diablomundo, the story is told in many ways beginning with a play that is performed on the day that the sun reaches the summer equinox--June 21. The theatre piece is developed by the Indians. Carlos Uriona elaborates:

> A group represents Atahuallpa and the Indians; another group represents the Spanish and Pizarro . . . It is in a big square in *Cajamarca* where the tragedy took place. A very important part of the ritual is that they capture several weeks before, a wild condor, which they keep in captivity and starve for three days. When the theatre piece ends, they spread all over the square and leave a bull in the center of the square. They set the condor free, and it is so hungry that it will attack the bull and tear apart the bull from the belly. And while it is eating everyone is celebrating the resurrection of Atahuallpa.[6]

The condor represents Atahuallpa and the bull is Spain. The condor represents the soul of Atahuallpa flying over the high peaks of the Andes. The idea of the play enacted every year in Peru served as the project's connection to history, both past and present. The three versions of Ocllo mentioned earlier, help to reinforce this connection of past to present.

The concept of the production also involved an interpretation of Shaffer's text as that of Old Martine's nightmare. Shaffer uses Martine as a narrator. He tells the story, now as an old man, but we also see his presence via Young Martine, the boy who, history says, accompanied Pizarro on his obsessive journey to acquire gold and establish "A name to be sung here for centuries in your ballads" (20).[7] The opening "prologue" is the representation of the nightmare where the cloth, discussed earlier, represents a cauldron where Pizarro is literally "spat out." The cauldron is not a part of Shaffer's visualization. Once Pizarro is spewed from the nightmare cauldron, Shaffer's lines are used, as written, to introduce the characters and plot. However, the concept is superimposed on the text, so that rather than being in real time, we remain in the nightmare with characters saying the lines, but not necessarily delivered to each other, nor in a realistic way. Cooke comments on this approach, explaining:

> We have tried to weave into the play, simultaneously a narrative action and a sense of the past, present, and future. Characters in the first scene, for example might have on clothes that they wore in their native village and they will be carrying armor that they have in the second act. They travel through the play as we travel through a dream . . . [8]

The action was set into place by contemporary Ocllo who entered the stage humming, knelt down with back to the audience on the downstage center area, and proceeded to enact a stylized "ritual" with kernels of corn. The opening movement of the production had a puppet-like condor fly from an eclipsed sun, thus attempting to establish the contemporary Peruvian ritual. The condor puppet, which was essentially cloth draped from large poles, symbolically "flew" over the cauldron and the nightmare began. This ritualized action was done in shadowy light and the cauldron was lit with hazy red; both actions were difficult to see and one wonders just how much the audience understood. Still, all three movements--the entrance of contemporary Ocllo, the flying condor, and the spewing cauldron--were attempts to layer Shaffer's text with additional meaning.

Unlike Shaffer's predecessors who wrote about the adventures of Pizarro and the Incas, the playwright remained truthful in his depiction of what is primarily William H. Prescott's narrative of the *History of the Conquest of Peru*.[9] Shaffer truthfully theatricalizes how, in the sixteenth century 167 Spaniards came to Peru and conquered the Inca empire, massacring 3,000 Indians in less than an hour, and thereby killing a race and a religion, supposedly for the sake of God, but in actuality for the sake of gold. But Shaffer weaves an additional layer to this historical tapestry, which reflects the playwright's particular perspective on universal issues such as God, faith and love. Shaffer's empathy, again, unlike previous depictions of the story, is clearly with Pizarro. Additionally, though Shaffer offers a good deal of stage direction and parenthetical description of the Incas and their movements, the dialogue is primarily given to the Spanish. Atahuallpa is the only Inca given a significant amount of lines. Originally, the idea was to develop the Spanish soldiers as extensions of Pizarro, and the Incas as extensions of Atahuallpa. This was an idea that never materialized, but one that would have helped to balance Shaffer's text.

By imposing a concept onto Shaffer's text, another kind of fiction emerged that often resulted in a complete departure from Shaffer's intent. Some would argue that this constitutes a revision of the text-- though Shaffer's actual words were not modified. The departures from the text were actually departures from the stage directions and descriptions of action. The "prologue" as discussed above is a good example, which adds movement and characters to Shaffer's text, but not dialogue. In a different vein, but nonetheless a "change" from Shaffer's intent, at the conclusion of the play our Pizarro was seen sitting in a burnt out sun, dejected over Atahuallpa's death and Atahuallpa's inability to become immortal. Shaffer calls for Pizarro to lie beside the body of Atahuallpa while the "SUN glares at the audience" (100). By the glaring Sun, Shaffer implies that the spirit of Atahuallpa lives on; with an eclipsed sun and Pizarro sitting in the midst of it, the audience is compelled to empathize with Pizarro, who has killed "the sun" and himself.

I mention these two examples for two reasons. They reflect the essence of the collaborative concept--which promoted a multi-layered perspective without the goal of a single unifying factor; but also they demonstrate a kind of contradiction in that concept. The prologue was an attempt to tie the present with the past, which it undeniably did, though it is doubtful that the audience comprehended such a relationship. The ritual of the condor as the successful conqueror-- symbolizing Atahuallpa's return--is at the heart of the contemporary ritual practiced in Peru today. Pizarro's presence in the burnt out sun implies just the opposite. It became apparent to me that the aesthetic choices did not always reinforce the concept. However, Diablomundo would argue that that notion is a Western idea and that aesthetic unity is not a necessary component for a theatrical production. Additionally, they would argue, and perhaps rightly so, that the audience will never realize all the aesthetic choices made in a production; nor will they realize to the fullest extent, how those choices work together or in counterpoint to advance the overall concept. In fact, Diablomundo's goal is to create a kind of "essence" of an event so that no one production element takes precedence over the other, including aesthetic unity (visual or theoretical), the comprehension of an actor's delivery of lines, and/or the understanding of a stylized or symbolic enactment of events. This philosophical approach embraces both the components cited from Shaffer's *Amadeus*--to take from the ordinary and create the legendary; and to take from the legends two men and reduce them to the ordinary of the human race. The portrayal was at once spectacular and small, metaphoric and concrete, stylized and realistic.

The Evolution of the Process--Deconstructing the Aesthetic

I've gone God-hunting and caught one.
Royal Hunt, Peter Shaffer

Deconstructing the aesthetic has to do with an examination of how meaning is conveyed to, and produced for an audience. Conveying meaning is primarily a function of content--the actor takes the playwright's lines and interprets them to provide a meaning or message to the audience. This is a traditional practice in Western theatre. Producing meaning, however, is not always a recognized or practiced strategy. While conveying meaning has to do with content, producing meaning has to do with form and style. Form refers to how the structure of the text is manipulated and ultimately portrayed on stage. Style refers to the exploitation of language, ritual and symbolic action as a means to layer meaning beyond the original content.[10]

As rehearsals evolved over a period of three weeks, which included both days and evenings, patterns emerged regarding the presentation of the two civilizations--the Incan and the Spanish. The goal was to "produce" a greater meaning than Shaffer's original content. With the exception of adding the prologue and the additional Ocllos, little else was exploited in the content of Shaffer's text. The allegiance to text was maintained, though Diablomundo often felt creatively stifled. Their practice is to begin with a text, but to exploit it in such a fashion that the text ultimately serves only as the impetus for the creative endeavor and never the final product. The structure of the text was manipulated by imposing distinct visual portrayals of the two societies. How these visual portrayals developed reflected inherent biases. For example, movement for the Spaniards was most often found through improvisation. Movement for the Incas was arbitrarily imposed, with little or no exploration save for the first week of rehearsals. Because of this practice, patterns emerged which highlighted the Spanish characters both individually and collectively, but which diminished any individuality among the Incas save for Atahuallpa, while collectively the Incas were so often physically dispersed on the stage that their "collective" presence rarely resonated.

This pattern evolved for a number of different reasons. First and foremost, the Spanish characters have all the lines and, therefore, by Western standards required more rehearsal. The major Spanish characters, such as De Soto, Miguel Estete, Pedro De Candia, and Young and Old Martine were all equity actors. Only two equity actors were cast as Incas, one as Atahuallpa and one as the Incan Priest Villac Umu. Equity rehearsals took place in the afternoon and evenings, so that basically the Spanish characters received twice as much rehearsal time. The assumption here, rightly or wrongly, is that characters with dialogue require more attention than those who have only movement and sound.

This hierarchal pattern ultimately reinforced the stereotype of class, which was also reinforced by the costumes. Even though the Spanish soldiers all had on similar "uniforms" they, nevertheless, were allowed distinct character portrayals with different hair styles, and individual mannerisms. However, the Incas were dressed alike, with both men and women wearing a tunic styled "uniform" with no individual distinctions. All wigs were the same color and basically the same length. In addition to Atahuallpa, Shaffer identified only five Incas with actual names, and two of those were non-speaking roles. There was no attempt on Shaffer's part to balance the portrayal of Incas and Spaniards in terms of individually drawn characters. He clearly views Incas as "types" and Spaniards as real people. However, this lack of recognition of "other" could have been addressed in the production, but traditional perspectives of how theatre should be developed slowly took precedence over the original goal of portraying two equally powerful civilizations. The standard Western concerns of "getting the show up"

Judy Lee Oliva

in a short period of time eventually won out, and it became clear to me how easily we lose sight of our aesthetic goals when the creative energy isn't balanced and when the creative engineers become victim of their own biases.

In terms of style, one of the most interesting aesthetic choices had to do with the exploitation of language, more specifically the exploitation of sound and dialect. One of the critiques of the original production of *The Royal Hunt of the Sun* centered around the use of strange accents or dialects. This was especially noted in reviews of the New York premiere.[11] Since Shaffer wrote the play for an English-speaking audience, the presentation of two non-English cultures presents a problem. The issue of dialect, accent and language is even more complex because Shaffer also includes a translator character for the Spaniards. This character, Felipillo, is an Indian who goes with Pizarro to translate the Inca language for the Spanish army. For this production, as in most, English is used as the accepted language. However, unlike some productions, here the Incas used a distortion of English to create a "foreign" effect, but not to suggest an accent. The Incas who had lines, distorted words by elongating the syllables, fluctuating the pitch and harshening the consonants. It had the effect of bird-like sounds at times, other times like animals, and usually it was understandable. John Ammerman, an Atlanta-based actor who played Atahuallpa, was the most successful at realizing this kind of "language." It created a kind of mystique that is necessary for this Incan God. Throughout rehearsals there was constant attention given over to the sounds of the Incas--mostly in the form of "you need to sound like birds here" or "where are the birds" or "I can't hear the birds." Little time was given over to the authenticity of the sound--it was the essence of the sound that the directing team wanted. Though probably not a feasible idea, I wondered what might have occurred had the Spaniards also explored a "sound" that was unique to them. Shaffer does provide the Catholic liturgy and music, which is used throughout, and it might be said that that was the essence of their sound.

Authenticity was an issue open for interpretation in this production. During rehearsals authentic rituals were explored alongside ritualized action--a distinction that both confused and intrigued me. I was looking for authenticity, whereas Diablomundo was seeking merely the essence of authenticity. Action by repetition became "ritual." Authentic ritual often blurred with ritualistic action, sometimes creating a kind of theatrical ritual that layered Shaffer's text with additional meaning. For example, in the second scene the playwright calls for the Spaniards to enter "bearing an immense wooden Christ" (20), and in its shadow, one by one the soldiers receive their blessing for a safe journey. The directing team not only used Shaffer's idea of a huge crucifix, but also used it as the center piece of the scene and then literally flew it out over the audience where it hung for the remainder of the production. In essence, "God" or the savior was "looking over" all--an ironic symbol to suggest that in the name of God, under his eyes and via his representatives, horrible things occurred; it also served as a visual contrast to the Inca God, Atahuallpa. The action might also be viewed as one in which the Spaniards literally relinquished their ties to the Church once they went in search of the gold. No matter what the interpretation, the action moved from the religious ritual of being blessed to a ritualistic act of letting religion "fly away."

Almost all the movement in the play was "ritualized" in some fashion, and much of the movement evolved from improvisations, notably with the Spanish characters and especially between Pizarro and Atahuallpa. The directing team suggested the feeling of a particular scene and what should ultimately result and then the actors were encouraged to improvise the movement, sometimes replacing Shaffer's words with sound that the movement evoked. These improvisations were videotaped and the directing team often made decisions about the final movements based on what they noticed in the taped improvisations. One of the most poignant and powerful moments during rehearsals occurred when the actors playing Pizarro and Atahuallpa improvised the capture of Atahuallpa. Neither actor knew quite what to do--just the feeling and the end result--but the spontaneity of the exploration, the tension in their uncertainty was explosive. The improvisation was done in a stylized fashion, in slow motion, and it was mesmerizing. The basic movement and stylization was maintained in performance, but the moment never quite resonated in performance as it did during the improvisation work. This is by no means the fault of the actors, but rather a by-product of what occurs when movement or blocking is "set" and done the same way over and over during the course of a production. A similar result occurred during the improvisation of Pizarro's reaction to the death of Atahuallpa. Here, however, the powerful movement and response from the actor portraying Pizarro was stymied by Shaffer's overwritten text. Some thought was given to cutting some of the lines and allowing the actor to substitute the movement and the sound that he had found in the improvisation. However, allegiance to the text was binding.

There is a close relationship between the portrayal of ritual and symbolic action, given that ritual is usually symbolic. Therefore, by symbolic action, I am referring to a kind of stylized movement employed by the actors to suggest a mood, an emotion, the passage of time and, in some cases, to suggest tension. The stylization was eclectic, but created a kind of unity in that the end result always reflected a specific energy. For example, many times the Spaniards moved in small and large circles, both as one group and as subgroups. In one instance they marched around Pizarro in a very small circle, shoulder to shoulder, picking up speed, as well as energy, with each rotation. This movement symbolized their uncertainty, then their frenzy, spurred on by Pizarro; and then finally, as the circle became one fast moving mass, it symbolized their agreement to stay with Pizarro at all costs and conquer the Incas.

The use of circles in the set and technical elements--the sun, the cloth which encircled the globe painted on the stage floor where much of the acting took place, the circles of light on the actors in the prologue--complemented the physical circles of movement employed throughout. Whenever actors moved in a circle, the movement was always symbolic. Likewise, whenever they moved en masse, the movement was symbolic; at least this was true of the Spanish characters. This fusion of symbolic movement with that of realistic blocking is a trademark of Diablomundo's work. It creates an interesting role for the audience, as the audience must be constantly aware of when movement takes on additional duties, such as to symbolize a larger act, create tension or initiate energy.

The use of symbolic action, in terms of creating a kind of energy via circles, was remarkably successful in almost every instance. However, there was one example where the use of symbolic action did not create the appropriate stage picture nor did it evoke the requisite emotional response. The massacre of the Incas at the end of Act one was the most disappointing aspect of the production. Shaffer calls for a fairly realistic portrayal, though done in mime and to "savage music." The directing team's decision to stylize the massacre was completely appropriate; but the focus was inherently inappropriate. The Spaniards stood in two descending lines on either side of center stage. With swords drawn they collectively lunged to the side, stepped back in line and then repeated the action. This movement was done to a steady beat that grew more and more frantic. The Incas entered one by one on all levels of the terraced stage set and with a small rope, mimed a strangulation death. The light was shadowy on the fringes of the set, so that most of the Incas were vaguely seen. The focus was clearly on the Spaniards. The capture of Atahuallpa took place; the Incas ran off to the wings; and then two Incas pulled a red cloth from upstage to downstage, finalizing the bloodbath. The red cloth, called for by Shaffer, is a fitting visual choice. However, it seems to me that in order to create any kind of empathy, the audience needed to focus on the Incas, not the Spaniards. And logically, had the same movement been done, but the positions been reversed, then the Incas would have been "killed" center stage where the cloth of blood "flowed." One could argue that to see the ruthless lunges of the Spaniards, done over and over, would automatically create a kind of empathy for the Incas. However, I maintain that in order for the audience to fully grasp the massacre, they must see the bodies or see the collective mass of death. The contradiction between the action of the Spaniards using swords and the Incas miming their death via strangulation also diminishes the horrific deeds of the Spaniards. Though it is interesting to explore the idea of killing one way and dying another, I did not feel that the idea worked here. Here the symbolism separated the acts of killing and dying when it should have brought them together. This is a good example of when the deconstruction of the aesthetic submerged the profundity of the action instead of substantiated it. The God Atahuallpa is caught, and that action engages attention; but the massacre is reduced to a portrayal of the Spaniards slaughtering the air.

The Performance--Finding the Light and the Shadow

The Normal is the good smile in a child's eyes . . . It is also the dead stare in a million adults.

Equus, Peter Shaffer

    The most exciting and the most perplexing aspect of experimentation is the notion of chance. There is the chance that the experiments will not work; but there is also an equal chance that they will. The lines between success and failure are often difficult to discern and always open to interpretation. The gulf between "the good smile" and "the dead stare" is the shadowy uncertain tension of life and art. Finding just where the light and shadow should go on this live portrait was the challenge for Diablomundo. The nuances of the members' artistic "strokes" were enlightening but it is their overall artistic philosophy that casts the most light on the Western theatre aesthetic.

This production of Shaffer's *The Royal Hunt of the Sun* was an experiment--to explore a way of working, a way of thinking, and a way of expressing. Experimentation is inherently productive. It helps us to redefine roles; to either accept or reject goals; and to reshape or restructure the medium. We learned in this collaboration with Diablomundo that the process of creating theatre cannot and should not exist in a vacuum--that culture, race, politics and economics are intrinsically tied to both the artist and the audience--and, therefore, any performance must be created and presented with that recognition. Specifically, I have concluded that even though our goal was to layer Shaffer's text with a different cultural perspective, our Western view of our own culture often confused the issue. There was, to cite one instance, a commonly accepted view that the "real" priests in the play were the Spanish ones, and the Inca priests were something foreign and not "religious."

The fuzzy lines between light and shadow remain: what should receive focus? How much should an audience understand from the words? What meaning can be produced through symbolic action and movement? To what extent do our own biases show up in our creative endeavors? The aesthetic choices in this production are not in and of themselves the pivotal culminating factors leading to success. For example, deciding how the massacre should be enacted is not as important as deducing what the difference is between the options. I suggest that the separation of the act of killing and dying is a viable creative choice only *if* the idea was simply to focus on killing and dying. However, in this case, there is an additional consideration and that is *who* is killing and dying; and that to me is more of a pivotal issue and *that* is where the focus should be placed.

Diablomundo introduced us to options--objects can grow and diminish onstage before our eyes; they can simultaneously function in a practical and a symbolic way. Sound can be language; and language can be sound. Movement can be energy and action can be ritualized. They made us aware of the relationship between authenticity and the perception of authenticity. Diablomundo helped us to understand how to theatricalize the emotional essence of a text. And, ultimately, we learned that there is a kind of unity and integrity that evolves when talented individuals who are politically, socially, economically, artistically and emotionally charged, allow themselves to dream, to push possibility and to imagine the impossible.

Notes

1. In addition to performing at both World Theatre Festivals, Diablomundo has also performed in New York, California, Georgia, Pennsylvania and Maryland. The troupe has toured throughout South America and most recently performed in Sweden and Finland in November 1994.

2. Cothran elaborated on his views during a panel entitled "The Diablomundo Project" at the Southeast Theatre Conference, on March 3, 1994, in Savannah, Georgia. Other members of the panel included myself; Dr. Tom Cooke, Head of the Department of Theatre at the University of Tennessee and director of the production of *The Royal Hunt of the Sun*; Phillip Arnoult, international liaison for the International Theatre Institute; and Carlos Uriona, founding member of Diablomundo.

3. For a review of the production of *Castaways* performed in Knoxville, see Doug Mason, "Castaways Creates Rich, Original Theatrical Banquet," *Knoxville News-Sentinel* 17 September 1993: ST6.

4. Gretchen Griffin, "Dancing with Diablo," *American Theatre* January 1994: 24.

5. See program notes, *The Royal Hunt of the Sun* in "The Round Table," Clarence Brown Theatre, Knoxville, Tennessee, 15 April 1994, 24.

6. Program notes, p. 25.

7. All quotes are from Peter Shaffer, *The Royal Hunt of the Sun* (New York: Samuel French, 1964).

8. Program notes, p. 28-29.

9. The story of Pizarro, the Spanish conquistador who captures the Inca God Atahuallpa has engaged the imagination of many writers since the conquest in 1532. German playwright Kotzebue wrote *The Spaniards in Peru* in 1796, a melodramatic version of the conquest. Kotzebue based his play on Frenchman Marmontel's two-volume book, *Les Incas*, written in 1772. English playwright Sheridan, remembered for his comedy of manners plays such as *The Rivals*, took Kotzebue's text and adapted it as *Pizarro* in 1799. Sheridan's version held the stage for some sixty years. French playwright Pixérécourt wrote his *Pizarro* in 1802. Shaffer bases *The Royal Hunt of the Sun* on William Prescott's *History of the Conquest of Peru*, two vols. (New York: Fred De Fau and Co., 1847).

10. I have written elsewhere about the use of content, form, and style as components for analysis of text in performance, though the definitions of each may vary. See my book, *David Hare: Theatricalizing Politics* (Ann Arbor: UMI Research P, 1990).

11. See Howard Taubman, "Pizarro, Gold and Ruin," *The New York Times* 27 October 1965: 36.

List of Contributors

DENNIS BARNETT is an actor, director, playwright, producer and teacher. He has a BA from Indiana University and an MFA from Florida State. His theatre, Upstart Stage, in Berkeley, California, contributed significantly to the development of nearly eighty plays, many of which have gone on to have successful runs in regional theatres.

NED BOBKOFF is a director and writer who has worked with performers from all walks of life throughout the United States and overseas. He has also been selected as an artist-in-residence in six states, and is currently developing a theatre project, "Journey Into Community Legends" that highlights acts of courage and triumph in community lives.

ALEXANDRA B. BONDS is a Professor of Costume Design at the University of Oregon, and a member of United Scenic Artists. In 1990 she received a Fulbright appointment at the National Institute of the Arts in Taipei, Taiwan. She has traveled throughout Europe and Asia researching theatrical costumes and imagery. Professor Bonds has studied the costumes of Chinese opera, Kabuki, and Balinese dance dramas. Her costume designs are regularly selected for the USITT Biennial Design Exposition.

SUZANNE BURGOYNE is an Associate Professor of Theatre at the University of Missouri/Columbia. Her translations appear in *Four Plays of Paul Willems: Dreams and Reflections* (Garland 1992) and *Paul Willems' The Drowned Land and La Vita Breve* (Peter Lang 1994). She has been a Fulbright fellow, a Kellogg National Fellow (for leadership training and interdisciplinary studies), editor of *Theatre Topics* and president of the Mid-America Theatre Conference.

KATHLEEN CIOFFI graduated in 1974 with a PhD in theatre history from New York University. She spent 1984-1987 and 1990-1991 in Gdańsk, Poland, where she directed the English Language Theatre Group of Gdańsk University. She has taught in New Mexico, Washington State and Poland. Professor Cioffi's scholarship has appeared most recently in *The Drama Review* and *Theatre Journal*.

BONNIE GOULD is a professional actress and an Associate Professor of Theatre at the University of Tennessee. She teaches performance and movement training to undergraduate and graduate students. Her interest in movement training has taken her to China where she studied Tai Ji Quan with Master Fu Zhong Wen and to Japan, where she studied Aikido at the Hombu Dojo. At the University of Tennessee, Professor Gould works on developing international theatre liaisons for the nascent International Theatre Research Center.

SUSAN VANETA MASON is an Associate Professor of Theatre Arts and Dance at California State University, Los Angeles. She served as theatre review editor for *Theatre Journal* from 1993-1995. Professor Mason was a Fulbright lecturer in American Studies at Utrecht University in 1993. She has a PhD from the University of Oregon (1980), has published performance criticism and several articles on Ibsen, and was a post-doctoral student in dramaturgy and criticism at the Yale School of Drama from 1983-1984.

VIVIAN K. MASON received her MFA in theatre from the University of Wisconsin/Madison. For over a decade she worked professionally as a production manager and technical director for theatre, opera and ballet companies in regional United States. She is currently on the faculty of the American University in Bulgaria.

YAEL NIR was a theatre student at Tel Aviv University in 1990 when she applied for the position of assistant director with Rina Yerushalmi's ensemble. Nir observed and eventually participated in the developmental work on *Woyzeck*, which was the subject of her MA thesis. Until 1993, Nir served in various positions with Yerushalmi's Itim Ensemble, including stage manager of *Woyzeck* and *Hamlet*, as well as executive producer.

Contributors

JUDY LEE OLIVA is an Assistant Professor of Theatre at the University of Tennessee. She holds an MFA in directing and a PhD in theatre and drama from Northwestern University. Professor Oliva has published in numerous journals including *Theatre Journal*, *Theatre Three*, *Theatre Topics* and *Theatre History Studies*. Her scholarship focuses on contemporary British and American Drama, with a special interest in Native American Performance. Oliva's book, *David Hare: Theatricalizing Politics* (UMI Research Press, 1991) remains the most comprehensive study of British playwright Hare's first two decades of work. Professor Oliva is currently writing a play based on three years of research in Native American Performance.

KENNETH ROBBINS is special assistant to the Dean, College of Fine Arts and Professor of Theatre at the University of South Dakota, where he teaches courses in playwriting, theory and criticism, and acting. His plays have been produced by the New Works Theatre, the Dallas Theatre Center and the Project Arts Center in Dublin, Ireland. An accomplished novelist, Robbins's works of fiction have appeared in *The North Dakota Quarterly*, *Briar Cliff Review* and *Southern Quarterly*. His new novel, *The Baptism of Howie Cobb*, received a 1994 publication by the USD Press. Professor Robbins has presented papers on playwriting at national and international conferences, including a presentation at the Eastern European Conference in 1993.

JONAH SALZ is co-founder and artistic director of the Noho Theatre Group established in 1981. He also serves as the director of traditional theatre training at Kyoto Performance Institute. Professor Salz has taught courses in Asian Studies, Performance Studies and Japanese theatre in the United States and Japan. In 1996 Salz joins the new faculty of the Intercultural Communications at Ryukoku University in Kyoto, teaching courses in world theatre.

RICHARD TROUSDELL is a Professor of Theatre at the University of Massachusetts at Amherst where he teaches directing and directing theory. An RCA-NBC Fellow at the Yale School of Drama where he earned a Doctor of Fine Arts degree in directing and dramatic literature, he has worked professionally at the New York Shakespeare Festival, the Dallas Theatre Center, the Quaigh Theatre in New York, and Glasgow's Clyde Unity Theatre. His articles on directing have appeared in *The Drama Review, Yale/Theatre, The Massachusetts Review* and *Theatre Topics*.

OHIO UNIVERSITY LIBRARY

Please return this book as soon as you have